The Law of Obligations: Connections and Boundaries

Edited by

Andrew Robertson
Faculty of Law
University of Melbourne

Routledge
Taylor & Francis Group
LONDON AND NEW YORK

First published in Great Britain 2004 by UCL Press

Published 2015 by Routledge
2 Park Square, Milton Park, Abingdon, Oxfordshire OX14 4RN
711 Third Avenue, New York, NY 10017

First issued in hardback 2015

Routledge is an imprint of the Taylor and Francis Group, an informa business

British Library Cataloguing in Publication Data
Robertson, A
The Law of Obligations: Connections and Boundaries
1 Obligations (Law)
I Title
346'.02

Library of Congress Cataloguing in Publication Data
Data available

ISBN 13: 978-1-138-83437-8 (hbk)
ISBN 13: 978-1-84472-012-5 (pbk)

Typeset by Phoenix Photosetting, Chatham, Kent

Acknowledgments

This book has developed from a conference of the same name held in February 2002 as part of a series of events to mark the opening of the new Law School building at the University of Melbourne. I would like to express my gratitude to all participants in the conference for making it such a stimulating forum. The chapters in this collection benefited from extensive discussion and debate at the conference. I would also like to thank the contributors to this volume for sharing the editorial burden by reading and commenting on one another's drafts, for their remarkable timeliness in revising their papers, and for their good-humoured co-operation throughout the process.

I am particularly grateful to the Faculty of Law at the University of Melbourne for providing financial support for the conference, and to Michael Crommelin, Dean of the Faculty of Law, for his encouragement. My thanks also go to Paris Paliouras, Wendy Beech and Lauren Holloway for their hard work in organising the conference and ensuring that it ran smoothly. This was a significant achievement given that the conference was held in a newly completed building, in the midst of the Law School's move from premises it had shared since 1873 (see Campbell, R, *A History of the Melbourne Law School 1857–1973*, Parkville: Faculty of Law, University of Melbourne, 1977, Chapter 6).

I owe an enormous debt to Michael Bryan, who was co-convenor of the conference and was instrumental in bringing it to fruition. He was a cheerful and tireless source of guidance throughout the process of organising the conference and putting this book together. It was intended for much of that process that Michael should be a co-editor of this book, but with characteristic modesty he declined that acknowledgment of his substantial contribution.

Finally, I would like to thank Anne Orford for her wise counsel, encouragement and good humour from the moment the conference was first proposed until submission of the final manuscript.

Andrew Robertson

List of Contributors

Michael Bryan is a Professor of Law at the University of Melbourne.

Robert Chambers is an Associate Professor in the Faculty of Law at the University of Alberta.

Ralph Cunnington is a Lecturer in the School of Law at the University of Birmingham.

Joachim Dietrich is a Senior Lecturer in the Faculty of Law at the Australian National University.

James Edelman is a barrister and Senior Lecturer in the Faculty of Law at the University of Western Australia.

Steve Hedley is a Professor of Law at University College, Cork.

Megan Richardson is an Associate Professor in the Faculty of Law at the University of Melbourne.

Andrew Robertson is an Associate Professor in the Faculty of Law at the University of Melbourne.

Michael Tilbury is the full-time New South Wales Law Reform Commissioner and Professorial Fellow at the University of Melbourne.

Contents

CONNECTIONS AND BOUNDARIES IN PRIVATE LAW

*Andrew Robertson**

The chapters of this book are based on papers presented and discussed at a conference on *The Law of Obligations: Connections and Boundaries* held at the University of Melbourne in February 2002. The papers collected here develop the central themes of the conference; namely, the relationships between the various branches of private law and the analysis of issues crossing the boundaries between the traditional categories within the law of obligations.

The mapping of private law has long been a controversial exercise. The efforts of Patrick Atiyah and Grant Gilmore in the 1970s continue to attract hostile attention.[1] Patrick Atiyah proposed 'some drastic redrawing of the lines' within the law of obligations.[2] He suggested that 'the new structure must ... rest on the three basic pillars of the law of obligations, the idea of recompense for benefit, of protection of reasonable reliance, and of the voluntary creation and extinction of rights and liabilities'.[3] Grant Gilmore argued that the enclave of contract law was gradually being swallowed up by the expanding empire of tort.[4] Scholars in the United States are still bristling at the suggestions of Atiyah and Gilmore, even though it might now be argued that Gilmore's prediction of a neo-classical reformulation of contract law has been realised.[5] Gilmore suggested that in law, as in the arts, we may experience 'alternating rhythms of classicism and romanticism'.[6] Gilmore saw his own era of private law scholarship as one of romantic agony; an ecstatic time of improvisation and experimentation, in which everything was 'confused, sprawling, formless and chaotic'.[7] But he predicted the return to a classical period in which everything would again be 'neat, tidy and

---

* I am very grateful to Anne Orford, Michael Bryan and Megan Richardson for their helpful comments on an earlier draft of this introductory chapter.

1 See, eg, Buckley, FH, 'Introduction' and Epstein, RA, 'Contracts Small and Contract Large: Contract Law through the Lens of *Laissez-Faire*', in Buckley, FH (ed), *The Fall and Rise of Freedom of Contract*, Durham, NC: Duke UP, 1999, 1 and 25 respectively.

2 Atiyah, PS, 'Contracts, Promises and the Law of Obligations' (1978) 94 LQR 193, 220.

3 Atiyah, PS, *The Rise and Fall of Freedom of Contract*, Oxford: Clarendon, 1979, 779.

4 Gilmore, G, *The Death of Contract*, Columbus, OH: Ohio UP, 1974, 95–96.

5 For recent irritated responses, see Buckley and Epstein, above n 1; Knapp, C, 'Rescuing Reliance: The Perils of Promissory Estoppel' (1998) 49 Hastings LJ 1191, 1332–33. A list of reviews and substantial responses to Gilmore's book can be found in the bibliography included in the 1995 re-issue, edited by Ronald Collins, 167–69.

6 Gilmore, above n 4, 111.

7 Gilmore, above n 4, 111–12.

logical' and 'formal rules of structure' would be stated.[8] It may be, Gilmore said in 1974, that 'some new Langdell is already waiting in the wings to summon us back to the paths of righteousness, discipline, order, and well-articulated theory'.[9] In the United States, as Peter Linzer has pointed out, 'we now know that the new Langdell, standing in the wings, was Gilmore's then-colleague at the University of Chicago, Richard Posner'.[10] For English legal scholars, the principal means of restoring or maintaining discipline and order in private law has been taxonomy, rather than economic analysis. In English private law scholarship, the metaphor of mapping has been used to express both romantic and classical inclinations.

Peter Birks and Andrew Burrows might be considered the chief English private law cartographers of the 1980s and 1990s. Their work clearly reflects 'the classical aesthetic' referred to by Gilmore.[11] Burrows has staunchly defended the division between contract, tort and restitution against the romantic experimentation of Atiyah.[12] Birks' work has developed in response to the romantic chaos not only of Gilmore and Atiyah,[13] but also of the legal realist and Critical Legal Studies movements.[14] Birks has led the movement for a new taxonomy of private law.[15] He has called for greater stability and consistency in the law and for the installation of 'new mechanisms against intellectual disorder'.[16] He has advocated the close mapping of the field of private law. Birks has himself promulgated a map derived from Justinian's Institutes, which divides private law into four categories according to the events from which rights arise. The essence of the Birksian scheme is that: 'The rights which people bear, whether *in personam* or *in rem*, derive from the following events: wrongs, consent, unjust enrichment, and others.'[17]

In their very different ways, Gilmore, Atiyah, Birks and Burrows have encouraged private law scholars to pay greater attention to the relations between private law obligations. Their contributions have enriched private law scholarship by provoking vigorous debate about the structure of private law and the ways in which particular obligations can be understood. This book contributes to that debate by offering a range of perspectives on the law of obligations. The papers collected here are concerned with the interaction between different parts of private law and the insights to be gained from looking across the traditional boundaries. This collection is principally concerned with the study of connections

---

8 Gilmore, above n 4, 111.

9 Gilmore, above n 4, 112.

10 Linzer, P, 'Rough Justice: A Theory of Restitution and Reliance, Contracts and Torts' [2001] Wisc LR 695, 703.

11 Gilmore, above n 4, 111.

12 Notably in Burrows, A, 'Contract, Tort and Restitution – A Satisfactory Division or Not?' (1983) 99 LQR 217; Burrows, A, *Understanding the Law of Obligations: Essays on Contract, Tort and Restitution*, Oxford: Hart, 1998.

13 Birks, P, *An Introduction to the Law of Restitution*, Oxford: Clarendon, 1985, 29.

14 See Birks, P, 'Equity in the Modern Law' (1996) 26 WALR 1, 4.

15 Notably with Birks, P (ed), *The Classification of Obligations*, Oxford: Clarendon, 1997 and Birks, P (ed), *English Private Law*, Oxford: OUP, 2000.

16 Birks, above n 14, 5.

17 Birks, above n 14, 8.

in private law: connections between contract, tort and restitution; connections between obligations and property rights; connections between obligations and remedies; connections between common law and equitable remedies. These chapters reconsider issues of classification in private law. They question the validity of the distinctions drawn between different branches of private law. They also explore some of the dangers that can arise from treating the boundaries within private law as fixed and impermeable.

This book covers three topics, and is organised accordingly. The first section is concerned with classification and the law of remedies. The chapters in this section deal with both the classification of remedies themselves and with remedial issues that cross classificatory boundaries within the law of obligations. The chapters in the second group reconsider some of the boundaries drawn by judges and scholars within the law of obligations. The third group deals with the relationship between obligations and property.

This classificatory scheme itself illustrates both the risks and the utility of taxonomy. It might be said, for instance, that the chapters do not fall neatly into the three categories. The categories overlap because they do not have the benefit of a common organising principle. It might be argued that a chapter put in one category would be better understood if placed in another. There may be illuminating connections between the chapters that are masked by the taxonomy that has been adopted. Similarities between approaches may be concealed. Differences of opinion might be overlooked. If the classificatory scheme breaks down it is because the subject matter of this book is too complex for an orderly, tripartite division. This does not mean that schemes for classifying complex subject matter serve no useful purpose, but only that their purpose is limited to offering an understanding of the subject matter. I am, of course, trying to make a broader point here about the utility of attempts to classify obligations and to map private law. If the law of obligations is too complex for orderly division, that does not mean that taxonomy is futile. The classification of private law obligations is a useful exercise, provided its goal is to aid understanding and contribute to debate, and not to devise a map that can be set in stone. The greatest achievement that can be hoped for in a new classificatory scheme or a radical redrawing of boundaries is to provide the starting point for a new discussion.

REMEDIES ACROSS THE BOUNDARIES

Chapters 2–4 deal with both the classification of remedies and with remedial issues that cross classificatory boundaries within the law of obligations. In Chapter 2, Michael Tilbury argues that the system of classification proposed by Peter Birks places too much emphasis on primary obligations at the expense of remedies.[18] Central to Birks' taxonomic scheme is a monist approach to the relationship between obligations and remedies. The monist approach is based on the idea of direct correspondence between obligation and remedy and the notion that remedies should simply mirror primary obligations. On this view remedial

18 Tilbury, M, 'Remedies and the Classification of Obligations'.

discretion is illegitimate. Tilbury argues that the monist approach is unsustainable. Some remedies, such as exemplary damages and reliance damages in contract, clearly do not simply reflect the primary obligation that has been breached. Remedies do not flow mechanically from obligations. Judges are required to make value judgments and policy choices and to balance a range of factors in determining the appropriate remedial response to a broken obligation.

Tilbury warns of two negative consequences of the monist approach to remedies. The first is that, by treating the remedy as a mirror of the obligation, the monist approach obscures the useful insights that remedies can provide in understanding the structure of the law of obligations. Although remedial issues do not line up precisely with liability issues, a consideration of remedies does provide a check on the way in which matters relating to liability might lead us to understand and classify obligations.[19] Tilbury's second concern is that the monist approach tends to oversimplify the law of remedies. Tilbury cites the proposals made by James Edelman in Chapter 3 of this volume as an example of this destabilising tendency. Edelman argues that all monetary awards for wrongs should be labelled as damages and we should move towards a greater consistency between the common law and equity by treating like damages awards alike. Tilbury suggests that symmetry between the common law and equity in relation to damages could only be achieved at the cost of an optimal fit between obligation and remedy. Approaches to causation and remoteness properly differ both between and within the common law and equity, according to the nature of the underlying obligation.

In Chapter 3 of this book, James Edelman develops his argument that the word 'damages' describes the monetary response to a wrong, and should not be understood as synonymous with 'compensation'.[20] There are, Edelman argues, several legitimate, non-compensatory measures of damages; namely, nominal, exemplary, restitutionary and disgorgement damages. The legitimacy of exemplary damages is a particularly interesting issue because it raises the question whether punishment is an appropriate goal of the law of obligations. This, in turn, forces us to consider the relationship between the law of obligations and the criminal law. As Edelman points out, the High Court of Australia has rejected the idea that there is a 'sharp cleavage between criminal law on the one hand and the law of torts and contract on the other'.[21] In the first part of his chapter Edelman argues that not only are awards of exemplary and gain-based

19 One example of this is to be found in the literature on equitable estoppel in Australia and promissory estoppel in the United States. The remedial consequences of estoppel provide a check on the understanding of estoppel we might derive from a consideration of liability issues. In particular, the prevalence of expectation-based relief gives pause to those who see estoppel as closely analogous to tort, and as essentially concerned to protect against harm resulting from reliance on inconsistent conduct. See Robertson, A, 'Situating Equitable Estoppel Within the Law of Obligations' (1997) 19 Syd LR 32 and Hillman, R, 'Questioning the "New Consensus" on Promissory Estoppel: An Empirical and Theoretical Study' (1998) 98 Col LR 580.

20 Edelman, J, 'The Meaning of "Damages": Common Law and Equity'. This argument was introduced in Edelman, J, *Gain-Based Damages*, Oxford: Hart, 2002, Chapter 1.

21 *Gray v Motor Accident Commission* (1998) 196 CLR 1, 7, quoting Street, H, *Principles of the Law of Damages*, London: Sweet & Maxwell, 1962, 34.

damages well supported by authority, but they are necessary for adequate protection of plaintiffs' interests.

The second part of Edelman's chapter focuses on the relationship between monetary awards at common law and their equivalents in equity. We should, Edelman argues, regard compensatory, disgorging and restitutionary awards made in response to equitable wrongs as damages, and should recognise the availability of exemplary damages to punish those who commit equitable wrongs. If we were to view each of these forms of equitable damages alongside their common law counterparts, this would foster the development of consistent principles relating to causation and remoteness. Edelman's response to the concerns expressed by Michael Tilbury in Chapter 2 is that adopting the nomenclature of damages does not obscure the differences of substance between the common law and equity, but invites more direct comparison. Calling equitable awards 'damages' draws our attention to the question of which damages rules are most appropriate in light of the underlying obligation in question.

In Chapter 4, Michael Bryan addresses a remedial problem lying at the intersection of contract, restitution and property law.[22] The question Bryan considers is whether a plaintiff seeking the restitution of money paid under a contract should be required to rescind the contract as a precondition to restitution. Three reasons have been given for such a precondition: first, to avoid double recovery; secondly, to protect vested property rights; and thirdly, to protect unsecured creditors by limiting the availability of proprietary restitution. Bryan argues that, although each of these considerations needs to be taken into account in determining whether rescission should be available in a particular case, none conclusively requires an election to rescind as a precondition to restitution. Moreover, the abolition of the election requirement is justified by the difficulty of determining what constitutes an election sufficient to satisfy the requirement and by the fact that gift transactions can be set aside without the donor giving notice of an intention to rescind to the donee. The ultimate question, Bryan suggests, is whether ordering the restitution of money paid under a subsisting contract upsets the contractual allocation of risk. It is this substantive question, rather than the formal requirement of contract termination, that should govern the availability of restitution for money paid under a contract.

CONTESTING THE BOUNDARIES

Chapters 5–7 consider issues relating to the classification of the law of obligations. In Chapter 5, Steve Hedley questions the utility of unjust enrichment, both as an organising idea and as a substantive legal principle.[23] He argues that there is no liability that can uncontroversially be said to be based on unjust enrichment or that cannot be justified on some other basis. He therefore sets about distributing the law of restitution into other categories. Few now claim that restitution for

---

22 Bryan, M, 'Rescission, Restitution and Contractual Ordering: The Role of Plaintiff Election'.
23 Hedley, S, '"Unjust Enrichment": The Same Old Mistake?'.

wrongs is based on unjust enrichment. Property claims can be justified without reference to the principle of unjust enrichment. In spite of the House of Lords' recognition in *Banque Financière de la Cité v Parc (Battersea) Ltd*[24] of unjust enrichment as a basis for subrogation, Hedley argues that unjust enrichment has nothing useful to add to the law of subrogation, recoupment and contribution. Hedley's main focus, then, is on the heart of the law of restitution: direct restitution for money paid, work done and goods delivered. The obligation to restore or pay for these benefits, Hedley suggests, arises from the law of contract or a category of obligation that is sufficiently close to contract that it might almost be called 'quasi-contract' if that expression were not so heavily laden with historical baggage. The idea that these actions cannot be described as contractual is, Hedley argues, based on an old-fashioned idea of contract in which all rights are created by the parties rather than the law.

Hedley suggests that insufficient attention has been paid in the literature to the task of justifying the principle of unjust enrichment in moral or public policy terms. Writers have tended to focus on what constitutes unjust enrichment. The fact that there is no unanimity either as to what constitutes an 'enrichment', or as to when an enrichment will be 'unjust' is no bad thing, Hedley suggests, because unjust enrichment is less harmful as a broad explanatory concept than as a 'definitive legal principle'.[25] It should come as no surprise that Hedley finds support for this view in the judgments of Gummow J, who has likened unjust enrichment to the umbrella concepts of proximity and unconscionability.[26] While accepting that these concepts are not without legal content, Gummow J has suggested that proximity, at least, 'used as a legal norm, has the uncertainty of a category of indeterminate reference, used with shifting meanings to mask no more than policy preferences'.[27]

Underlying Hedley's analysis in Chapter 5 is the idea that the march of unjust enrichment has in part been facilitated or necessitated by the adoption of an overly restrictive understanding of contract. I scrutinise that restrictive conception of the law of contract in Chapter 6.[28] The classical understanding of the law of obligations was founded on the idea that a sharp distinction could be drawn between contract and tort. Contractual obligations were believed to be voluntarily assumed, while obligations in tort were thought to be imposed by the courts. Although the principal flaws in the classical model are widely understood, many judges and scholars still insist that at some fundamental level contract and tort can be distinguished. Chapter 6 is the first step in my attempt to understand that insistence and its implications. The goal of Chapter 6 is to demonstrate the persistence of the idea that contract can be sharply distinguished from tort and to provide a detailed account of the reasons why that distinction does not stand up

---

24 [1999] 1 AC 221. Hedley criticises elsewhere the utility of unjust enrichment in this context; see Hedley, S, *A Critical Introduction to Restitution*, London: Butterworths, 2001, 330–31.

25 *Roxburgh v Rothmans of Pall Mall* (2001) 185 ALR 335, [74] (Gummow J).

26 *Hill v Van Erp* (1997) 188 CLR 159, 237–39.

27 *Ibid*, 238, citing The Hon Justice McHugh, 'Neighbourhood, Proximity and Reliance' in Finn, PD (ed), *Essays on Torts*, Sydney: Law Book Co, 1989, 5, 13.

28 Robertson, A, 'On the Distinction between Contract and Tort'.

to close scrutiny. A close consideration of the principles of contract law shows that obligations in contract, like those in tort, are to a significant extent shaped by community standards. It is a serious misconception to suggest that obligations in contract can be distinguished from those in tort on the basis that the former are voluntarily assumed while the latter are imposed by law. This conclusion casts doubt on the idea that contractual obligations can be regarded as the core of a 'consent' category within the law of obligations. It calls into question the appropriateness of adopting consent as an organising principle within private law.

In Chapter 7, Joachim Dietrich focuses on obligations that might be thought to lie within the 'other' category in the Birksian taxonomic scheme.[29] The principles of estoppel, Dietrich suggests, exhibit elements of contract and tort. The complexity of estoppel, however, makes it very difficult to identify within it an 'other causative event' that might allow us to place it in the fourth category. The cause of action in estoppel seems, Dietrich argues, to lie between the categories of consent and wrongs. Dietrich makes a similar argument in the relation to precontractual liability, which not only involves obligations arising from consent and legal and equitable wrongs but also unjust enrichment. For Dietrich, the taxonomist's response to precontractual liability should not be to distribute it amongst those categories of obligation, though, because the cases can only be explained by looking across the boundaries drawn between those categories. The elements of precontractual liability identified by Dietrich in previous writing cross the boundaries between contract, tort and unjust enrichment.[30] Like the estoppel cases, therefore, the precontractual liability cases do not fit comfortably in the 'other events' category, and tend to undermine any attempt to create a rigid scheme for the classification of obligations.

PROPERTY AND OBLIGATION

The relationship between property rights and private law obligations is explored in several chapters in this collection. In Chapter 4, Michael Bryan considers the proprietary consequences of rescission and raises the question whether a plaintiff entitled to the return of property under a rescinded contract is also entitled to the profits derived by the defendant from the use of that property. The final three chapters of this volume examine further the relationship between obligation and property. This relationship is explored at its broadest level by Robert Chambers, who argues in Chapter 8 that the law of obligations cannot, and should not, be considered separately from property law.[31] Chambers argues that we must break down the boundary between the law of obligations and the law of property in order to treat like cases alike. A particular fact situation may yield one result if considered as a problem of unconscionability or unjust enrichment and an entirely different result if considered as a problem relating to indefeasibility of

29 Dietrich, J, 'The "Other" Category in the Classification of Obligations'.
30 Dietrich, J, 'Classifying Precontractual Liability: A Comparative Analysis' (2001) 21 LS 153.
31 Chambers, R, 'Integrating Property and Obligations'.

title to land. The concept of 'property' is strained in disputes arising from the breakdown of marriage and other relationships of cohabitation because the potential of obligations arising by way of estoppel or unjust enrichment has not been adequately explored. We can overcome this problem, Chambers argues, by classifying all private law rights, including property rights, according to the source of those rights in accordance with the Birksian scheme. Chambers explains how the source of all property rights can be found within Birks' four categories of consent, wrongs, unjust enrichment and other events. This provides us with a means of bringing obligations and property together and thus provides a means of understanding all of private law.

In Chapter 9, Megan Richardson analyses the property/obligations divide in relation to confidential information.[32] She points out that an interest in confidential information has long been endowed with what might be seen as a characteristic of property, which is that it can be asserted against an indefinite class of persons, subject only to the requirement of notice. She suggests, however, that the legal concept of property does not offer a complete understanding of the obligation of confidence, which is informed by a range of considerations. Moreover, not all kinds of confidential information have been accorded proprietary status. It is trade secrets – which can be the subject of market transactions – that are most commonly identified as property. Richardson suggests that the economic understanding of 'property' as a tradeable commodity offers a useful perspective on the treatment of confidential information under the equitable confidentiality doctrine. Government secrets were, in effect, treated as property in the economic sense in *Attorney-General v Blake* when an account of profits was ordered for the misuse of those secrets in breach of contract.[33] The remedy of an account of profits, granted at the election of the plaintiff, can be seen as equivalent to a compulsory licence. Does this mean that an individual entitled to claim breach of confidence may elect to treat personal information as a tradeable asset, even if it is not a trade secret? So far there is little judicial support for such commodification of private personal information, although Richardson suggests that there are sound liberal and utilitarian arguments for doing so. Richardson demonstrates in Chapter 9 that a reading of economic and philosophical literature on property and commodification can enrich our understanding of the legal regime for the protection of secrets and can shed light on the use of property concepts in relation to obligations of confidence. While the economic concept of property provides some useful insights, Richardson suggests that it is ultimately trust, rather than ownership, that reveals most about the confidentiality obligation.

The question whether contract rights should be regarded as property is considered by Ralph Cunnington in Chapter 10.[34] Cunnington shows that the tort of inducing breach of contract provides better protection for contracting parties against interference by third parties than the law of contract provides against

32 Richardson, M, 'Owning Secrets: "Property" in Confidential Information?'.

33 [2001] 1 AC 268.

34 Cunnington, R, 'Contract Rights as Property Rights'.

interference by the contracting parties themselves. The tort of inducing breach of contract protects the interest of contracting parties in performance of contractual obligations, and is inconsistent with the idea that a contracting party may choose to break a contract and pay damages. The law of contract should, Cunnington argues, provide a remedial response consistent with that provided by the law of tort. The characterisation of contract rights as property could help to achieve this goal, since this would provide a justification for the general availability of restitutionary damages for the infringement of those rights. Although an argument can be made for characterising contract rights as property, Cunnington argues, there is no need to introduce confusion by taking this intermediate step. It is far better to recognise openly that restitutionary damages are needed to protect the performance interest in contract and, accordingly, that restitutionary damages should be available where compensatory damages are inadequate and specific relief is unavailable.

CONCLUSION

These chapters reveal the rich insights to be gained from debate about connections and boundaries in private law. Taxonomy is not a dry technical exercise. Each time we adopt or redraw a boundary, we are offering a particular conception of the underlying obligations. Classification forces us to think about the nature of each of the underlying obligations, how they relate to one another, and how they can be distinguished from one another. These essays show that there is a great deal to be learned from a consideration of the connections between obligation and remedy, between different categories of obligation and between obligation and property. A consideration of those connections takes us to the very heart of private law: the values that inform it and the goals it seeks to achieve.

2

REMEDIES AND THE CLASSIFICATION OF OBLIGATIONS

Michael Tilbury

The inspiration for this chapter comes from what, for convenience, I will call 'taxonomy scholarship', by which I mean that species of legal scholarship concerned with the classification or divisions of the legal system. In modern times, taxonomy scholarship originates, essentially, in the advocacy of the recognition of the restitutionary obligation following the publication of Professor Birks' magisterial *Introduction to the Law of Restitution* in 1985.[1] This scholarship is not limited solely to the identification and recasting of restitutionary obligations, but seeks to discover an overall taxonomy for the common law, of which the law of obligations forms only a small part.[2]

In the context of the law of obligations, Nicholas McBride has written that:

> any academic who is seriously concerned to teach others about what our obligations are needs a good list of our obligations. The classification of obligations is an integral part of the production of good lists of our obligations. The classification of obligations is therefore central to the work of any academic who is concerned to teach others about what our obligations are.[3]

Leaving aside for the moment any comment on the central importance of the enterprise suggested in the assertions of this syllogism,[4] the assertions should at least provoke those interested in the law of remedies to contemplate the relationship between the law of remedies and the debates about the taxonomy of the common law. In particular two questions spring to mind:

- the first is the extent to which a remedial perspective can contribute to the classification of obligations;
- the second, the other side of the coin, is the importance of classification for the law of remedies itself.

Crucial to a discussion of these two questions is a determination of the relationship between 'obligation' and 'remedy', an inquiry which itself necessarily gives rise to the further questions of the meaning and use of the words 'obligation' and 'remedy'.

---

1 Birks, P, *An Introduction to the Law of Restitution*, Oxford: Clarendon, 1985.

2 For a proposed overall taxonomy of the common law, see Birks, P, 'Introduction', in Birks, P (ed), *English Private Law*, Oxford: OUP, 2000, vol 1, xxxv–li.

3 McBride, NJ, 'The Classification of Obligations and Legal Education', in Birks, P (ed), *The Classification of Obligations*, Oxford: Clarendon, 1997, 88–89.

4 See 'Conclusion', below.

Consideration of the central question of the relationship between obligation and remedy has occurred principally in the context of identifying and separating the content and role of proprietary 'rights' and 'remedies', especially as manifest in the constructive trust, where the issue is sharply drawn and difficult to avoid.[5] This chapter attempts to address the issue principally in the context of non-proprietary 'rights' and 'remedies'. It does so by addressing the questions listed above in the following order:

- the meaning and use of obligation and remedy;
- the relationship between obligation and remedy;
- the importance of a remedial perspective in the classification of obligations; and
- the importance of the modern classification movement for the law of remedies.

OBLIGATION AND REMEDY

I do not propose to dwell unduly on the different meanings that these terms can bear in the varying contexts in which they are used in law. This task is addressed at length in the taxonomy literature.[6] What I do want to do is to highlight those aspects of our understanding of the terms that are essential to this chapter.

Obligation

The word 'obligation', whose root derives from the Latin verb 'to bind',[7] refers to the legal nexus that ties the defendant to the plaintiff in private or civil law.[8] The circumstances in which that legal tie arises – that is, the bases of obligation – have been variously described in Western systems of law. For our purposes, it is sufficient to accept the now common view that obligations arise from contract (or consent), from wrongs, from unjust enrichment and from other events, a view that

---

5 See especially Waters, DWM, 'Liability and Remedy: An Adjustable Relationship' (2001) 64 Saskatchewan L Rev 429; Evans, S, 'Defending Discretionary Remedialism' (2001) 23 Syd LR 463. And consider Wright, DM, *The Remedial Constructive Trust*, Sydney: Butterworths, 1998. Compare Barker, K, 'Rescuing Remedialism in Unjust Enrichment Law: Why Remedies are Right' [1998] CLJ 301 (dealing more generally with unjust enrichment).

6 Especially Birks, P, 'Rights, Wrongs, and Remedies' (2000) 20 OJLS 1; Barker, above n 5, 312–15.

7 In Latin the word describes that tie from both the defendant's and the plaintiff's point of view: see Zimmermann, R, *The Law of Obligations: Roman Foundations of the Civilian Tradition*, Cape Town: Juta & Co, 1990, 1. By contrast, English usage views the 'tie' only from the defendant's perspective. We speak of the defendant's obligation to render performance. We do not speak of the plaintiff's obligation to claim that performance. Rather, we speak of the plaintiff's 'right' to it. Thus, as Birks points out, when I refer in English to 'my obligations', I refer to my duties, not to my rights: Birks, P, 'Obligations: One Tier or Two', in Stein, PG and Lewis, ADE (eds), *Studies in Justinian's Institutes in Memory of JAC Thomas*, London: Sweet & Maxwell, 1983, 19f.

8 For discussion of Justinian's famous definition in *Inst* 3.13 pr, see Birks, P, 'Definition and Division: A Meditation on *Institutes* 3.13', in Birks (ed), above n 3, 1, 6–12.

(in its essentials) boasts a Roman lineage.[9] Leaving aside for the moment the 'other events' category, the three-fold classification into consent, wrongs and unjust enrichment reflects, broadly, the way in which private law is translated in most law school curricula into courses in contract, tort and restitution respectively. But only broadly, because 'contract' is narrower in the three-fold classification of obligations than it is for most academic courses in contract, which usually, and naturally, contain a discussion of breach of contract. In the three- or four-fold classification, 'contract' refers to those obligations of the defendant that arise from the contract itself – for example, to the obligation to pay the contract price – rather than to the obligations which arise from breach of contract. The reason is that breach of contract is a civil wrong, so the obligations arising from such breach are in the category of wrongs. Thus, for the purposes of this classification, the category of 'wrongs' is wider than 'tort', even though 'wrong' and 'tort' may have been synonymous in 19th century law, particularly 19th century statutory law.[10]

Notwithstanding the seeming need to classify obligations, we often hear the call these days for a unified or coherent law of obligations,[11] sometimes with reference to the authority of civilian systems of law with their long tradition (derived from Roman law)[12] of treating 'obligation' at least as an 'umbrella concept'.[13] These calls are made in a number of contexts and have a variety of meanings. First, in the context of curriculum development, the plea is usually no more than for the replacement of 'Contracts' with 'Obligations 1', 'Torts' with 'Obligations 2' and 'Unjust Enrichment' (if offered or not subsumed elsewhere) with 'Obligations 3'.[14] By itself, an appeal of this sort is no more than cosmetic, save that its implementation would serve to indicate without more that there is some sort of relationship between contract, tort and unjust enrichment. The implementation of such a proposal would neither break down the barriers between the nominate obligations nor suggest how problems should be solved on the boundaries.

More substantially, the appeal for a unified law of obligations may be made for the purpose of ensuring, or advocating, that concepts should, generally, receive like treatment in the law, regardless of the source of obligation in question. An example, fuelled perhaps by a realisation that obligations in tort and contract are

---

9 See Thomas, JAC, *Textbook of Roman Law*, Amsterdam: North Holland, 1976, 219–23 (dealing with the differing classifications of Gaius and Justinian).

10 See Meagher, RP, Heydon, JD and Leeming, MJ, *Equity: Doctrine and Remedies*, Sydney: Butterworths, 4th edn, 2002, [23–105] ('wrongful acts' synonymous with 'torts' under Lord Cairns' Act).

11 See Justice Thomas, 'An Endorsement of a More Flexible Law of Civil Remedies' (1999) 7 Waikato L Rev 23, 36–37 (arguing for an integrated law of obligations which identifies the 'essential obligation').

12 See, eg, Wieacker, F, *A History of Private Law in Europe with Particular Reference to Germany*, Oxford: Clarendon, 1995, 186–89.

13 See Vranken, M, *Fundamentals of European Civil Law*, Sydney: Federation, 1997, 83–84. But, in French law for example, this does not mean much since substantive law continues to differ significantly according to the source of obligation: see Bell, J, Boyron, S and Whittaker, S, *Principles of French Law*, Oxford: OUP, 1998, 304–05.

14 For an example, see Birks, above n 8, 15–17 (dealing with (English) Law Society and Council of Legal Education, *Notice to Law Schools regarding Full-Time Qualifying Law Degrees* (1995)).

not as disparate as they once were regarded,[15] is a call for the uniform operation of contributory negligence in contract and in tort, at least in circumstances where the obligation breached looks similar, if not identical (such as where a contractual duty of care is on all fours with the duty of care existing in the circumstances in tort).[16] The High Court of Australia rejected just such a call in *Astley v Austrust Ltd*,[17] but was swiftly overruled by legislatures in all relevant States and Territories.[18]

The like treatment of like situations regardless of source of obligation is, obviously, a compelling argument in favour of the call for a unified law of obligations. But it needs careful application. It is not simply a question of saying, for example, that contributory negligence should apply whatever the obligation breached. Rather, it is a question of analysing whether or not uniform treatment is justified given the differing natures of the obligations in question. There is, undoubtedly, a real danger of overlooking the implications flowing from the reasons for the imposition of obligation in the first place. The High Court highlighted this danger in *Astley v Austrust*[19] by refusing to apply contributory negligence in an action for breach of contract. The court reasoned that there is a real difference in applying contributory negligence in a context in which liability is imposed by law to that in which it arises from consent.[20] It is not simply transportable from the one to the other. Whether this is right or not,[21] it illustrates the point that it is futile to argue for uniform treatment of concepts such as 'intention', 'causation' and 'remoteness' without regard to the reason why obligation exists in the first place. The question inevitably arises: which version of the concept should be taken and why?

Remedy

Because 'remedy' is peculiarly susceptible of a variety of meanings in law,[22] it is necessary to state at the outset how I propose to use it. For the purposes of this

---

15 See Robertson, A, 'On the Distinction between Contract and Tort', Chapter 6 of this volume.

16 See Tilbury, M and Carter, JW, 'Converging Liabilities and Security of Contract: Contributory Negligence in Australian Law' (2000) 16 J Cont L 78, especially at 80–93.

17 (1999) 197 CLR 1.

18 Law Reform (Miscellaneous Provisions) Act 1955 (ACT), s 15(1) (read with the definition of 'wrong' in s 14); Law Reform (Miscellaneous Provisions) Act 1965 (NSW), s 9(1) (read with the definition of 'wrong' in s 8); Statutory Duties (Contributory Negligence) Act 1945 (NSW), s 2; Law Reform (Miscellaneous Provisions) Act 1955 (NT), s 16(1) (read with the definition of 'wrong' in s 15(1)); Law Reform Act 1995 (Qld), s 10 (read with the definition of 'wrong' in s 5); Law Reform (Contributory Negligence and Apportionment of Liability) Act 2001 (SA), s 7 (read with the definition of 'fault' in s 3); Wrongs Act 1954 (Tas), s 4(1) (read with the definition of 'wrong' in s 2); Wrongs Act 1958 (Vic), s 26(1) (read with the definition of 'wrong' in s 25). Western Australia's Law Reform (Contributory Negligence and Tortfeasor's Contribution) Act 1947, which is differently drawn to the legislation in other jurisdictions, achieves the same result in this respect by reason of s 4(1) ('any claim for damages founded on an allegation of negligence') and its proviso (a): see *Craig v Troy* (1997) 16 WAR 96, 152–55 (Malcolm CJ), 199–200 (Franklyn J).

19 (1999) 197 CLR 1.

20 *Ibid*, especially at [84]–[87].

21 On which, see Tilbury and Carter, above n 16, and literature there cited.

22 See Birks, above n 6, 9–12, though the hope that the word will be expunged from our legal vocabulary will almost certainly not be realised!

chapter, 'remedy' is the legal response to events that constitute a wrong or to events that, while not constituting a wrong, still give rise to legal liability.[23] If we adopted Birksian terminology, we would put this shortly as: a remedy is the legal response to a wrong or a not-wrong.[24] This understanding of remedy cuts across the Austinian division of rights into primary and secondary.[25]

Where a remedy is a response to a wrong, then, according to John Austin, the plaintiff's remedial right is 'secondary' since it is triggered by, and dependent on, the defendant's breach of a prior or 'primary' right. Thus, in the standard examples, the plaintiff's right to damages (the plaintiff's secondary right) arises from the defendant's breach of the plaintiff's primary right to the performance of a contract or the observance of a duty under tort law breached by the defendant. Since our law currently operates through nominate remedies, we can identify as responses to wrongs (and hence as 'remedies') at least the money remedies of damages, account of profits, restitutionary damages and equitable compensation. We can also now confidently include the injunction in the category of 'remedies', since, as the High Court held in *ABC v Lenah Game Meats Pty Ltd*,[26] it is only possible for an interlocutory injunction to go in aid of a recognised legal, equitable or statutory right. This applies, *a fortiori*, to a permanent injunction and puts paid to suggestions that there could be such a thing as an 'autonomous injunction' in our law – that is, especially, an interlocutory injunction which simply preserved the status quo even in circumstances where there was no recognisable legal, equitable or statutory right to protect.[27]

By contrast, in the case of 'not-wrongs', the 'remedial response' is primary in the Austinian sense, there being no 'wrong' in the equation. Uncontroversial examples are: my right to demand the defendant's disgorgement of a sum of money which he or she has received unjustly (as under a mistake of fact) at my expense; and my right to demand a sum due under a contract (the action for the agreed sum).[28] Professor Birks, implicitly drawing on classical equitable doctrines, also makes the point that specific performance is a primary right arising from the not-wrong of making a contract which is realised when the court orders, and enforces, the decree.[29] But this view is at once too narrow and too wide. Technically, the view is too narrow because the making of the contract is only one of the factors that establishes the equity to relief.[30] While the equitable remedy of

---

23 I have adopted this understanding of 'remedy' elsewhere: Tilbury, MJ, *Civil Remedies*, Sydney: Butterworths, 1990, vol 1, [1002]–[1004]. See also Tilbury, M, Noone, M and Kercher, B, *Remedies: Commentary and Materials*, Sydney: LBC Information Services, 3rd edn, 2000, 4. And consider Barker, above n 5, 319–22.

24 Birks, above n 6, 27–29.

25 Austin, J, *Lectures on Jurisprudence*, 5th edn, Campbell, R (ed), London: John Murray, 1885, Lecture XLV.

26 (2001) 185 ALR 1, especially at [15]–[21] (Gleeson CJ), [61] (Gaudron J), [91] (Gummow and Hayne JJ); cf at [156]–[167] (Kirby J), [278]–[287] (Callinan J). See also *Siskina v Distos Campania Naviera SA* [1979] AC 210, 254 (Lord Diplock).

27 See Tilbury, above n 23, [6055].

28 Especially Birks, P, 'Equity in the Modern Law: An Exercise in Taxonomy' (1996) 26 UWA L Rev 1, 10–12, 40–42. But compare Barker, above n 5, 318–22.

29 Birks, above n 6, 27.

30 Especially *Hasham v Zenab* [1960] AC 316, 329 (PC) (Lord Tucker).

specific performance generally depends on the plaintiff's ability to establish a contract enforceable at law, courts of equitable jurisdiction sometimes allow specific performance after preventing the setting up of facts that are inconsistent with the existence of an enforceable contract at law and then charge the defendant upon the equities that dictate the availability of specific performance.[31] An example is where a decree of specific performance is made against a defendant charged upon the equities arising from the plaintiff's part performance of an unwritten contract unenforceable by reason of the Statute of Frauds.[32] Practically, the view is too wide because, in the vast majority of cases, breach of contract is the equity that renders it equitable to intervene by way of specific performance,[33] even where the breach is merely threatened,[34] the position being analogous to *quia timet* relief in the case of injunctions.[35]

Does Austin's distinction between primary and secondary rights matter for our purposes? An answer to this question must begin from the realisation that, as Austin himself tells us, the distinction 'rests exclusively upon a difference between the events from which the rights and duties respectively arise'.[36] So regarded, the crucial importance of the distinction is its recognition that secondary rights and duties arise from events that constitute a breach of duty (a 'wrong'). The effect of this recognition is that it locates a greater remedial potential in secondary than in primary rights. As Professor Birks explains:[37]

> Wrongs have a wide-open remedial potential ... A victim of a wrong can be given such remedial rights as the system thinks good. The victim of a wrong of battery ... could be given the right both to be compensated in money and to be satisfied further by having the wrongdoer's ears cut off. The system has a choice.
>
> Quite differently, at the primary level, the causative event, in itself, has a much more limited potential. The reason is that it is only the characterisation of the defendant's conduct as a breach of duty which makes it possible to contemplate pursuing a policy of deterrence or retribution. Those ideas cannot be brought to bear on the primary causative events. Apart from any other consideration, the primary events are often composed of facts which are not within the control of the defendant at all ... In short, if I show that you have committed a wrong, a brand new system with all its choices still before it might think of attaching all sorts of dire remedial consequences. But if I show that I have recovered a judgment against you for $100, my allegation suggests nothing but that you ought to pay me $100.

Beyond this, the distinction between primary and secondary rights is not of much importance and, indeed, contains the danger that it may be thought to create a

---

31 See especially Spry, ICF, *The Principles of Equitable Remedies: Specific Performance, Injunctions, Rectification and Equitable Damages*, Sydney: LBC Information Services, 6th edn, 2001, 52–53. See also Burrows, A, *Remedies for Torts and Breach of Contract*, London: Butterworths, 2nd edn, 1994, 335.

32 The *locus classicus* is the Earl of Selborne's speech in *Maddison v Alderson* (1883) 8 App Cas 467, 475–76. See also *McBride v Sandland* (1918) 25 CLR 69, 77; *JC Williamson v Lukey and Mulholland* (1931) 45 CLR 282, 300, 309; *Steadman v Steadman* [1976] AC 536, 552, 559.

33 Burrows, above n 31, 335.

34 Especially *Turner v Bladin* (1951) 82 CLR 463, 472 (Williams, Fullagar and Kitto JJ).

35 Birks regards such injunctions as probably secondary: see Birks, above n 28, 40.

36 Austin, above n 25, 763.

37 Birks, above n 28, 12–13.

paradigm to which all causes of action should conform. One effect of the application of the paradigm is, for example, to obliterate or confine the category of not-wrongs by attempting to discover a 'wrong' in cases of autonomous unjust enrichment (that is, restitution where there is no wrong).[38] Another would be to suggest that only responses to wrongs are remedies.[39] The barrenness of such an approach is demonstrated by considering the categorisation as primary rights of the action for the agreed sum and (less securely) specific performance.[40] The problem is that both are 'remedies' in normal speech and are clearly, functionally, secondary – in short, a part of the law of remedies. Indeed, the availability of specific performance is, theoretically at least,[41] dependent on the inadequacy of the *remedy* at law, usually damages.[42] And the inadequacy of the damages test has even been applied to the non-equitable action for the agreed sum.[43] Again, law and economics scholars oppose specific performance and damages in a search for the most efficient remedy in given situations.[44] This shows, in short, that we need to avoid reifying the Austinian distinction between primary and secondary rights, recognising both its limits and those of a taxonomy that seeks to build on it.

THE RELATIONSHIP BETWEEN OBLIGATION AND REMEDY

Two opposed views of the relationship between 'obligation' and 'remedy' have emerged. Following the writings[45] and judicial utterances[46] of Justice Hammond in New Zealand, I refer to these as the 'monist' and 'dualist' views of remedies. I also state the distinction between the two approaches in Justice Hammond's terms. Put shortly, the monist view is that obligation and remedy are congruent rights: the dualist view is that, after a court has made a determination of the obligation it is asked to uphold, it then (and only then) makes a context-specific evaluation of the remedy that is most appropriate in all the circumstances. A simple illustration of the divergence of these views is that a monist would regard a proprietary remedy as supporting only a proprietary obligation:[47] a dualist

---

38 See Barker, above n 5 (replacing 'wrong' with 'primary injustice'). Compare Birks, above n 6, 28.

39 Though the assumption may be made for pragmatic reasons, including pedagogical purposes: see Tilbury, Noone and Kercher, above n 23, 4.

40 See text to n 29–35 above.

41 Consider especially Laycock, D, *The Death of the Irreparable Injury Rule*, New York: OUP, 1991.

42 See Spry, above n 31, 59–74.

43 See *Attica Sea Carriers Corp v Ferrostaal Poseidon Bulk Redderei GmbH (The Puerto Buitrago)* [1976] 1 Lloyd's Rep 250, 255 (Lord Denning MR).

44 See Tilbury, Noone and Kercher, above n 23, 753–58, and literature there cited.

45 Especially Hammond, G, 'Rethinking Remedies: The Changing Conception of the Relationship Between Legal and Equitable Remedies', in Berryman, J (ed), *Remedies: Issues and Perspectives*, Scarborough: Carswell, 1991, Ch 4; Hammond, G, 'The Place of Damages in the Scheme of Remedies', in Finn, P (ed), *Essays on Damages*, Sydney: Law Book Co, 1992, Ch 9.

46 *Butler v Countrywide Finance Ltd* [1993] 1 NZLR 623 especially at 631–33; *Brown v Pourau* [1995] 1 NZLR 352 especially at 368. See also *Dickie v Robay Pharmacy (1986) Ltd* [1995] 3 NZLR 429, especially at 441.

47 Consider Birks, P and Mitchell, C, 'Unjust Enrichment', in Birks (ed), above n 2, [15.182]–[15.211].

would not regard the non-proprietary nature of the obligation as necessarily precluding the award of a proprietary remedy.[48]

Monism

The monist view that obligations and remedies are congruent bears three closely related shades of meaning in the literature. First, and most generally, 'congruency' means that remedy is a mirror image of the right it supports. Clear and uncontroversial illustrations are the specific performance of a contract (where the defendant is ordered to perform the very promise made to the plaintiff); and the restitutionary response in cases of autonomous unjust enrichment (where I have unjustly received $1000 at your expense, I must, then, restore $1000 to you). The same point is sometimes made, but with greater linguistic difficulty, where a court orders compensation pursuant to a wrong. Compensation aims to put the injured party in the position which would have obtained had no wrong occurred. By restoring the status quo and reversing (at least theoretically) the effect of the defendant's wrong, compensation can be seen to be the mirror image of the plaintiff's right. Thus, using the examples of negligence and breach of contract generating a claim for damages, Birks writes: 'The secondary obligation to pay compensatory damages is ... the same thing as the right, looked at from the other end.'[49]

Secondly, and relatedly, congruency can suggest that remedy is no more than a reflex or response to the right it supports.[50] The subtle difference in meaning between this aspect of congruency and the meaning in the last paragraph is that emphasis shifts from the general to the particular – the particular here being the function of remedy in the context of the particular right.[51] Here the meaning of congruency stresses that remedy should go no further than effectuating the purpose(s) of the plaintiff's obligation. If it does, it ceases to be a mirror image of that obligation.

Thirdly, 'congruency' can mean that remedy is inherent in the plaintiff's cause of action, the theory of the plaintiff's case. Where the facts allow the plaintiff to bring a particular action, the law ascribes (in advance) the right to one type of response or allows the plaintiff to elect between a plurality of responses.[52] This aspect of congruency can be said to have the following advantages:

- it alerts the plaintiff to what must be pleaded;
- it avoids any gap in the right/remedy structure by assuring the plaintiff of the availability of a particular remedy or remedies in given situations; and

48 *Pettkus v Becker* [1980] 2 SCR 834; *Lac Minerals Ltd v International Corona Resources Ltd* [1989] 2 SCR 574; and *Cadbury Schweppes Inc v FBI Foods* [1999] 1 SCR 142 are perhaps the best examples of this approach. See also *Rawluk v Rawluk* [1990] 1 SCR 70. And consider *Re Stephenson's Nominees* (1987) 76 ALR 485, 502 (Gummow J).

49 Birks, above n 8, 24.

50 See Weinrib, E, 'The Juridical Classification of Obligations', in Birks (ed), above n 3, 37, especially at 46.

51 *Ibid*, especially at 42 ('the reason for taking damages from the defendant is the same as the reason for awarding damages to the plaintiff').

52 Eg, Birks, above n 6, 34.

- it empowers the plaintiff by giving him or her the certainty of knowing what remedy or remedies are available in particular situations and, in particular, of knowing that such remedies are not dependent on the discretion of the court.

Reasons such as this give the monist view an immediate appeal for they seem to suggest that remedy is performing its natural function, namely, giving effect to the reason for the imposition of liability in the first place. In short, the monist view is 'rights maximising'. Unfortunately, the monist view simply cannot be sustained. Even in the simplest of cases, remedy does tend to do more than mirror, or be a reflex of, the primary right in question with the result that right and remedy are not necessarily in perfect alignment. There are at least five reasons pointing to this conclusion.

First, the remedy granted in any case may serve purposes unrelated to the reason(s) for the imposition of liability in the first place. Exemplary damages are the clearest example of this. Generally parasitic on compensatory damages,[53] the object of exemplary damages is simply to punish, independently of the plaintiff's cause of action,[54] the defendant's 'conscious wrongdoing in contumelious disregard of the plaintiff's rights'.[55] Conduct satisfying this description will, invariably, be different, at least in degree, to the conduct that the plaintiff must prove to establish the cause of action. Another example may be the award of reliance damages in contract,[56] if such damages represent (at least in some cases) a measure independent of expectation damages[57] (rather than a manifestation of them).[58] Expectation damages, the normal recovery in contract, seek to put the plaintiff in the position that he would have obtained if the contract had been performed.[59] So regarded they can thus be seen to mirror the very obligation breached by giving effect to the injunction that promises are to be kept. But it is otherwise with reliance damages, at least so far as they seek simply to compensate the plaintiff for loss suffered by reliance on the defendant's promise, rather than to capture the essence of the obligation breached.

Secondly, because remedy necessarily crystallises at some time after the defendant's breach of the plaintiff's primary rights, there will inevitably be issues

53 See *XL Petroleum (NSW) Pty Ltd v Caltex Oil (Aust) Pty Ltd* (1985) 155 CLR 448, 468–69 (Brennan J).

54 *Gray v Motor Accident Commission* (1998) 196 CLR 1; *Kuddus v Chief Constable of Leicestershire Constabulary* [2002] 2 AC 122, [21] (Lord Slynn), [44] (Lord Mackay), [89] (Lord Hutton), overruling *AB v South West Water Services Ltd* [1993] QB 507. But compare *Harris v Digital Pulse Pty Ltd* [2003] NSWCA 10 (7 February) (Heydon JA) (no power to issue exemplary damages in equity). But see Edelman, J, 'The Meaning of "Damages": Common Law and Equity', Chapter 3 of this volume.

55 *Whitfield v De Lauret & Co Ltd* (1920) 29 CLR 71, 77; *Gray v Motor Accident Commission* (1998) 196 CLR 1, [14] (Gleeson CJ, McHugh, Gummow and Hayne JJ).

56 But only 'may' because this necessarily involves assumptions about the purpose(s) of the law of contract.

57 See *Restatement of the Law Second, Contract 2d*, St Paul: American Law Institute, 1981, sec 349. Consider also *Anglia TV v Reed* [1972] 1 QB 60; *Bowlay Logging Ltd v Domtar Ltd* [1978] WWR 105. But compare *Commonwealth of Australia v Amann Aviation Pty Ltd* (1991) 174 CLR 64.

58 See *Commonwealth of Australia v Amann Aviation Pty Ltd* (1991) 104 ALR 1.

59 Especially *Robinson v Harman* (1848) 1 Exch 850, 855; 154 ER 363, 365 (Parke B).

surrounding the remedy which reflect not the plaintiff's right as such but the fact of its later determination. Issues such as compensation (in the form of interest) for the delay and for the effect of inflationary trends and of foreign currency liabilities on the award are obvious examples. Not only do these issues abound in contract and tort cases,[60] but they are just as capable of arising in cases of autonomous unjust enrichment,[61] while interest may be payable in the context of specific performance and injunction,[62] even as a condition of granting relief.[63] Yet these are often cited as the best illustrations of the congruency of right and remedy.

Thirdly, remedial entitlement is simply not routine on a finding of liability. Orthodox doctrine tells us that remedies derived from common law are available as of right or as a matter of course. The purpose of the doctrine is to emphasise that, unlike the position in equity, common law remedies are not dependent on the court's discretion.[64] But, whatever meaning is attributed to 'discretion',[65] doctrinal orthodoxy cannot conceal the fact that the rules governing common law remedies are often stated at such a level of generality or are often expressed in such weasel words (such as the rules relating to remoteness of damage)[66] or involve, on their face, such flexibility (such as the rules for determining the date of assessment of damages[67] or of assessing the value of a lost chance),[68] that the courts have a wide measure of freedom in the determination of the availability of relief. Indeed, it would not be out of place to say, perhaps loosely, that, even at common law, the courts have wide 'discretion' in determining the availability of remedy.[69]

As everyone knows, the position with respect to equitable remedies is straightforward: they are available only in the discretion of the court. The monist claim that, in this context, equitable discretion has long since withered into some rule-based application, or ought to,[70] is overstated, at least in Australia with its robust equity jurisprudence.[71] It is true that some discretionary factors governing

---

60 See Burrows, above n 31, 107–20, 256–62.

61 Eg, *Westdeutsche Landesbank Girozentrale v Islington LBC* [1996] AC 669 (simple or compound interest?); *Yorkshire Insurance Co v Nisbet Shipping Co Ltd* [1962] 2 QB 330, 340–41 (Diplock J) (gain from foreign currency conversion not recoverable via subrogation), but note the reservations of Megaw LJ in *L Lucas Ltd v Export Credits Guarantee Department* [1973] 1 WLR 914, 924.

62 See Spry, above n 31, 623, n 4 (which draws attention to the inherent equitable jurisdiction to award interest).

63 *Harvela Investments Ltd v Royal Trust Company of Canada (CI) Ltd* [1986] AC 207. See Spry, above n 31, 200–01.

64 Eg, Jordan, F, *Chapters on Equity in New South Wales*, Sydney: Government Printer, 6th edn, 1947, 15.

65 See text to nn 100–04 below.

66 Especially *Parsons (Livestock) Ltd v Uttley Ingham & Co Ltd* [1978] QB 791, 802 (Lord Denning MR, dissenting: 'I cannot swim in this sea of semantic exercises ...'). And see Burrows, above n 31, 55 ('It may well be that considerable discretion must be allowed to the courts, for example in dividing up the type of loss').

67 *Dodd Properties Ltd v Canterbury City Council* [1980] 1 WLR 433 is a particularly good example.

68 Eg, *Howe v Teefy* (1927) 27 SR (NSW) 301.

69 See Beatson, J, *The Use and Abuse of Unjust Enrichment*, Oxford: Clarendon, 1991, 250–51.

70 Eg, Birks, above n 28, 39.

71 Consider *Harris v Digital Pulse Pty Ltd* [2003] NSWCA 10 (7 February) at [15] (Spigelman CJ).

equitable relief have at times been restated as more or less conclusive defences,[72] particularly under the pressure of 19th century positivism.[73] But, even so restated, these defences are often framed in such indeterminate terms or involve such imprecise standards that they remain at least weakly discretionary, reserving to the courts a large measure of freedom in their application.[74] The great 20th century cases dealing with the availability of specific performance or injunctions in situations involving 'personal services'[75] or 'constant supervision'[76] are eloquent testimony to this, as, more generally, is Dr Spry's seminal treatise on equitable remedies.[77]

More tellingly, courts retain discretion to refuse to grant equitable relief in circumstances where its grant would cause an unconscionable hardship to the defendant that is not, in all the circumstances of the case, outweighed by the unfairness to the plaintiff of refusing to grant relief. The discretion here is a strong one, exercisable having regard to the facts and circumstances of each case. Unsurprisingly, it is a discretion applied sparingly. A modern illustration is the decision of Goulding J in *Patel v Ali*:[78] specific performance was refused of a contract relating to the sale of land where, following the conclusion of the contract, the defendant suffered a series of catastrophes in her life which would only be compounded by a court order requiring her to sell her house in a neighbourhood in which she was settled. That hardship was not outweighed by the unfairness to the defendant in refusing relief and confining the defendant to an action in damages. Another illustration is the refusal of specific performance in cases where the defendant would have to lay out large amounts of money in circumstances that would cause him or her considerable financial distress.[79] In these cases, the relegation of plaintiffs to their remedy at law is a clear manifestation of equitable discretion as remedial choice.

Fourthly, equitable remedies are available on terms. This 'moulding' of relief 'may produce a final result not exactly representing what either side would have wished', but rather a result that follows from 'the balancing of competing interests to which, in the particular circumstances, weight is to be given'.[80] The most famous example is from American public law, where structured injunctions can effectively

---

72 Consider, eg, *Ryan v Mutual Tontine Westminster Chambers Association* [1893] 1 QB 116; *JC Williamson Ltd v Lukey and Mulholland* (1931) 45 CLR 282 ('constant supervision').

73 See Berryman, J, 'The Specific Performance Damages Continuum: A Historical Perspective' (1985) 17 Ottawa L Rev 295.

74 Eg, *ANZ Executors and Trustees Ltd v Humes Ltd* [1990] VR 615; *Argyll v Argyll* [1967] Ch 302 ('clean hands' defence).

75 *CH Giles & Co Ltd v Morris* [1972] 1 WLR 307; *Posner v Scott-Lewis* [1987] Ch 25; *Hill v CA Parsons & Co Ltd* [1972] Ch 305.

76 *Patrick Stevedores Operations No 2 Pty Ltd v Maritime Union of Australia* (1998) 195 CLR 1, [78]–[81]; *Co-operative Insurance Society v Argyll Stores (Holdings) Ltd* [1998] AC 1, though note the reservations of Dr Spry, above n 31, 668–75.

77 Above n 31, *passim*.

78 [1984] Ch 283.

79 Eg, *Dowsett v Reid* (1912) 15 CLR 695.

80 *Bridgewater v Leahy* (1998) 194 CLR 457, [127] (Gaudron, Gummow and Kirby JJ). See also *Vadasz v Poineer Concrete (SA) Pty Ltd* (1995) 184 CLR 102, 114.

grant prospective relief against future constitutional violations by spelling out, sometimes in great administrative and other detail, the terms on which the court orders are to be granted and effected.[81] In *Brown v Board of Education*,[82] the US Constitution required the court to declare that segregation was impermissible and this the Supreme Court did in *Brown (No 1)*.[83] Remedially, this ruling would seem to call simply for the court to order desegregation. In *Brown (No 2)*[84] it did so, but on terms. Since immediate desegregation was impossible and could, in any event, give rise to severe social dislocation (such as 'white flight'), the remedy was fashioned so that desegregation was ordered only 'with all deliberate speed'.[85] Some American commentators see this separation of 'right' and 'remedy', in somewhat colourful if not romantic terms, as reflecting a duality in which 'rights' represent principled and normative ideals difficult to attain in the real world. Remedies, by contrast, attempt to close the gap between the ideal and reality by giving as great effect to the right as is possible in all the circumstances.[86]

Fifthly, there are well known situations where the same set of facts gives rise either to more than one cause of action with differing remedial consequences or to one cause of action that supports a variety of remedial responses.[87] In these situations, the monist concedes – and may indeed welcome[88] – the existence of remedial choice, but assigns the choice to the plaintiff rather than to the court (thus avoiding any danger of judicial discretion in choice of remedy).[89] This is consistent with existing authority in cases of concurrent liability in tort and breach of contract[90] and of overlapping remedies in tort and restitution.[91] But it proves nothing as far as remedial choice in general is concerned. Just as a rule of law gives free reign to the plaintiff's choice in these circumstances, so it may well curb them in other circumstances. This is, after all, effectively what happens when the courts refuse to award an equitable remedy and leave the plaintiff to his or her remedy at law.[92] Further, it is arguable that the plaintiff's choice should be limited where the policies underlying the imposition of liability on one possible basis require application notwithstanding the potential existence of liability on some other basis not attracting like policy reasons.[93]

---

81 See Wood, R (ed), *Remedial Law: When Courts Become Administrators*, Amherst, MA: Massachusetts UP, 1990.

82 347 US 483 (1954); 349 US 294 (1955).

83 347 US 483 (1954).

84 349 US 294 (1955).

85 349 US 294, 301 (1955).

86 Especially Gewirtz, P, 'Remedies and Resistance' (1983) 92 Yale LJ 585; Jeffries, JC, 'The Right-Remedy Gap in Constitutional Law' (1999) 109 Yale LJ 87.

87 See Tilbury, above n 23, Ch 2.

88 Eg, Birks, above n 6, 33.

89 Birks, above n 6, 33.

90 *Central Trust Co v Rafuse* [1986] SCR 147; *Henderson v Merrett Syndicates Ltd* [1995] 2 AC 145; *Astley v Austrust Ltd* (1999) 197 CLR 1.

91 The best known cases are *United Australia Ltd v Barclays Bank Ltd* [1941] AC 1 and *Tang Man Sit v Capacious Investments Ltd* [1996] AC 514.

92 See text to nn 78–79 above.

93 Consider Tilbury and Carter, above n 16, 83–93.

Dualism

The necessary disjuncture between right and remedy emerging from the above five considerations inescapably points us in the direction of the dualist analysis of remedies. Justice Hammond's analysis involves two limbs. First, it requires the court to make a context-specific evaluation of the remedy that is the most appropriate in the circumstances. Secondly, it requires that this be done only after the initial determination of whether or not an obligation has been breached. I want to take these two points separately. The first illuminates the nature of the discretion in question. The second prescribes a sequence for the determination of obligation and remedy that, because I do not consider it to be generally correct, suggests a via media – at least at first blush.

Assuming the court has determined there has been a breach of obligation, how does the court make a context-specific determination of the remedy to award in the circumstances? The search is for the most appropriate remedy in a basket in which all potential remedies are available – as is clearly the case in trade practices law[94] and Native Title law.[95] Justice Hammond suggests a number of factors generally relevant to appropriateness. I refer to these, broadly, as 'factors that advance the justice of the case'. According to Justice Hammond, they include: the plaintiff's choice of remedy; the relative severity of the remedy on the parties; economic efficiency; the nature of the right recognised by the court; the moral view to be attached to the interests at stake; the effect of a given remedy on a third party or the public; difficulties of calculation of loss; the practicability of enforcement; and the conduct of the parties.[96] For Professor Birks, whatever the content of the considerations relevant to remedial choice, the objection to them is simply the discretion they invest in courts to select the appropriate remedy. Such a discretion, he argues, is always a strong one, not 'bedded down' by precedent and kept fresh from case to case,[97] though his analogy to sentencing discretion (which is always informed by sentencing principles developed in case law)[98] suggests that it is not completely unbounded. In any event, in Birks' version of dualism, a 'discretionary remedialism' based on intuitive law-finding replaces a certain jurisprudence. This, in turn, threatens the neutrality of decision-making and ultimately the rule of law itself, thereby placing in jeopardy the survival of a pluralist society.

Birks' 'discretionary remedialism' does not reflect the arguments of dualists to the extent that it exaggerates the type of discretion claimed.[99] The word

94 Where the court has access to a 'remedial smorgasbord' provided by the legislation: see *Akron Securities v Iliffe* (1997) 41 NSWLR 353, 364, 366 (Mason P), Trade Practices Act 1974 (Cth) s 87.

95 Especially *Mabo v Queensland (No 2)* (1992) 175 CLR 1, 61 (Brennan J) (a Native Title recognised by the common law may be protected by such legal or equitable remedies as are appropriate to the particular rights and interests established). Compare Native Title Act 1993 (Cth), Pt 2 Div 5 (compensation).

96 Hammond, 'Rethinking Remedies', above n 45, 102–06; Hammond, 'The Place of Damages', above n 45, 223–25.

97 Especially Birks, P, 'Three Kinds of Objection to Discretionary Remedialism' (2000) 29 UWA L Rev 1, 3.

98 See New South Wales Law Reform Commission, *Sentencing* (Discussion Paper 33, 1996), Chapters 3, 5 and 6.

99 See also Tilbury, M, 'Teaching Remedies in Australia' (2001) 39 Brandeis LJ 587, 593–94.

'discretion' is used in many senses in law.[100] It refers, widely, to the choice arising between two or more courses of action (or inaction). That choice may be completely unbounded (that is, it may be an arbitrary or uncontrolled discretion). More commonly, it is limited. Like Justice Hammond, most dualists find that limitation in considerations relevant to the identification of remedial appropriateness in the context. The application of those considerations in any case necessarily requires a balancing of standards, interests or principles. Precedent and tradition will invariably play a part in that application. The force of these factors will vary from time to time along a continuum which, at one extreme, represents strong discretion; at the other, weak discretion. Justice Hammond's considerations of remedial choice are located somewhere along this continuum. Ever since the publication, in 1969, of Kenneth Culp Davis' seminal study of discretion,[101] we have been as aware of the dangers of arbitrariness and inequality that inhere in the exercise of strong discretionary powers as we have of the peril of insufficient individualisation arising from narrow discretionary powers. Finding the right balance is not always easy, but it must surely be one of the burdens of remedies scholarship.

Of course, when remedies are first made available in breach of existing jurisdictional patterns[102] or in new circumstances, the court may be said, inelegantly, to be exercising a strong discretion in developing the law and (perhaps) departing from existing precedent. But, even on their first application, Justice Hammond's approach requires the articulation of the context-specific considerations that compel the court to pick out, from its basket of remedies, the one that is the most appropriate. The court would be exercising a discretion no stronger, and arguably much less strong, than that currently exercised in refusing to grant a plaintiff equitable relief and relegating the plaintiff to an action in damages in circumstances where the grant of equitable relief would cause an unconscionable hardship to the defendant not outweighed, in all the circumstances of the case, by the unfairness to the plaintiff of refusing equitable relief.[103] Further, in the course of time, precedents would be established and these would determine in which contexts particular remedies are, and are not, appropriate. What may have once been a stronger discretion would now be exercised according to established principles. In any event, the assumption that a dualist analysis would effect a radical change in the present law is unfounded, since current law, with its emphasis on the de facto primacy of compensation, 'reflects sensible, painfully evolved insights of enduring value'.[104]

---

100 See especially Waddams, SM, 'Judicial Discretion' (2001) 1 Oxf U Commonwealth LJ 59.

101 See Davis, KC, *Discretionary Justice: A Preliminary Inquiry*, Baton Rouge, LA: Louisiana State UP, 1969.

102 Advocacy of the 'appropriate remedy' approach first occurred in the context of arguments favouring the 'cross-over' of legal and equitable remedies: see Thomas, above n 11, 29–33.

103 See text to nn 78–79 above.

104 Hammond, 'The Place of Damages', above n 45, 229.

A via media?

The other part of Justice Hammond's analysis of dualism states a requirement that the court make a determination of liability before its consideration of remedy. But, as a practical matter, remedial issues are, in the vast majority of cases, considered together with the determination of liability, not after liability has been determined. In civil law, there is generally no equivalent to a sentencing hearing. And, it is impossible to read most common law cases without being conscious of the strong connection between obligation and remedy. Courts generally define obligations in the light of the remedy or remedies available and the remedy in the light of the obligation that is to be found. The one influences, but does not control, the other. As Goulding J put it in *Chase Manhattan Bank NA v Israel-British Bank (London) Ltd*:[105]

> Within the confines of a single legal system, right and remedy are indissolubly connected and correlated, each contributing in historical dialogue to the development of the other, and, save in very exceptional circumstances, it is as idle to ask whether the court vindicates the suitor's substantive right or gives the suitor a procedural remedy as to ask whether thought is a mental or cerebral process. In fact the court does both things by one and the same act.

Many remedies scholars, including Professor Ken Cooper-Stephenson,[106] Professor Paul Gerwitz[107] and Mr David Wright,[108] accept this pragmatic view of the relationship between obligation and remedy. This is hardly surprising since the view represents what Justice Thomas calls the 'descriptive perception of what presently happens in practice'.[109] Although Justice Thomas dismisses the approach as simply 'alluring ... in its self-defined moderation',[110] it does, in my view, accurately state the relationship between obligation and remedy.

The remedy of equitable compensation, which has been developing apace of late, provides a current illustration of how the determination of obligation and remedy are inextricably related. Equitable compensation is, in principle, available in response to a breach of an equitable obligation, such as a breach of fiduciary duty. In *Brickenden v London Loan & Savings*,[111] the Privy Council, on appeal from Canada, held that a breach of fiduciary duty by non-disclosure of material facts did not entitle the person in breach to argue that the victim of the breach had suffered no loss since the victim would have proceeded with the transaction in any event. The nature of the right breached thus dictated that the remedy should not be proscribed by a notion of causation which speculated about what the victim would have done if disclosure had been made. Since then courts,

---

105 [1981] Ch 105.

106 Cooper-Stephenson, K, 'Principle and Pragmatism in the Law of Remedies', in Berryman, J (ed), *Remedies: Issues and Perspectives*, Scarborough: Carswell, 1991, Chapter 1.

107 Gewirtz, above n 86.

108 Especially Wright, D, 'Wrong and Remedy: A Sticky Relationship' [2001] Singapore J Leg Stud 1.

109 Justice Thomas, above n 11, 26.

110 Justice Thomas, above n 11, 26.

111 (1934) 3 DLR 465, 469.

particularly in Canada and New Zealand, have extended the category of 'fiduciary' putting pressure on the *Brickenden* principle by reason of the potentially extensive liability imposed on defendants whose 'trust-like' relationship with the plaintiff rests, in the circumstances, on slender or dubious grounds. There are three possible solutions:

- to hold that, in the light of the *Brickenden* principle, the notion of 'fiduciary' should generally be carefully drawn, an example of remedy influencing the content of right;
- to hold that the *Brickenden* principle does not apply to all fiduciaries, but only to those falling within a carefully defined class and/or who commit particular breaches, an example of a clarification of principle having regard to both the right and remedy involved; and
- to hold that, in the light of the expanded concept of fiduciary, the *Brickenden* principle no longer applies, an example of right influencing the content of remedy.

In *Maguire v Makaronis*,[112] the joint judgment of Brennan CJ, Gaudron, McHugh and Gummow JJ showed a definite preference for the first or second approaches, while rejecting the third. Their Honours said:

> It may be that concern with respect to the apparent rigour of the reasoning in *Brickenden* reflects what has been seen as the tendency in some recent decisions too readily to classify as fiduciary in nature relationships which might better be seen as purely contractual or as giving rise to tortious liability. Whilst that may be so, it is not self-evident that the response should rest in a general denial of the applicability of the reasoning in *Brickenden* to delinquent fiduciaries, particularly solicitors and other professional advisers.

This pragmatic understanding of the relationship between obligation and remedy is not a via media. It is a manifestation of the dualist view without the requirement of an independent determination of obligation and remedy.[113] Once the monist analysis is rejected, as I believe it must be, only an approach conceding control of remedial choice to the court is possible.[114] But the pragmatic understanding of the relationship between obligation and remedy means that any statement of the dualist view is incomplete, even misleading, unless it acknowledges that the nature of the obligation breached is the starting point and generally the most important factor (while not necessarily the only one) determining the appropriate remedy in any particular case. This draws attention to the obvious facts that remedy cannot exist without obligation; that there is an unbreakable relationship between obligation and remedy; and that it is essential to obtain the optimal 'fit' between obligation and remedy.[115] On this view, the appropriate remedy in any particular

---

112 (1997) 188 CLR 449, 474. See further Edelman, J, 'The Meaning of "Damages": Common Law and Equity', Chapter 3 of this volume.

113 Justice Thomas, above n 11, 26.

114 This assumption underlies two important papers by Professor Waters and Justice Finn: see Waters, above n 5, and Finn, P, 'Equitable Doctrine and Discretion in Remedies', in Cornish, W *et al* (eds), *Restitution: Past, Present and Future*, Oxford: Hart, 1998, Chapter 17.

115 See text to nn 15–21 above.

case is that which the court, in a context-specific evaluation, determines best supports the obligation in question and otherwise advances the justice of the case.[116]

REMEDIAL PERSPECTIVE AND THE CLASSIFICATION OF OBLIGATIONS

On the monist approach, a remedial perspective would seem to add nothing to the task of classifying obligations since the remedy is a mere mirror or reflex of the obligation in question, generalised remedial responses being regarded simply as the realisation of rights.[117] In contrast, the dualist approach, which allows an independent operation to remedial law, holds out, at least potentially, a more robust role for remedies in informing the classification of obligations. However, there are strong analytical reasons for believing that the role for a remedies perspective in the classification of obligations itself is limited to providing a check on, or supplement to, the classification of obligations. This is so regardless of whether one is a monist or a dualist.

The reason is simple: remedial concerns are not necessarily the same as those addressed in the imposition of liability. Very roughly, the facts isolated from events that ground liability (and hence determine obligation) include: the conduct of the defendant; the intention with which it was done; the relationship between the parties; and the nature of the damage suffered.[118] So far as remedial concerns in any case focus on matters other than these – such as considerations relevant in the selection of the appropriate remedy[119] – they are unlikely to shed light on the reason(s) for the imposition of liability in the first place and so are unlikely to add anything to the juristic classification of the obligation in question.

Indeed, so far as remedial concerns traverse the very matters relevant to the determination of liability, it may be thought that the remedial perspective can add nothing to what is already known or being investigated. But this would be a mistake, for experience shows that analysis of remedy may reveal insights about obligation that, until then, were hidden. Thus, Professor Stapleton's analysis of the measures of money remedies in contract and tort tells us much about the classification of obligations on the borderland of contract and tort.[120] Just as Fuller and Perdue's famous isolation of the so called 'reliance interest' in damages awards for breach of contract called into question the whole basis of liability in contract, showing that the full enforcement of promises via an award in contract of expectancy damages did not preclude more limited relief based on reliance.[121] As Fuller himself was to write to Karl Llewellyn in 1938: 'I consider the

---

116 This includes (but is not limited to) the proportionality of remedy: Finn, above n 114, 270.

117 See Birks, P, 'The Law of Restitution at the End of an Epoch' (1999) 28 UWA L Rev 13, 17.

118 Consider Birks, P, 'The Concept of a Civil Wrong', in Owen, DG (ed), *Philosophical Foundations of Tort Law*, Oxford: Clarendon, 1995, 37–42 (in the context of tort).

119 See text to n 96 above.

120 Stapleton, J, 'A New "Seascape" for Obligations: Reclassification on the Basis of Measure of Damages', in Birks (ed), above n 3, Chapter 8.

121 Fuller, LL and Perdue, WR, 'The Reliance Interest in Contract Damages' (1936 and 1937) 46 Yale LJ 52 and 374.

contribution made in my article on the reliance interest to lie, not in calling attention to the reliance interest itself, but in an analysis which breaks down the Contract-No-Contract dichotomy and substitutes an ascending scale of enforceability.'[122]

TAXONOMY AND THE LAW OF REMEDIES

Just as taxonomy dictates a classification of obligations, so it may also be thought to require a classification of remedies. As a legal subject, the focus of remedies is on what the plaintiff gets, namely, damages, specific performance, and so on. Looking beyond their form, these nominate remedies are, I suggest, only sensibly classifiable according to their goals or functions.[123] These can be variously described. Prominent among them are compensation, restitution, punishment, prevention and fulfilment. For the dualist, this may seem obvious. Faced with the task of identifying the remedy in the basket that, in all the circumstances, best effects the obligation in question, it is essential to know what the remedies in the basket can do. Even a monist finds it useful, as an aid in classification of obligations, to identify remedial goals as the goals of rights.[124] But there is a hidden danger in the monist approach. Its view that remedy is a mirror or reflex of obligation can lead to a neglect of any taxonomy of remedies – a neglect reinforced by the emphasis since the 19th century on the importance of studying the development of liability.[125]

I suggest that this neglect is evident in the most important contribution that modern taxonomy has made to the law of remedies, namely, the argument for the disassembling of the law of damages. Both Professor Birks[126] and Dr James Edelman[127] argue that all money awards for wrongs should be 'damages' so that the general equation of damages with 'compensation' will come to an end. I say 'general' because it is commonly accepted[128] that damages may, exceptionally, serve other goals, such as punishment in the case of exemplary damages, or restitution in the case of restitutionary damages.[129] If the argument succeeds, these exceptional cases will continue to be referred to as 'damages' and account of profits will also be brought within the category. This will destabilise the law of damages in two important respects. First, in order to avoid their degeneration into a meaningless category and to allow their proper assessment, damages will need to be categorised at least by goal (which is made obvious in the current law by the

122 Cited in Summers, RS, *Lon L Fuller*, Stanford, CA: Stanford UP, 1984, 133.

123 Tilbury, above n 23, [1028]–[1029].

124 Especially Birks, above n 117, 17.

125 See Waters, above n 5, 435.

126 Especially Birks, above n 28, 27–29.

127 Edelman, 'The Meaning of "Damages": Common Law and Equity', Chapter 3 of this volume. See also Burrows, A, 'We Do This at Common Law but That in Equity' (2002) 22 OJLS 1, 15.

128 But see *Harris v Digital Pulse Pty Ltd* [2003] NSWCCA 10 (7 February), [2] (Spigelman CJ, criticising the extension of damages beyond compensation).

129 See McGregor, H, *McGregor on Damages*, London: Sweet & Maxwell, 16th edn, 1997, [12]–[18].

label of the remedy in question)[130] and by effect (since a remedy that is either an account of profits, or one so resembling it as to need differentiation from it, may have a proprietary effect).[131] *Pace* Birks, this is not simply a contrast of measures.[132] Secondly, a determination will have to be made as to whether or not all the current rules of damages (such as the once-and-for-all rule, the rules of remoteness, and so on) are to apply to the monetary remedies now brought within the category, and, if so, how.[133]

The need to confound the law of damages in this way is by no means obvious.[134] If the objective is to promote the greater availability of a range of monetary (or other) remedies that serve purposes other than compensation, that objective should not – and I predict will not – be achieved by a simple relabelling of those remedies as 'damages'. So far as the purpose of doing so is to overcome existing jurisdictional or other restraints that impair the availability or development of monetary remedies other than damages, those restraints must be addressed explicitly[135] rather than by making an attempt to overcome them surreptitiously. So far the objective is to achieve a standardisation of existing, but seemingly analogous, rules applying in differing nominate remedies; the danger of across-the-board standardisation is that it runs the risk of ignoring the nature of the rights in issue and of failing to achieve the optimal 'fit' of obligation and remedy.[136] There are, for example, very sound reasons why the rules of remoteness and causation should vary between equitable compensation and damages if the former are aimed at enforcing the trust that lies at the heart of the fiduciary relationship,[137] while the latter are aimed at simple compensation for loss flowing from a tort.[138] Indeed, pushing the point further, there are equally sound reasons why the rules of causation and remoteness should vary between the tort of negligence on the one hand and the tort of deceit on the other.[139] The rights breached are simply different and call for different remedial responses. We would do well to recall Fullagar J's warning, in another context, of 'the temptation, which is so apt to assail us, to import a meretricious symmetry into the law'.[140]

---

130 As Birks, above n 28, 29–30 admits.

131 Especially *Scott v Scott* (1963) 109 CLR 649, 663–64; *Attorney-General for Hong Kong v Reid* [1994] 1 AC 324 (PC), disagreeing with *Lister v Stubbs* (1890) 45 Ch D 1. And see Edelman, J, *Gain-Based Damages*, Oxford, Hart, 2002, 258–60, 262–64.

132 Birks, above n 28, 29.

133 Consider Edelman, above n 131, 103–11.

134 See also McGregor, H, 'Restitutionary Damages', in Birks, P (ed), *Wrongs and Remedies in the 21st Century*, Oxford: OUP, 1996, Ch 9.

135 Consider *Harris v Digital Pulse Pty Ltd* [2003] NSWCA 10 (7 February 2003).

136 See text to nn 15–21 above.

137 *Canson Enterprises Ltd v Boughton & Co* [1991] 3 SCR 534, especially McLachlin J. And consider Rickett, C, 'Compensation for Loss in Equity – Choosing the Right Horse for Each Course', in Birks, P and Rose, F (eds), *Restitution and Equity*, London: Mansfield, 2000, vol 1, Chapter 10.

138 McGregor, above n 129, [9]–[11].

139 *South Australia v Johnson* (1982) 42 ALR 161, 167–70 (Gibbs CJ, Mason, Murphy, Wilson and Brennan JJ); *Smith New Court Securities Ltd v Citibank NA* [1997] AC 254.

140 *Attorney-General (NSW) v Perpetual Trustee Co (Ltd)* (1952) 85 CLR 237, 285 (affirmed (1955) 92 CLR 113).

CONCLUSION

The modern taxonomy movement has done a great service to the law by reawakening interest in doctrinal research, which, in the 1970s and 1980s, was in danger of being sacrificed on the altar of a number of '-isms'. However, the lesson of the law of remedies with its warning against appealing but misleading standardisations is that taxonomy is not, and cannot ever be, an end in itself. We need constantly to be aware of its limitations.

The first is the real danger of reifying categories, with the potential injustice flowing from decisions impelled by categories, rather than by broader considerations of justice, common sense and the traditions of the common law and its method. In this respect, it may be that the now common four-fold classification of obligations is simply drawn at too high a level of generality to be really useful in a system of law that develops incrementally, primarily by analogical reasoning.[141]

The second is that categories vary from legal system to legal system and may be culture-specific. A noticeable feature of the categories identified in modern taxonomy is that they are derived from Roman law and imposed on the common law with all the difficulties to which that is giving rise. Indeed, we must ask whether a taxonomy that may now be appropriate for England as a member of the European Union is also fitting in Australia. In particular, can an Australian taxonomy ignore the very fundamental impact of the Trade Practices Act 1974 (Cth), especially its all-important s 52, on the common law of Australia?[142]

Finally, and *a priori*, we should not be surprised if it turns out that the classification of law, and its concepts, does not (and cannot) proceed in the same manner, or as smoothly, as classification in the natural sciences. After all, we are not identifying observable species. Law is solely the product of the human mind and, as such, is subject to constant revision, reinterpretation and reinvention.

---

141 Consider, especially, *Harris v Digital Pulse Pty Ltd* [2003] NSWCCA 10 (7 February), [12] (Spigelman CJ) (identification of a principle at a high level of abstraction, from which a rule of particular application is then derived, is incompatible with traditional common law judicial method).

142 See Finn, above n 114, 253–56.

3

THE MEANING OF 'DAMAGES': COMMON LAW AND EQUITY

James Edelman

INTRODUCTION

One of the most common terms in the law is the word 'damages'. In many of the instances in which the term is used, it is interchanged as a synonym for 'loss compensation'. This is potentially very misleading. The simplest lesson from this chapter is that the word 'damages', unqualified, is meaningless. 'Damages' simply means a 'money award' given for a wrong.[1] This definition is justified, explored and its consequences considered in this chapter.[2] One significant consequence of this conclusion is that arbitrary boundaries should not be drawn between money awards for wrongs at common law and in equity. Both are 'damages'.

An immediate objection is that 'damages' is commonly understood by most lawyers and judges as a synonym for 'compensation' for loss. But this common understanding of 'damages' as meaning compensation for loss is dangerous and misleading. It ignores, and/or suggests the illegitimacy (or at least the unique or anomalous nature) of all forms of non-compensatory damages such as exemplary damages, nominal damages, restitutionary damages and disgorgement damages.[3]

This chapter is divided into two parts. The first is concerned with advancing a definition of damages at common law. The thesis is that, at common law, 'damages' means a monetary response to a breach of duty (or 'wrong'). That breach of duty might be a breach of contract or it might be a tort. The importance of this approach is that it involves the rejection of a prevalent view that 'damages' is synonymous with 'compensation'. The thesis of the first part of this chapter is demonstrated by showing the legitimacy of several forms of non-compensatory monetary awards

---

1 Undoubtedly, wrongs exist in equity and tort has no monopoly on the category of wrongdoing. However, determining which causes of action, both at common law and in equity, amount to 'wrongs' is an extremely difficult task and requires detailed consideration to be given to the content of the rival category of 'unjust enrichment'. See Edelman, J, *Gain-Based Damages*, Oxford: Hart, 2002, Chapter 2.

2 For other discussion of this definition, see Birks, P, *Restitution – The Future*, Sydney: Federation, 1992, 23; Birks, P, 'Rights, Wrongs and Remedies' (2000) 20 OJLS 1; Stapleton, J, 'A New "Seascape" for Obligations: Reclassification on the Basis of Measure of Damages', in Birks, P (ed), *The Classification of Obligations*, Oxford: Clarendon, 1997, 193; Cane, P, 'Exceptional Measures of Damages: A Search for Principles', in Birks, P (ed), *Wrongs and Remedies in the Twenty-First Century*, Oxford: Clarendon, 1997, 300.

3 For a full discussion of the existence and nature of the latter two types of damages and their history at common law and in equity, see Edelman, above n 1.

for wrongs that are acknowledged to be forms of 'damages': exemplary damages, restitutionary damages and disgorgement damages.

The second part applies this understanding of damages to equitable wrongs. It is shown that each of these forms of common law damages has counterparts in equity. By this approach, awards of 'equitable compensation' or 'accounts of profits', which respond to wrongs in equity, are really just different forms of 'damages'. This is more than an exercise in nomenclature. With recognition that the former are simply equity's 'compensatory damages' and the latter are equity's 'disgorgement damages', an understanding of rules of causation and remoteness in equity can be developed by comparison with the common law counterparts. This is *not* to say that one set of rules will always apply. The common law has different rules of remoteness for different wrongs and different rules for negligent and intentional conduct. The same is true of equitable wrongs. The nature of the wrong is always relevant. But where the nature of the wrong is the same at common law and in equity (for example, the wrong of fraudulent representation in equity is identical to the tort of deceit) then the same tests of remoteness and causation should apply and analogy is helpful.

One cautionary footnote must be made at the start, to which reference will be made at the conclusion of this chapter. It will be seen that the term 'equitable compensation' is often used in different senses. It is only where it is used properly to mean *compensation for loss suffered from wrongdoing* that it should be recognised as an award of compensatory damages in equity – the doppelganger of common law compensatory damages. The award of 'equitable compensation' which operates to 'restore' a trust estate or 'effect restitution to the trust estate' is not comparable to compensatory damages or to restitutionary damages; it is a different species of money award entirely. It is an award that operates to give effect to a primary obligation to maintain the trust fund.

THE MEANING OF 'DAMAGES'

The compensation illusion

'Compensatory damages' are money awards which aim to compensate a plaintiff for financial loss suffered.[4] So common are compensatory damages at common law that it is sometimes thought, and an illusion sometimes created, that 'where no loss has been suffered no substantial damages of any kind can be recovered'.[5] Dr McGregor begins his seminal treatise on damages with the statement that '[d]amages are pecuniary compensation'.[6] Such a coterminous relation between 'damages' and 'compensation' is axiomatic in German law.[7] However, 'damages'

4 Naturally non-pecuniary loss can be quantified as financial loss and in exceptional circumstances an injury to feelings or enjoyment is also *quantified* as financial loss: *Baltic Shipping Company v Dillon* (1993) 176 CLR 344; *Ruxley Electronics and Construction Ltd v Forsyth* [1996] AC 344 (HL); *Farley v Skinner* [2001] 3 WLR 899.

5 *Stoke-on-Trent City Council v W & J Wass Ltd* [1988] 1 WLR 1406 (CA), 1410 (Nourse LJ).

6 McGregor, H (ed), *McGregor on Damages*, London: Sweet & Maxwell, 16th edn, 1997, 1.

7 §823 BGB; Markesinis, BS, *The German Law of Obligations: Vol II, The Law of Torts: A Comparative Introduction*, Oxford: Clarendon, 3rd edn, 1997, 12.

at common law have never been restricted to compensation for loss. At common law, 'damages' can have goals completely independent from compensation. The term 'damages' at common law means nothing more specific than a monetary award given for a wrong.

The etymology of 'damages' itself is ambiguous, deriving perhaps from the Latin *damnum* or the French *domage*, and suggesting an association with loss.[8] But the earliest legal usages of the term referred to 'damages' in a sense that was clearly not compensatory; including as a reference to a monetary award quantified by three times the loss suffered by the defendant.[9] Yet, a perception that damages were coterminous with compensation began to take root in the 19th century. In modern times, this view is almost inevitably accompanied by a reference to the classic judicial statement of the nature of damages by Lord Blackburn in *Livingstone v Rawyards Coal Co*:[10]

> It is a general rule that, where any injury is to be compensated by damages, in settling the sum of money to be given for reparation of damages you should as nearly as possible get at that sum of money which will put the party who has been injured, or who has suffered, in the same position as he would have been in if he had not sustained the wrong for which he is now getting his compensation or reparation.

This statement has been referred to and paraphrased again and again, sometimes just as 'general principle'[11] but, on other occasions, as a 'fundamental principle'[12] or even as an absolute rule, a 'principle that is absolutely firm, and which must control all else'.[13]

The fallacy and illusion that damages are coterminous with compensation can ironically be seen in *Livingstone v Rawyards Coal Co* itself. The *Livingstone* appeal came to the House of Lords from the First Division in Scotland. Both the appellant and respondent had assumed that coal under the appellant's property was reserved to the respondent and the respondent had mined that coal. The appellant later realised that this was an error. The coal had not been reserved and he sued to recover the value of the profits that the respondent had reaped from his coal.

The appellant argued that the loss suffered was the value of the coal and should be measured by the net profit from the sale of the coal by the respondents. The House of Lords held this was not a compensatory award. The appellant could not have worked the land himself and the only loss to the appellant was the lost ability to offer the right to mine the coal for a price and an element for damage done to the land.[14] However, all members of the House of Lords indicated that

---

8 *Oxford English Dictionary*, 2nd edn, 1989.

9 Act 8 Hen VI, c 9 (1430) *'Le pleyntif recovera ses damages au treble vers le defendant'*.

10 (1880) 5 App Cas 25 (HL), 39 (*'Livingstone'*).

11 *British Transport Commission v Gourley* [1956] AC 185 (HL) 197, 212.

12 *British Westinghouse Electric and Manufacturing Co Ltd v Underground Electric Railways Co of London Ltd* [1912] AC 673 (HL), 689; *Tai Hing Cotton Mill Ltd v Kamsing Knitting Factory* [1979] AC 91 (PC), 104; *Ruxley Electronics and Construction Ltd v Forsyth* [1996] AC 344 (HL), 355, 365–66; *Dodd Properties (Kent) Ltd v Canterbury City Council* [1980] 1 WLR 433 (CA), 451.

13 *Skelton v Collins* (1966) 115 CLR 94, 128.

14 The size of the land was so small that the expense of sinking a pit to mine only that land would have been far greater than the value of the coal.

further (non-compensatory) damages might have been awarded in different circumstances. Each speech acknowledged that if there had been evidence of 'bad faith or sinister intention'[15] the appellant could have recovered the market value of the coal, the very damages award which they had explained was *not* compensatory, without even a deduction for the respondent's cost of working the coal. The nature of such an award is considered below in the sections on disgorgement damages and exemplary damages.

The House of Lords has recently made this point explicitly. The majority of the Law Lords, in *Attorney-General v Blake*,[16] affirmed that the statement concerning compensation in the *Livingstone* case is only a 'general principle'. Lord Nicholls, in the leading speech, stated that 'the common law, pragmatic as ever, has long recognised that there are many commonplace situations where a strict application of this [compensatory] principle would not do justice between the parties'.[17] At common law the award of exemplary damages (and perhaps nominal damages) has been the most prominent (and well recognised) of these situations but the maturity and development of the modern law now commonly also recognises restitutionary damages and disgorgement damages.

The species of non-compensatory damages

If it were correct, as an absolute proposition, that damages are only concerned with compensating for loss, *exemplary* damages, *nominal* damages, *restitutionary* damages and *disgorgement* damages could not exist.[18] None of these awards are concerned to compensate a claimant for loss. The English Law Commission, in its Consultation Paper, *Aggravated, Exemplary and Restitutionary Damages*,[19] observed that, at least empirically, claims that tort law is exclusively concerned with compensation are 'simply false'. The existence of exemplary damages especially, anomalous or not, in different forms for thousands of years[20] shows the express concern of the civil law with matters beyond compensation.

In *Smith New Court Securities Ltd v Scrimgeour Vickers (Asset Management) Ltd*[21] Lord Steyn confronted a submission that the only purpose of the law of tort should be to compensate. In a passage subsequently approved by the Court of Appeal, he said that this is 'far too narrow a view' and preferred the broad view of Professor Glanville Williams.[22] Professor Williams had noted that tort law is concerned with

---

15 *Livingstone* (1880) 5 App Cas 25, 31 (Earl Cairns LC), 34 (Lord Hatherley), 39 (Lord Blackburn).

16 [2001] 1 AC 268 ('*Blake*') (Lord Nicholls; Lords Browne-Wilkinson, Goff and Steyn concurring, Lord Hobhouse dissenting).

17 *Ibid*, 278.

18 This chapter does not consider awards of aggravated damages as there is a powerful view that these are really just another species of compensatory damages: see Law Commission, *Aggravated, Exemplary and Restitutionary Damages* (Law Com No 247, 1997). Cf Beever, A, 'The Structure of Aggravated and Exemplary Damages' (2003) 23 OJLS 87.

19 Consultation Paper No 132, 1993, 5.31.

20 The earliest known case being in Babylonian Law in the Code of Hammurabi about 4000 years ago.

21 [1997] AC 254 (HL).

22 *Ibid*, 280. See *Standard Chartered Bank v Pakistan National Shipping Corp (No 4)* [2000] 3 WLR 1692 (CA), 1724.

the normative role of regulating conduct.[23] Professor Williams listed four broad goals: appeasement, compensation, deterrence and justice,[24] goals also referred to on several recent occasions by the Court of Appeal in New Zealand.[25] Compensation is the most common remedy in tort because it often achieves all of these goals. But as the Canadian Supreme Court has recently recognised, although compensatory damages are usually sufficient to deter wrongdoing, other remedies are needed when compensatory damages cannot so deter.[26]

Nominal damages

Nominal damages have been described by the House of Lords in the following manner:[27]

> A technical phrase which means that you have negatived anything like real damage, but that you are affirming by your nominal damages that there is an infraction of a legal right which, though it gives you no right to any real damages at all, yet gives you the right to the verdict or judgment because your legal right has been infringed.

Dr McGregor has argued that 'nominal damages ... are not really damages' and are unnecessary, either as a 'peg on which to hang costs' as costs are now in the court, or to assert that a right has been infringed since a court can make such an assertion by a declaration.[28] However, whether needed or not, it is an empirical fact that nominal damages still remain to serve these two non-compensatory functions.

Exemplary damages

Exemplary damages 'are essentially different from ordinary [compensatory] damages [because] ... the object ... is to punish and deter'.[29] With this object, 'compensation is not the purpose of exemplary damages. A perceived need for compensation, or further compensation, is not a proper basis for making an award of exemplary damages'.[30] The issue arose before the House of Lords in *Broome v Cassell & Co Ltd*.[31] The *Broome* case involved a jury award of exemplary damages against the publishers and authors of a book that was libellous of a retired navy officer. The defendants had known that passages in the book were libellous prior to publication but had proceeded nevertheless. The trial judge instructed the jury that an award of exemplary damages could be made if the conduct fell within

---

23 Cane, P, *The Anatomy of Tort Law*, Oxford: Hart, 1997, 5.

24 Williams, G, 'The Aims of the Law of Tort' (1951) 4 CLP 137; see also *Restatement of the Law (Second) Torts*, St Paul, MN: American Law Institute, 1979, §901.

25 *Daniels v Thompson* [1998] 3 NZLR 22, 68; *Donselaar v Donselaar* [1982] 1 NZLR 81, 90.

26 *Royal Bank of Canada v W Got & Associates Electric Ltd* (2000) 178 DLR (4th) 385, 394–95.

27 *Owners of the Steamship 'Mediana' v Owners, Master and Crew of the Lightship 'Comet'* [1900] AC 113, 116.

28 McGregor, H, 'Restitutionary Damages', in Birks (ed), *Wrongs and Remedies*, above n 2, 203–04.

29 *Rookes v Barnard* [1964] AC 1129, 1221 ('*Rookes*').

30 *A v Bottrill* [2002] UKPC 44, [65].

31 [1972] AC 1027 ('*Broome*').

Lord Devlin's second limb (where exemplary damages were permissable) in *Rookes v Barnard*, as wrongful conduct cynically aimed at profit where the profit exceeds any loss suffered. The jury held that the conduct was calculated for gain and awarded £15,000 compensatory damages and £25,000 exemplary damages against the defendants. The Court of Appeal affirmed this ruling, as did the House of Lords. In the process of the discussion of exemplary damages, two Law Lords dealt with the question of whether exemplary damages, with their non-compensatory goals, were illegitimate and reached diametrically opposed conclusions.

Lord Reid emphasised that exemplary damages were an 'anomaly' in that they allowed a measure of damages that was not based upon compensation. Lord Reid argued that the 'objections to allowing juries to go beyond compensatory damages are overwhelming'.[32] He only retained exemplary damages out of respect for precedent, considering them too firmly embedded in the law.[33] Lord Wilberforce, however, took the opposite approach considering exemplary damages legitimate and useful. His Lordship emphasised that 'anomaly' is a question-begging word and that the function of tort law is not limited to compensation.[34] This division of views was noted by the English Law Commission,[35] which concluded after detailed consultation, in its final report, that 'it is coherent to pursue the aims of punishment (retribution, deterrence, disapproval) through the civil law'.[36]

In 1998 the High Court of Australia considered the nature of an award of exemplary damages in the context of a question of whether exemplary damages could be awarded in an action for negligence resulting from the intentional driving of a motor car into the appellant. In *Gray v Motor Accident Commission*[37] a central issue was whether a criminal conviction (and hence criminal punishment) was a bar to exemplary damages. However, in the joint judgment of Gleeson CJ, McHugh, Gummow and Hayne JJ, it was affirmed that exemplary damages were not illegitimate simply because of their non-compensatory purposes. In a passage which footnoted and rejected the contrary views of Dr McGregor the following was said:[38]

> There is an appearance of tension between using criminal proceedings to compensate a party who is wronged and using the same proceedings to punish a wrongdoer. But there is a tension only if it is assumed that '... a sharp cleavage between criminal law on the one hand and the law of torts and contract on the other is a cardinal principle of our legal system'.[39] As Windeyer J points out in *Uren*,[39a] the 'roots of tort and crime' are 'greatly intermingled'.

32 *Ibid*, 1087.

33 *Ibid*, 1086.

34 *Ibid*, 1114.

35 *Law Commission*, above n 18, 5.16–5.18.

36 *Ibid*, 5.22.

37 (1998) 196 CLR 1.

38 *Gray v Motor Accident Commission* (1998) 196 CLR 1, 7.

39 Street, H, *Principles of the Law of Damages*, London: Sweet & Maxwell, 1962, 34. See also McGregor, above n 6, [430].

39a *Uren v John Fairfax & Son Pty Ltd* (1966) 117 CLR 118, 149.

In *Kuddus v Chief Constable of Leicestershire Constabulary*,[40] the House of Lords revisited this issue. The question of legitimacy was raised in the context of the rule, established by the Court of Appeal in 1993,[41] and peculiar to England, that exemplary damages are only available for causes of action for which they had been awarded prior to *Rookes v Barnard* in 1964.[42] The tort committed in the *Kuddus* case was misfeasance in public office, a tort for which exemplary damages had not been awarded prior to 1964. In considering whether the cause of action limitation should be rejected, all the Law Lords thought that the logical anterior question was whether exemplary damages were themselves legitimate. If exemplary damages were illegitimate then, if they must be maintained because of respect for precedent, there would be a strong case for retaining the cause of action limitation, however illogical, to limit their availability. However, the parties to the case had agreed that exemplary damages were legitimate and should not be abolished and the argument focused instead upon whether the cause of action test proposed in the *Rookes* case commanded the support of a majority of the Law Lords in the *Broome* case. Nevertheless, all the Law Lords commented upon the anterior question of the legitimacy of exemplary damages.

Three of the Law Lords did not express concluded opinions but were strongly in favour of exemplary damages and their legitimacy. Lord Slynn thought that 'as the law now stands' the agreement of the parties that exemplary damages are legitimate was 'well founded'[43] although he 'did not consider it right to consider reopening the whole question' in that case.[44] Lord Mackay referred to the views of the Law Commission that exemplary damages should not be removed as 'derived from a very full and careful consultation' and the 'best indication ... on the desirability of retaining the power to award exemplary damages'.[45] Lord Hutton referred to decisions from his jurisdiction in Northern Ireland that led him to the conclusion that 'exemplary damages serve a valuable purpose in restraining the arbitrary and outrageous use of executive power and in vindicating the strength of the law'.[46]

Lord Nicholls did express a conclusive opinion. He expressly stated that exemplary damages were legitimate and 'continue to discharge a role, perceived to be useful and valuable, in other common law jurisdictions' and he sided with Lord Wilberforce's powerful views in favour of exemplary damages.[47] More recently, delivering the advice of a majority of the Privy Council in *A v Bottrill*,[48]

---

40 [2001] 2 WLR 1789 ('*Kuddus*').

41 This 'rule' arose from an interpretation of the speeches in *Broome v Cassell & Co* [1972] AC 1027 by the Court of Appeal in *AB v South-West Water Services Ltd* [1993] QB 507. In fact, in *Kuddus*, Lords Slynn, Mackay and Hutton considered that the decisions in *Rookes* and *Broome* had not unequivocally laid down such a 'cause of action' limitation: *Kuddus* [2001] 2 WLR 1789, 1796 (Lord Slynn), 1802 (Lord Mackay), 1815 (Lord Hutton).

42 The Law Commission, above n 18, 4.4, 5.49, referred to this as the 'cause of action' limitation, considering it 'rationally indefensible' to limit the availability of exemplary damages by reference to the existence of precedent prior to the arbitrary date of the decision in *Rookes*.

43 *Kuddus* [2001] 2 WLR 1789, 1791.

44 *Ibid*, 1796.

45 *Ibid*, 1800, 1802.

46 *Ibid*, 1809, 1811.

47 *Ibid*, 1807.

48 [2002] UKPC 44.

Lord Nicholls considerably expanded the scope of exemplary damages by holding that, in New Zealand, intentional wrongdoing or conscious recklessness is not a prerequisite for an award of exemplary damages.

Only Lord Scott in *Kuddus* thought exemplary damages were illegitimate. Lord Scott sided with Lords Devlin and Reid and argued that the award of exemplary damages is an anomaly because it offends against the 'fundamental principle of damages' which is to compensate for loss.[49] Ironically, as will be seen below, Lord Scott acknowledged the need for non-compensatory awards in cases where a defendant has committed a wrong with a view to material gain. However, Lord Scott considered that in such cases profit could be stripped by 'restitutionary damages' (such an award is described in this chapter as 'disgorgement damages').[50] Lord Scott did not explain why such 'restitutionary damages', which also offend against his so called 'fundamental principle of damages', should be legitimate while exemplary damages should not.

Restitutionary damages

Modern English and Australian courts have finally recognised the maturity of restitutionary awards in the law of wrongs and have acknowledged that damages can be awarded which focus not upon the loss to the claimant but upon the gain made by the defendant. One such award of damages which focuses upon gain made by a defendant from a wrong is 'restitutionary damages'.[51] In *Atlantic Shipping & Management v Finagrain*,[52] Toulson J said, in an *ex tempore* judgment, that: 'there seems to have been an assumption that the plaintiffs would be limited in damages to any pecuniary loss which they might be able to prove. If that assumption has been made, it seems to me likely, at the least, that the assumption is wrong.' Similarly, in the course of the leading speech in *Attorney-General v Blake*,[53] Lord Nicholls said that: 'when awarding damages, the law does not adhere slavishly to the concept of compensation for financially measurable loss. When the circumstances require, damages are measured by reference to the benefit obtained by the wrongdoer.'[54]

Restitutionary damages for a wrong are the counterpart to restitution for an unjust enrichment. The award of restitutionary damages, like the award of restitution, focuses upon reversing a transfer of value. In the case of restitutionary damages it is because the transfer was made pursuant to a wrong rather than an unjust enrichment. In *Roxborough v Rothmans of Pall Mall Australia Ltd*,[55] in a joint judgment in the High Court of Australia, Gleeson CJ, Gaudron and Hayne JJ

---

49 [2001] 2 WLR 1789, 1816.
50 *Ibid*, 1819.
51 Edelman, above n 1.
52 (1999) unreported, 15 January (HC).
53 [2001] 1 AC 268 (HL).
54 *Ibid*, 285.
55 (2001) 185 ALR 335, 343 [26]. See also a similar statement in *Hill v Van Erp* (1997) 188 CLR 159, 226–27 (Gummow J).

approved comments of Mason CJ[56] explaining the operation of restitution in the context of unjust enrichment:

> Restitutionary relief, as it has developed to this point in our law, does not seek to provide compensation for loss. Instead, it operates to restore to the plaintiff what has been transferred from the plaintiff to the defendant whereby the defendant has been unjustly enriched ... The subtraction from the plaintiff's wealth enables one to say that the defendant's unjust enrichment has been 'at the expense of the plaintiff'.

The Supreme Court of Canada has made the same point also in relation to unjust enrichment.[57] And where restitutionary damages are given for a wrong, the award operates in exactly the same way as where restitution is given for an action in unjust enrichment. Just as the value transferred might be a monetary benefit or a non-monetary benefit where the award is made in the law of unjust enrichment requiring restitution to reverse that transfer, so too the same effect is made by restitutionary damages in the law of wrongs. As Mance LJ, in the leading judgment in the English Court of Appeal in *Experience Hendrix v PPX Enterprises Inc*, said:[58]

> [In cases of restitutionary damages] the law gives effect to the instinctive reaction that, whether or not the appellant would have been better off if the wrong had not been committed, the wrongdoer ought not to gain an advantage for free, and should make some reasonable recompense.

In the case of money wrongfully transferred from a plaintiff to a defendant, restitutionary damages were often pleaded as an action in *indebitatus assumpsit* for money had and received. As the Lord Chancellor stated in *United Australia v Barclays Bank Ltd*,[59] in cases involving wrongdoing 'an action in [*indebitatus*] *assumpsit* ... lies only because the acquisition of the defendant is wrongful and there is thus an obligation to make restitution'.

Non-monetary transfers could also be reversed with an award of restitutionary damages. Different labels were again often used. One example is *Yakamia Dairy Pty Ltd v Wood*.[60] The defendants had wrongfully depastured cattle upon land belonging to the plaintiff. The District Court of Western Australia held that the plaintiff had suffered no financial loss and could therefore recover no substantial damages. The plaintiff appealed directly to the Full Court of the Supreme Court of Western Australia and the court unanimously affirmed a line of authority that allowed recovery based upon a 'wayleave' although no financial loss had been suffered. It was held that a 'reasonable remuneration' should be awarded to represent the value of the beneficial use wrongfully transferred from the plaintiff.[61]

---

56 *Commissioner of State Revenue (Vict) v Royal Insurance Australia Ltd* (1994) 182 CLR 51, 75.

57 *Citadel General Assurance Co v Lloyds Bank Canada* [1997] 3 SCR 805, 824 (La Forest J, delivering the judgment of himself, Gonthier, Cory, McLachlin, Iacobucci and Major JJ).

58 [2003] EWCA Civ 323, [26].

59 [1941] AC 1, 18. See also 34 (Lord Romer): 'What was waived by the judgment was not the tort but the right to recover [compensatory] damages for the tort.'

60 [1976] WAR 57 (SCWA). For a more recent example concerning the tort of passing off, see *Irvine v Talksport Ltd* [2003] 2 All ER 881.

61 *Ibid*, 58 (Jackson CJ).

Historically, these restitutionary damages were described by numerous different labels: wayleaves, common counts of *indebitatus assumpsit*[62] (as well as *quantum meruit* and *quantum valebant* awards),[63] *mesne* profits, reasonable royalties, monetary rescission or even awards simply labelled 'damages' and assessed according to a 'user principle'. The Supreme Court of Canada has also referred to awards of restitutionary damages as 'the monetary equivalent of a rescissionary remedy',[64] and the United States Supreme Court has described them as 'rescissory damages'.[65] Each of these awards, when made for wrongs, operated to reverse wrongful transfers.[66]

Much can be said in support of the legitimacy of restitutionary damages but that is beyond the scope of this chapter.[67] It suffices to observe here that the form of gain-based damages known as 'restitutionary damages' is well recognised in England[68] and in Australia.[69] In *Hospitality Group Pty Ltd v Australian Rugby Union Ltd*[70] in the majority joint judgment of Hill and Finkelstein JJ in the Full Federal Court of Australia it was said that:

> So far as pecuniary remedies are concerned, it should be noted that damages may be either compensatory or non-compensatory. In the latter category are contemptuous damages, nominal damages, exemplary damages and restitutionary damages. Restitutionary damages may be limited to cases involving the misuse of a plaintiff's property.[71]

Although their Honours were, with respect, right to recognise 'restitutionary damages', the limitation they suggested has never been imposed by any of the different labels used to effect restitutionary damages. In the common counts of *indebitatus assumpsit* courts made such awards to effect restitutionary damages,

---

62 Lawes, E, *Practical Treatise on Pleading in Assumpsit*, London: W Reed, 1810, 418–503.

63 From the mid-19th century these forms were pleaded as *indebitatus assumpsit*: Baker, JH, 'The History of Quasi-Contract in English Law', in Cornish, WR *et al* (eds), *Restitution: Past Present and Future*, Oxford: Hart, 1998, 37, 41.

64 *Hodgkinson v Simms* [1994] 3 SCR 377, 384, also referring to this approach as 'restitutionary': [1994] 3 SCR 377, 383.

65 *Randall v Loftsgaarden*, 478 US 647, 657 (1986).

66 Although, as seen below, the count of money had and received in *indebitatus assumpsit* was also sometimes used in the 20th century as disgorgement damages.

67 See, eg, Edelman, above n 1, Ch 3.

68 See, for instance, recognition of restitutionary damages in *Freeman v Niroomand* (1996) 52 Con LR 116 (CA) (Millett LJ); *Porter v Magill* [2000] 2 WLR 1420 (CA), 1497 (Robert Walker LJ); *Gondal v Dillon Newsagents Ltd* [2001] RLR 221; *Attorney-General v Blake* [1998] Ch 439 (CA), 457–59; *Jaggard v Sawyer* [1995] 1 WLR 269 (CA), 281 (Bingham MR); *Kuddus* [2001] 2 WLR 1789, 1819 (Lord Scott); *Alfred McAlpine Construction Ltd v Panatown Ltd* [2001] 1 AC 518, 588 (Lord Millett). Other cases have referred to the award simply as 'restitution' for the wrong: see, eg, *Ministry of Defence v Ashman* [1993] 2 EGLR 102 (CA), 106; *Ministry of Defence v Thompson* [1993] 2 EGLR 107 (CA).

69 *Gaba Formwork Contractors v Turner Corp* (1991) 32 NSWLR 175; *Commissioner of State Revenue (Vic) v Royal Insurance Australia Ltd* (1994) 182 CLR 51, 73 (Mason CJ); *Winterton Constructions Pty Ltd v Hambros Australia Ltd* (1991) 101 ALR 363 (FCA), 374 (Gummow J); *Bryson v Bryant* (1992) 29 NSWLR 188, 222 (Sheller JA); *LPJ v Howard Chia Investments Pty Ltd* (1990) 24 NSWLR 499, 505 (Hodgson J); *Hospitality Group Pty Ltd v Australian Rugby Union Ltd* (2001) ATPR 41-831 (Hill and Finkelstein JJ); *Anthanasopoulos v Moseley* (2001) 52 NSWLR 262.

70 (2001) ATPR 41-831 ('*Hospitality Group*').

71 *Surrey County Council v Bredero Homes Ltd* [1993] 1 WLR 1361.

irrespective of any interference with property in cases such as fraud and deceit[72] or for the value of work and labour transferred due to the tort of 'seduction'.[73] Recently restitutionary damages have been awarded for a breach of contract.[74]

Although some commentators also support this view that restitutionary damages are only available for proprietary torts,[75] it is also logically flawed.[76] Restitutionary damages for wrongs are the corresponding money award to restitution in unjust enrichment (such as for a mistaken payment, duress or failure of consideration).[77] In many instances a set of facts is capable of alternative analysis as either restitutionary damages for a wrong or restitution for a cause of action in unjust enrichment.[78] But there is no 'property' restriction where restitution is given for unjust enrichment. For example, an award of restitution was allowed in *Pavey & Matthews Pty Ltd v Paul*[79] for unjust enrichment where the defendant refused to make payment of a reasonable remuneration for building work done as promised. The award of restitution of the value of the work done by builders (under an unenforceable contract) was made despite the fact that the case involved no interference with the property of the defendant. In the same way there is no justification for such a restriction on restitutionary damages for a *wrong*.[80] Finally, even if there were no authority in relation to non-proprietary torts, it would be anomalous to allow restitutionary damages for a tort involving interference with property (such as trespass) even when committed innocently, but to deny recognition for a tort such as deceit because the deceit did not interfere with the defendant's property.

Disgorgement damages

The final form of non-compensatory damages to be examined here is damages that operate to strip – or disgorge – profits wrongfully made. I have discussed this remedy, as well as restitutionary damages, in detail in another work.[81] This form of damages can be referred to as 'disgorgement damages'. In *Dubai Aluminium Co Ltd v Salaam*,[82] Lord Millett said that 'it is increasingly recognised today that the ends of justice sometimes go beyond compensating a plaintiff for his loss and may extend to stripping a defendant of his profits'.

---

72 *Russell v Bell* (1842) 10 M & W 340, 352; 152 ER 500; *Hill v Perrott* (1810) 3 Taunt 274; 128 ER 109; *Bristow v Eastman* (1794) 1 Esp 172, 173; 170 ER 317; *Holt v Ely* (1853) 1 E & B 794, 799; 118 ER 634, 636; *Clarke v Dickson* (1858) El Bl & El 148; 120 ER 463.

73 *Lightly v Clouston* (1808) 3 Taunt 112; 127 ER 774; *Foster v Stewart* (1814) 3 M & S 191; 105 ER 582. This was the precursor to the modern tort of interference with contractual relations. For a view that this tort is a 'proprietary tort' (although also arguing that restitutionary damages are not confined to such torts), see Cunnington, 'Contract Rights as Property Rights', Chapter 10 of this volume.

74 *Experience Hendrix LLC v PPX Enterprises Ltd* [2003] EWCA Civ 323.

75 See, eg, Jackman, I, 'Restitution for Wrongs' [1989] CLJ 302.

76 See also the discussion of Cunnington in Chapter 10 of this volume.

77 *David Securities Pty Ltd v Commonwealth Bank of Australia* (1992) 175 CLR 353, 379.

78 See, eg, *Kettlewell v Refuge Assurance Company* [1908] 1 KB 545 (CA).

79 (1987) 162 CLR 221.

80 As for equitable wrongs, see below.

81 See, eg, Edelman, above n 1, Chapter 3.

82 [2003] 1 All ER 97, 135, [164].

The term 'disgorgement damages' has only been used recently in judicial decisions.[83] It is used in this chapter as a term that encompasses all profit-stripping awards at common law and in equity. For common law wrongs it includes awards described as an 'account of profits', the 'formula'[84] of a liability to account for profits as a 'constructive trustee',[85] as well as awards sometimes described as 'money had and received'[86] and on other occasions simply as 'damages'.[87] Lord Millett has suggested that, at common law, the term 'disgorgement damages' is preferable to 'account of profits': 'The Court makes the order because it is prepared to make an award of gain-based damages.'[88]

Disgorgement damages differ from exemplary damages in that an award disgorging only the profit only operates to strip the profit made from the wrong and does not leave the defendant any worse off. As a result, disgorgement damages are not subject to all the objections to exemplary damages such as indeterminacy. Since the non-compensatory award of exemplary damages has been recognised as legitimate, there cannot be any objection to gain-based damages awards such as disgorgement damages, which are subject to fewer objections.

In the House of Lords case of *Attorney-General v Blake*,[89] disgorgement damages were recently awarded for a breach of contract. In that case the House of Lords awarded an account of profits for a breach of contract committed by the British double-agent George Blake. Blake had written, in breach of secrecy

---

83 See *Hospitality Group Pty Ltd v Australian Rugby Union Ltd* (2001) ATPR 41-831; see also *Experience Hendrix LLC v PPX Enterprises* [2002] EWHC 1353 (QB), [50] ('I decline to order an assessment of damages, either on a compensatory approach or an assessment of profit basis.')

84 This phrase in such circumstances is now recognised as merely a formula recognising a liability to account for profits rather than any true proprietary relief in such circumstances: *Giumelli v Giumelli* (1999) 196 CLR 101, 112 (Gleeson CJ, McHugh, Gummow and Callinan JJ); *Dubai Aluminium Co Ltd v Salaam* [2003] 1 All ER 97, 135, [164]; *Coulthard v Disco Mix Club Ltd* [2000] 1 WLR 707, 731 (this 'type of trust is merely the creation by the court … to meet the wrongdoing alleged: there is no real trust and usually no chance of a proprietary remedy'); *Selangor United Rubber Estates Ltd v Cradock (No 3)* [1968] 1 WLR 1555, 1582 (Ungoed-Thomas J: the expressions are 'nothing more than a formula for equitable relief').

85 *Hospital Products Ltd v US Surgical Corp* (1984) 156 CLR 41 (Deane J); *Reid-Newfoundland Co v Anglo-American Telegraph Co Ltd* [1912] AC 555 (PC); *Lake v Bayliss* [1974] 1 WLR 1073. These cases involved profit-stripping following a breach of contract.

86 Especially in cases described as 'fraud' or the 'tort of fraud' at common law: *Reading v Attorney-General* [1951] AC 507 (HL); *Mahesan S/O Thambiah v Malaysian Government Officers Co-operative Housing Society* [1979] AC 374 (PC), 376; *Armagas Ltd v Mundogas SA* [1986] AC 717, 742–43 (Robert Goff LJ); decision affirmed [1986] 1 AC 717 (HL); *Petrotrade Inc v Smith* [2000] 1 Lloyd's Rep 486, 490; *Federal Sugar Refining Co v US Sugar Equalization Board Inc*, 268 F 575 (DCNY, 1920). For an argument that all common law awards for 'fraud' should really be seen as awards for 'deceit' rather than a broader concept of fraud, see Handley, K, 'Civil Liability for Bribery (No 2)' (2001) 117 LQR 536.

87 *Powell v Aiken* (1858) 4 K & J 343, 351; 70 ER 144, 147 (the award of 'damages' for trespass effected 'an account of profit realised … by the working of coal to give relief in respect of wrongs attended with profit to the wrongdoer' (Sir Page Wood V-C)); *Jegon v Vivian* (1871) LR 6 Ch App 742, 762 (the 'damages' award stripped profits because 'this Court never allows a man to make a profit by a wrong' (Lord Hatherley LC)). See also *Attorney-General v Blake* [2001] 1 AC 268, 284 citing cases including *British Motor Trade Association v Gilbert* [1951] 2 All ER 641 for other awards of 'damages' which operated to strip profits.

88 Lord Millett, 'Book Review: *Gain-based Damages*' (2003) 4 Oxf U Commonwealth LJ 291. See also Elliot, S and Edelman, J, 'Target Holdings Considered in Australia' (2003) 119 LQR 545.

89 [2001] 1 AC 268.

provisions in his employment contract with the Crown, a book that discussed his time as an agent for the Secret Intelligence Services. Whilst in hiding in Russia, Blake was sent profits from the publishers (who were joined as a third party). But the Crown had suffered no loss from Blake's disclosures. The information was no longer confidential. In delivering the leading speech, Lord Nicholls stated that 'normally' the remedies of compensatory damages, injunctions and specific performance will be the only remedies available for a breach of contract. However, 'in exceptional cases, where those remedies are inadequate' the question of accounting for profits will arise.[90] Lord Nicholls considered that it would be 'difficult and unwise' to be too specific in providing the exact circumstances in which disgorgement should be available for a breach of contract[91] and Lord Steyn considered that the 'remedy for disgorgement of profits against a contract breaker [is] best hammered out on the anvil of concrete cases'.[92] However, Lord Nicholls did lay out broad guidelines which suggested that an account of profits would be available where two conditions were satisfied.[93]

Unfortunately in the *Hospitality Group* case the majority of the Full Federal Court, although accepting that damages for torts can be non-compensatory, held that:

> ... under presently accepted principles, an injured plaintiff cannot claim a windfall to prevent a wrongdoer profiting from his wrong, except in those cases where exemplary damages are available and it is proper that illicit profits are taken into account in assessing the quantum of the award.[94]

This is simply incorrect. Disgorgement damages have long been available for torts. The problem is that they have rarely been referred to by a single term. Sometimes they are called an 'account of profits';[95] on other occasions they are hidden within a reference simply to 'damages' or 'money had and received'.[96] In this respect the dissent of Emmett J in the *Hospitality Group* case is more satisfying. Although conflating disgorgement damages and 'restitutionary damages' (a different remedy which is discussed above), Emmett J would have allowed

---

90 *Ibid*, 285.

91 *Ibid*.

92 *Ibid*, 291.

93 The claimant must have a 'legitimate interest in performance' and other monetary remedies must be 'inadequate'. These conditions are examined in detail in Edelman, above n 1, Chapter 5. The reference to 'inadequacy' should be seen in the same sense as the term is used by Lord Nicholls in *A v Bottrill* [2002] UKPC 44, [22]: 'Exceptionally, a defendant's conduct in committing a civil wrong is so outrageous that an order for payment of compensation is not an adequate response. Something more is needed from the court, to demonstrate that such conduct is altogether unacceptable to society.'

94 Referring to *McMillan v Singh* (1984) 17 HLR 120, 125 and *John v MGN Ltd* [1997] QB 586, 619.

95 One exception is a case where an account was allowed for a trespass: *Phillips v Homfray* (1883) 24 Ch D 439 (CA). This case is discussed in detail in Gummow, W, 'Unjust Enrichment, Restitution and Proprietary Remedies', in Finn, P, *Essays on Restitution*, Sydney: Law Book Co, 1990, 60–67; Swadling, W, 'The Myth of *Phillips v Homfray*', in Swadling, W and Jones, G (eds), *The Search for Principle: Essays in Honour of Lord Goff of Chieveley*, Oxford: OUP, 1999, 277.

96 See above nn 86 and 87.

disgorgement of profits in order to deter that plaintiff or others from committing the tort of inducing breach of contract. He referred to a case in the United States in which an award of 'money had and received' was given to strip profits made in consequence of the tort of inducing breach of contract,[97] and (although describing them as awards of an 'account of profits') referred to several English cases where an award of money had and received was given for the tort of inducing breach of contract.[98]

DAMAGES IN EQUITY

The first part of this chapter has shown that the link between 'damages' and 'compensation' must be broken, and that 'damages' can mean nothing more than a money award given for a wrong. Thus, we have (at least) 'compensatory' damages, 'exemplary' damages, 'nominal' damages, 'restitutionary' damages and 'disgorgement' damages. This part focuses upon equity. It is shown that the same type of damages awards exist in equity and are regularly awarded for equitable wrongs. The difficulty that will be seen is that although courts are now acknowledging that 'damages are a monetary payment awarded for the invasion of a right' the sentence is often concluded with 'at common law'.[99]

Are equitable remedies more 'discretionary' or 'flexible' than common law remedies?

The most common form of argument that equitable remedies are somehow different and should not be assimilated in any classification with the common law is that they are 'discretionary' and 'flexible' and focus upon 'justice to the individual'.[100] It is argued that equitable remedies are insufficiently settled for a successful plaintiff to claim a right to any equitable remedy in the same way as a plaintiff has a right to 'damages' at common law.[101]

The common assumption that equity has a degree of flexibility that the common law does not possess is perhaps related to the famous maxim that equity is as long as the Chancellor's foot. This maxim is generally attributed to John Selden who opined the view that this ridiculous measure would be the case if the measure of equity *were to be* based only upon the Chancellor's conscience.[102] Lord

---

97 *Federal Sugar Refining Co v United States Sugar Equalisation Board*, 268 F 575 (SDNY, 1920), 582.

98 Emmett J referred to the cases of *Lightly v Clouston* (1808) 3 Taunt 112; 127 ER 774; *Foster v Stewart* (1814) 3 M & S 191; 105 ER 582. Although he was, with respect, quite right to say that these cases were concerned with the benefit to the wrongdoer from the tort, they were cases of the common count of work done and are better seen as restitutionary damages.

99 *Canson Enterprises Ltd v Boughton & Co* (1991) 85 DLR (4th) 129, 145 (La Forest J).

100 *Day v Mead* [1987] 2 NZLR 443, 451; Finn, P, 'Equitable Doctrine and Discretion in Remedies', in Cornish *et al* (eds), above n 63, 251, 267 *et seq*; cf Birks, P, 'The Remedial Constructive Trust' (1999) 115 LQR 681.

101 Gummow, Justice WMC, 'Equity: Too Successful?'(2003) 77 ALJ 30, 41. Cf Birks, P, 'Rights, Wrongs and Remedies' (2000) 20 OJLS 1, 16; Birks, above n 100, 684–88.

102 Pollock, F (ed), *Table Talk of John Selden*, London: Selden Society, 1927, 43.

Eldon was well aware of this when he stated, in 1818, that 'nothing would inflict on me greater pain in quitting this place than the recollection that I had done anything to justify the reproach that the equity of this court varies like the Chancellor's foot'.[103]

Despite this, rhetoric that equitable remedies are 'discretionary' is common. But on close examination, this rhetoric is usually qualified by an acknowledgment that such 'discretion' is not a pure 'discretion' but is exercised according to fixed rules. As Harman LJ has noted, 'since the time of Lord Eldon ... equitable jurisdiction is exercised only upon well-known principles'.[104] Thus, 'the jurisdiction to compel specific performance [which has] always been treated as discretionary [is] confined within the well-known rules'.[105] Or 'the discretion [to grant an injunction] is not one to be exercised according to the fancy of whoever is to exercise the jurisdiction of equity'.[106] Again, 'although an account of profits, like other equitable remedies, is said to be discretionary, it is granted or withheld according to settled principles'.[107]

Further, the *rhetoric* of discretion does not set equitable remedies apart from the common law. The fear of an unguided discretion has also long existed at common law. Coke wrote of 'the incertain and crooked cord of discretion'.[108] In relation to exemplary damages at common law, the High Court of Australia has observed that: 'reported cases usually speak of a "discretion" to award exemplary damages. Standing alone, such a description, even if followed by the expression "to be exercised judicially", is of little assistance. At best, it invites attention to what are the criteria that are to inform the exercise of that discretion'.[109]

The point of the remaining part of this chapter is to show that the compensatory, disgorging and restitutionary money awards for wrongs in equity should be considered alongside their common law counterparts and likewise recognised as species of 'damages'. Such an approach will have the great benefit that, when considering rules of causation and remoteness, courts can strive toward the desirable goal of '*adopting a single rule (applicable both at law and in equity)*'[110] that treats such like responses alike. As Professor Hohfeld argued almost 100 years ago, to treat equity as a system of law to be considered separately and independently from the common law is 'unscientific, both from the point of view of analysis and from that of educational expediency'.[111]

---

103 *Gee v Prichard* (1818) 2 Swan 402, 414.

104 *Bridge v Campbell Discount Co Ltd* [1961] 2 WLR 596, 605.

105 *Ryan v Mutual Tontine Westminster Chambers Association* [1893] 1 Ch 116, 126.

106 *Doherty v Allman* (1878) 3 App Cas 709, 728–29.

107 *Warman International Ltd v Dwyer* (1995) 182 CLR 544, 559.

108 Coke, 4 Inst 41.

109 *Gray v Motor Accident Commission* (1998) 196 CLR 1, 10 (Gleeson CJ, McHugh, Gummow and Hayne JJ), footnotes omitted.

110 *Tinsley v Milligan* [1994] 1 AC 340, 375.

111 Hohfeld, WN, 'Relations between Equity and Law' (1913) 11 Mich LR 537, 538 quoting from Professor Cook who referred to the fact that equitable 'modifications' such as specific performance should be taught as part of contract and not as part of 'equity'.

Damages in equity

Compensatory damages

It is sometimes thought that the award of compensatory damages in equity was only made possible by the passage of Lord Cairns' Act in 1858.[112] That Act provided that where the Court of Chancery had jurisdiction to entertain an application for an injunction or for specific performance the court could award damages either in addition to or in substitution for the injunction or specific performance. In 1980 the House of Lords affirmed that such damages were to be measured in the same way as damages at common law[113] and Lord Nicholls has recently said that these 'damages' under Lord Cairns' Act, like common law 'damages', include both compensatory damages and gain-based damages.[114]

But equity was not historically so restricted. From the time of Richard II, the Chancellor awarded compensatory damages in equity.[115] Between 1559 and 1646, Tothill noted 11 cases in the courts of Chancery where 'damages' were awarded to compensate for loss.[116] But the notion developed that these money awards in equity were not 'damages' because over time the courts of Chancery used different language and different procedures to describe and give effect to awards which had precisely the same functions and goals as common law damages. For example, a trustee was required to pay over money in order to put beneficiaries in the position as if a breach had not occurred if trust money had been lost as a result of deliberate or careless breaches of trust.[117] Although this action was 'analogous to proceedings at law'[118] for negligence against a mortgagee or executor,[119] the award was described as a remedy consequent upon an 'account for wilful default' and never described as 'damages'. After the decision of Lord Eldon in *Todd v Gee*[120] in 1810, the view became commonplace that if a suitor wanted 'damages' he or she must seek them at common law only.

At this point one qualification should be made. There *was* one common money award in equity which did *not* correspond to any form of common law damages. An award of money following an account of administration in common form (a

---

112 21 & 22 Vict c 27 s 2. Eg, *Phillips v Homfray* (1871) LR 6 Ch App 770, 780 (Lord Hatherley LC: 'this Court has now the power to grant compensation').

113 *Johnson v Agnew* [1980] AC 367, 400 (Lord Wilberforce).

114 *Attorney-General v Blake* [2001] AC 268, 281 (Lord Nicholls), citing *Bracewell v Appleby* [1975] Ch 408 (CA) and *Jaggard v Sawyer* [1995] 1 WLR 269 (CA).

115 17 Ric II c 6 (1393). For the history of the medieval jurisdiction of Chancery awards of damages until the mid-19th century reforms, see McDermott, PM, 'Jurisdiction of the Court of Chancery to Awards Damages' (1992) 108 LQR 652.

116 Tothill (1559–1646) 51–52; 21 ER 121.

117 Stannard, JH, 'Wilful Default' [1979] Conv 345; *Re Chapman, Cocks v Chapman* [1896] 2 Ch 763; *Armitage v Nurse* [1998] Ch 241, 252 (Millett LJ: 'A trustee is said to be accountable on the footing of wilful default when he is accountable not only for money which he has in fact received but also for money which he could with reasonable diligence have received. It is sufficient that the trustee has been guilty of a want of ordinary prudence.')

118 *Ex Parte Bax* (1751) 2 Ves Sen 388; 28 ER 248.

119 *Bulstrode v Bradley* (1747) 3 Atk 582; 26 ER 1136; *Re Salmon* (1889) 42 Ch D 351, 369.

120 (1810) 17 Ves 273, 277–78; 34 ER 107.

'*common* account', described in the later 19th century as 'restitution to the trust estate') did not require any pleading of fault or loss and was an award concerned with performance of the trustee's duty. It was not concerned with compensation for any loss suffered by the beneficiaries or the trust. The award requiring payment of money found owing on a 'common account' was equity's equivalent to the common law action for 'debt' arising from a contract. It required that the defendant be called upon to account for any deficiency in the trust[121] which the defendant had promised to maintain and involved an account of the property actually received and what had become of it.[122] If the account showed that money had been improperly disbursed (falsification) or that money had been received for which account had not been made (surcharge) a money award for those missing sums was given.

Although the award of the common account often results in the same quantum as a compensatory award its overt concern is 'performance' of the trustee's promise to maintain the trust estate or apply the fund in an authorised manner. Questions of loss are irrelevant in the same way as they are irrelevant in an action at common law for a debt owing arising from a contractual promise. As Justice Gummow has noted, 'the fundamental point remains that the obligation to make restitution which is imposed on defaulting trustees is of a more absolute nature than the common law obligations to pay damages for tort or breach of contract'.[123] Questions of causation and remoteness that enter into damages assessments at common law are therefore as irrelevant to this equitable remedy as they are in an action for a contractual debt.[124] As Bacon VC has stated, this obligation 'cannot be called a tort, nor is this an action for damages'.[125] A related point is made by Professor Tilbury in this volume.[126] Professor Tilbury endorses the reasoning of the joint judgment of the High Court in *Maguire v Makaronis*,[127] tentatively supporting the decision of the Privy Council in *Brickenden v London Loan & Savings*,[128] which held that 'but-for' causation was irrelevant to a breach of fiduciary duty. Where the remedy sought is a common account for restoration or performance of a trustee's obligations to maintain the trust fund or apply it as authorised, then, naturally, 'but-for' notions of

121 *Partington v Reynolds* (1858) 4 Drew 253, 255–56; 62 ER 98. ('There are two different modes of accounting ... and accordingly there are two different forms of decree in use to compel him to account ... They proceed on totally distinct grounds. The one supposes no misconduct [common account]; the other is entirely grounded in misconduct.' Kindersley V-C.) See also Haddan, TH, *Outlines of the Administrative Jurisdiction of the Court of Chancery*, London: W Maxwell, 1862, 229–42; Elliott, S, 'Remoteness Criteria in Equity' (2002) 65 MLR 588.

122 *Read's Case* (1603) 5 Co 33b, 34a; 77 ER 103; *Pybus v Smith* (1790) 1 Ves 189; 30 ER 294.

123 Gummow, W, 'Compensation for Breach of Fiduciary Duty', in Youdan, TG (ed), *Equity, Fiduciaries and Trusts*, Toronto: Carswell, 1989, 71; *Ferrari v Ferrari Investments (Townsville) Pty Ltd* [1999] QCA 230.

124 *Re Windsor Steam Coal Co (1901) Ltd* [1929] 1 Ch 151 (CA); *Magnus v Queensland National Bank* (1888) 37 Ch D 466 (CA).

125 *Flintcroft's Case* (1882) 21 Ch D 519 (CA) 527. See also *Re Windsor Steam Coal Co (1901), Ltd* [1929] 1 Ch 151 (CA) 156, 166–67.

126 Tilbury, M, 'Remedies and the Classification of Obligations', Chapter 2 of this volume.

127 (1997) 188 CLR 449, 474.

128 (1934) 3 DLR 465, 469.

causation should not apply. No one would ever suggest that such causation tests would apply in an action seeking recovery of a liquidated contractual debt. These are not instances where the remedy is referable to the 'wrong' of breach of trust (or breach of contract).

The most powerful example of compensatory damages in equity can be seen in cases of fraudulent misrepresentation. In such cases, courts of equity have long acknowledged that their awards of compensation were identical to compensatory damages at common law.[129] In fraudulent misrepresentation cases, courts of common law and chancery courts had concurrent jurisdiction.[130] Although there was some conflict between different tests at common law and in equity it was accepted that it was no objection to an action for fraudulent misrepresentation in equity that the same cause of action arose at common law, 'for in cases of fraud … the court of equity has a concurrent jurisdiction with the common law'.[131] In *Peek v Gurney*,[132] for example, Lord Chelmsford stated that the loss suffered as a result of fraudulent misrepresentations could be recovered in an action brought by a Bill in equity. Although the action in that case failed, Lord Chelmsford stated that the action in equity 'is a suit instituted to recover damages' and 'is precisely analogous to the common law action for deceit'.[133]

This point that Lord Chelmsford made in 1873 is now well established.[134] Lord Browne-Wilkinson has stated that, 'although the historical development of the rules of law and equity have, in the past, caused different labels to be stuck on different manifestations', the duties of care at common law and in equity should be treated as the same.[135] And the distinction between the award of equitable compensation, which is truly equity's compensatory damages, and the award in equity which is not truly compensatory but which operates as a performance award is becoming appreciated in modern times (although the latter award is often still referred to as 'compensation'). Millett LJ stated in *Bristol and West Building Society v Mothew*:[136]

---

129 *Schroeder v Mendl* (1877) 37 LT 452, 454. See also cases of compensation for loss awarded to a plaintiff also seeking specific performance of a contract of sale: *Todd v Gee* (1810) 17 Ves Jun 274; 34 ER 106; *Phelps v Prothero* (1855) 7 De G M & G 722; 44 ER 280. Maxwell, 1862, 229–42; Elliott, S, 'Remoteness Criteria in Equity' (2002) 65 MLR 588.

130 'Where there is a claim for damages on the ground of fraud … it is immaterial whether it is framed or considered as an action in tort or a claim for equitable relief': Sheridan, LA, *Fraud in Equity*, London: Pitman, 1956, 36; *Canson Enterprises Ltd v Boughton & Co* (1991) 85 DLR (4th) 129, 141.

131 *Colt v Woollaston* (1723) 2 PW 154, 156; 24 ER 679, 680; *Metropolitan Bank v Heiron* (1880) 5 Ex D 319, 343; *Boston Deep Sea Fishing & Ice Co v Ansell* (1888) 39 Ch D 389, 367–68.

132 (1873) LR 6 HL 377.

133 *Peek v Gurney* (1873) LR 6 HL 377, 390, 393; *Ramshire v Bolton* (1869) 8 LR Eq 294; *Slim v Croucher* (1860) 1 De G F & J 518, 524; 45 ER 462, 465 (Lord Campbell LC).

134 *Warman International Ltd v Dwyer* (1995) 182 CLR 544; *Target Holdings Ltd v Redferns (A Firm)* [1996] 1 AC 421, 434; *Bristol and West Building Society v Mothew* [1998] Ch 1, 17; *Aquaculture Corp v New Zealand Green Mussel Co Ltd* [1990] 3 NZLR 299, 301; Rickett, C, 'Equitable Compensation: The Giant Stirs' (1996) 112 LQR 27.

135 *Henderson v Merrett Syndicates Ltd* [1995] 2 AC 145, 205.

136 [1998] Ch 1, 17.

> Although the remedy which equity makes available for breach of the equitable duty of skill and care is equitable compensation rather than damages, this is merely the product of history and in this context is in my opinion a distinction without a difference. Equitable compensation for breach of the duty of skill and care resembles common law damages in that it is awarded by way of compensation to the plaintiff for his loss. There is no reason in principle why the common law rules of causation, remoteness of damage and measure of damages should not be applied by analogy in such a case.[137]

The only difference between compensatory awards in equity and those at common law is the tendency to call the equitable compensatory award 'equitable compensation' and the common law award 'compensatory damages'. It is commonly acknowledged that the different labels are really a 'distinction without a difference'[138] and many courts are now beginning to refer to the equitable award, as Lord Chelmsford did, as compensatory damages as well. This is entirely logical, especially once it is considered that not only do the two awards have precisely the same compensatory goal but that references to this award of compensation in equity for breach of fiduciary duty have also been used as a basis to extend liability for compensatory damages at common law for the tort of negligence.[139]

Although some Australian courts have followed the logical trend and referred to compensatory awards in equity as 'damages',[140] as have courts in England,[141] Australia has not yet been prepared to acknowledge that compensatory damages in equity are just equity's counterpart to common law compensatory damages. As a result it is suggested that methods for assessment of the loss suffered in equity is not necessarily the same as at common law (although there has yet to be a test pronounced for remoteness of damage in equity). In *Youyang Pty Ltd v Minter Ellison Morris Fletcher*,[142] after quoting the above extract from Lord Millett, a unanimous High Court of Australia raised doubts about its correctness:

---

137 The later reference by Millett LJ to 'equitable compensation in lieu of rescission or specific restitution' should be seen as a reference to the 'common account' or primary obligation of accountability. This monetary obligation arises independently of any wrong. See Millett, above n 88, 294.

138 In *Seager v Copydex (No 2)* [1969] 1 WLR 809 Lord Denning described equitable compensation as 'damages'. The difficulty however is that sometimes the term 'equitable compensation' is used in the context of awards which effect restitution and on other occasions in the context of 'performance' measures such as the common account.

139 *White v Jones* [1995] 2 AC 207, 270–74, 285–86; *Henderson v Merrett Syndicates Ltd* [1995] 2 AC 145, 179, 204–05. See also *Hedley Byrne & Co Ltd v Heller & Partners Ltd* [1964] AC 465 (HL).

140 *Mordecai v Mordecai* (1988) 12 NSWLR 58; *Ferrari v Ferrari Investments (Townsville) Pty Ltd* [1999] QCA 230; *Harpur v Ariadne Aust Ltd* [1996] QCA 483 (29 November).

141 *Tang Man Sit v Capacious Investments Ltd* [1996] AC 514, 520; *United Pan-Europe Communications NV v Deutsche Bank AG* [2000] 2 BCLC 461 (CA). See also the reference by Lord Nicholls to 'compensatory damages' for a breach of confidence in equity: *Attorney-General v Blake* [2001] 1 AC 268.

142 [2003] HCA 15, [39] ('*Youyang*'). See also *Pilmer v Duke Group Ltd* (2001) 180 ALR 249, 273.

> However, there must be a real question whether the unique foundation and goals of equity, which has the institution of the trust at its heart, warrant any assimilation even in this limited way with the measure of compensatory damages in tort and contract. It may be thought strange to decide that the precept that trustees are to be kept by courts of equity up to their duty has an application limited to the observance by trustees of some only of their duties to beneficiaries in dealing with trust funds.

The answer to this concern, addressed in more detail below as a response to Professor Tilbury, can be put simply: there is no reason why protection of this 'trust' cannot allow a stricter remoteness measure. Different rules of remoteness and causation[143] will apply according to the nature of the tort or breach of contract.[144] Most obviously, the remoteness rules that apply to intentional torts such as deceit or injurious falsehood differ from those that apply to negligence or torts of strict liability.[145] The remoteness rule for deceit, 'any direct consequences', also differs from the less strict rule of 'reasonably foreseeable' kinds of harm arising from negligence.[146] For equitable wrongs, such as breach of trust or fiduciary duty, there is no reason why unique (perhaps even stricter) remoteness rules could not also be applied to supposedly 'unique' equitable wrongs that have 'the institution of the trust at [their] heart'.[147] Indeed, despite the antipathy toward 'assimilation' with the common law, in the joint judgment in *Youyang* the High Court itself uses the language of common law damages in describing the award, saying that 'by analogy with common law terms, the damage was then suffered; subsequent events went to quantification'.[148] Similarly, statutory wrongs, such as breaches of s 52 of the Trade Practices Act 1974 (Cth) have been held to be 'closely analogous' to actions for the tort of deceit for the purposes of choosing a remoteness rule.[149]

---

143 Until amending legislation was introduced, contributory negligence in Australia was held only to apply to torts and not to breach of contract (*Astley v Austrust Ltd* (1999) 197 CLR 1) or equitable wrongs (*Pilmer v Duke Group Ltd* (2001) 180 ALR 249, 273).

144 Although it has been suggested that the 'standard' test for breach of contract and torts is the same, the question is far from resolved: see, for instance, the reference by Deane J in *The Commonwealth v Amann Aviation Pty Ltd* (1991) 174 CLR 64, 116 to 'the gradual assimilation of the tests of "within the contemplation of the parties" (in contract) and "reasonably foreseeable" (in tort)'. See also *Hungerfords v Walker* (1989) 171 CLR 125, 149. Cf *Parsons Ltd v Uttley Ingham & Co* [1978] QB 791, 802, 806; *BDC Ltd v Hofstrand Farms Ltd* (1986) 26 DLR (4th) 1, 13–15; cf *C Czarnikow Ltd v Koufos* (1969) 1 AC 350, 383–87, 425.

145 *Palmer Bruyn & Parker Pty Ltd v Parsons* [2001] HCA 69 (6 December 2001); *Smith New Court Securities Ltd v Scrimgeour Vickers* [1997] AC 254.

146 *Smith New Court Securities Ltd v Scrimgeour Vickers* [1997] AC 254.

147 *Youyang Pty Ltd v Minter Ellison Morris Fletcher* [2003] HCA 15, [39].

148 *Ibid* [69].

149 In *Kizbeau Pty Ltd v W G & B Pty Ltd* (1995) 184 CLR 281, 290–91, the High Court saying also that 'in assessing damages under s 82 of the Act, the rules for assessing damages in tort ... are the appropriate guide in most, if not all, cases'.

On the other hand, like the authorities in England,[150] the Court of Appeal in New Zealand[151] and the Supreme Court of Canada[152] all suggest that, in cases of compensatory damages in equity, courts should follow principles of causation and remoteness of damages analogous to those applied at common law. As the Supreme Court of Canada stated of compensatory damages in equity: 'why should it not borrow from the experience of the common law? Whether the courts refine the equitable tools such as the remedy of compensation, or follow the common law on its own terms, seems not particularly important where the same policy objective is sought.'[153]

Disgorgement damages

Disgorgement damages are abundant for equitable wrongs. The only confusion is a matter of nomenclature. The profit-stripping effected under various different names at common law has only ever been referred to in equity as an 'account of profits'. Equity's nomenclature has the potential to confuse. The 'account' of profits refers simply to a process of determining profits that have been made as a consequence of wrongdoing. It says nothing about the disgorgement of those profits. The true order is one of account and payment over. However, although nomenclature of 'disgorgement damages' might be simpler and is used in this chapter to highlight the symmetry between the common law and equity, courts are unlikely to abandon the long-term use of the term 'account of profits' to describe equity's process of disgorgement of the profits of wrongdoing.

Disgorgement of profits is a standard remedy in equity for wrongs such as breach of fiduciary duty, breach of confidence or knowing participation in a breach of fiduciary duty. In *Boardman v Phipps*,[154] for example, the appellants were the solicitor to a trust and a beneficiary under that trust. The trust owned shares in a company. In the course of representing the interests of the trust, information was acquired which allowed the appellants to obtain a large number of shares (amounting to a controlling interest) in the company for themselves. Although there was no possibility that the trust would have acquired further shares,[155] and although the trust *benefited* from the increase in value of the shares from the appellants' acquisition, the House of Lords held that the appellants' acquisition

150 *Bristol and West Building Society v Mothew* [1998] Ch 1, 17; see also Vos, G, 'Linking Chains of Causation: An Examination of New Approaches to Causation in Equity and the Common Law' [2001] CLJ 337.

151 'Compensation or damages in equity were traditionally said to aim at restoration or restitution, whereas common law tort damages are intended to compensate for harm done; but in many cases, the present being one, that is a difference without a distinction': *Day v Mead* [1987] 2 NZLR 443, 451. See also *Bank of New Zealand v New Zealand Guardian Trust Co Ltd* [1999] 1 NZLR 664 (CA). Note also the recognition that, as discussed above, there are instances in which equitable awards are truly made for restoration but such awards, aimed at securing performance of an obligation, are not compensatory and for which rules of remoteness do not apply.

152 Quoting the passage in the footnote above: *Canson Enterprises Ltd v Boughton & Co* (1991) 85 DLR (4th) 129, 151.

153 *Canson Enterprises Ltd v Boughton & Co* (1991) 85 DLR (4th) 129, 153 (La Forest J with whom Sopinka, Gonthier and Cory JJ concurred).

154 [1967] 2 AC 46.

155 *Ibid*, 119 (Lord Upjohn).

amounted to a breach of fiduciary duty. The breach of fiduciary duty consisted of an unauthorised action based on information obtained in a fiduciary capacity. Informed consent of the beneficiaries had not been properly obtained. The appellants were held liable to disgorge the profits with an order for an account of the profits represented by the higher value of the shares as well as the more remote (but still reasonably foreseeable) profits made from capital distributions from the shares.

There is one obstacle to referring to the 'account of profits' in equity as disgorgement damages. In *Watson v Holliday*[156] Kay J held that an account of profits was not an award of damages. The claim for an account of profits was brought against a defendant for breach of patent. Because the defendant was bankrupt the claimant had to prove his claim in the bankruptcy. But s 31 of the Bankruptcy Act 1869 excluded from proof in the bankruptcy 'demands in the nature of unliquidated damages arising otherwise than by reason of a contract'. Kay J held that an account of profits was not excluded because it was not 'damages'.[157] This view should be rejected. Kay J himself recognised that the award of money had and received can operate in exactly the same manner as an account of profits.[158] And in the United States that award of money had and received, where operating to strip a profit from a wrong, has been acknowledged as an award of damages. In *Hart v E P Dutton & Co Inc*,[159] Hart sued the publisher of a book which suggested he was a World War II traitor for libel. He sought the profits the publisher had made through the sale of the book. But an action for damages for libel was subject to a one year limitation period. In order to evade this period, which had expired, Hart argued that the profits could be stripped in an action not for 'damages' but for 'money had and received'. The New York Supreme Court rejected this argument stating:

> ... whatever the plaintiff may call the action ... in the absence of any statute or common law authority, it must be considered as an action for damages ... In applying the statute of limitations the Court should look for the reality and the essence of the action and not its mere name.[160]

As explained in part one, the term 'damages' cannot mean anything more than a money award for a wrong, and the epithet 'disgorgement' should be used to describe those different varieties of award at common law and in equity that operate to strip profits from wrongdoing. As Lord Nicholls in *Attorney-General v Blake* (in accepting that 'damages' at common law could be awarded based upon the profit a defendant had made from wrongdoing) acknowledged:

> Despite the niceties and formalities once associated with taking an account, the amount payable under the account of profits need not be any more elaborately or precisely calculated than damages.[161]

---

156 (1882) 20 Ch D 780, 784.

157 *Ibid*.

158 In *Watson v Holliday* Kay J followed Lord Westbury LC from *Neilson v Betts* (1871) LR 5 HL 1, 22 and stated that the account is like an equitable claim for money had and received.

159 93 NYS (2d) 871 (DCNY, 1949).

160 *Ibid*, 878; affirmed *Hart v EP Dutton & Co Inc*, 98 NYS (2d) 773 (SCNY App, 1950).

161 [2001] 1 AC 268, 288.

However, Lord Nicholls insisted upon calling the profit-stripping award given for the breach of contract an 'account of profits' (rather than 'damages' qualified by the epithet 'disgorgement'). But this was because he considered the use of the only other epithet proffered during the hearing, 'restitutionary' (damages), to be an 'unhappy expression' in a case of profit disgorgement.[162] On the other hand,[163] Lord Steyn refrained from using the term 'account of profits' and referred to 'disgorgement of profits'. Further, the term 'disgorgement' is not judicially unknown: the Supreme Court of Canada has referred to an account of profits as 'disgorgement',[164] Lord Diplock has used disgorgement to refer to an award of money had and received when it operates to strip profits[165] and the English Court of Appeal have recently referred to an account of profits and 'disgorgement' interchangeably.[166] Perhaps most accurately, the Full Court of the Federal Court of Australia recently referred interchangeably to 'disgorgement damages' and 'account of profits' to refer to a money award stripping profits for torts or breach of contract.[167]

Restitutionary damages

As noted above, in discussing the award of 'damages' under Lord Cairns' Act, the House of Lords has acknowledged that these damages in equity include restitutionary damages. The most common example of restitutionary damages in tort law, and one of the examples used above, is the use of the property of another. The value of the use is transferred from the plaintiff to the defendant even though no actual financial loss might be suffered by the plaintiff. This exact award, for trespass, was made by the Lord Chancellor in the leading case of *Phillips v Homfray*. That case has been discussed at great length in a searching article by Mr Swadling, devoted exclusively to it.[168]

The case concerned a partnership, the Tredegar Iron Company, which in 1859 negotiated with the plaintiffs for rights to mine the coal under their farm. The negotiations failed but the partnership secretly began mining the coal under the plaintiffs' land without their consent. After agreeing to sell the property to Tredegar Iron in 1863, the plaintiffs became aware of this and refused to proceed with the sale. *Inter alia*, the defendants brought a suit for specific performance of the contract of sale and a cross-suit was brought by the plaintiffs for a declaration that the contract was binding and an injunction and damages. The matter came before the Vice Chancellor, Sir John Stuart, in 1871. The Vice Chancellor declared that the contract for sale of the property was not binding and ordered it to be

162 *Ibid*, 284.

163 *Ibid*, 291, 292.

164 *Hodgkinson v Simms* [1994] 3 SCR 377, 383; *Cadbury Schweppes Inc v FBI Foods Ltd* [1999] SCR 142, 155.

165 *Mahesan S/O Thambiah v Malaysian Government Officers Co-operative Housing Society* [1979] AC 374 (PC), 376.

166 *United Pan-Europe Communications NV v Deutsche Bank AG* [2000] 2 BCLC 461 (CA).

167 *Hospitality Group Pty Ltd v Australian Rugby Union Ltd* (2001) ATPR 41-831 (Hill and Finkelstein JJ).

168 Swadling, above n 95, 277.

delivered up for cancellation. In relation to the injunction and associated orders the Vice Chancellor granted the injunction and directed that inquiries be taken as to damages. One of the inquiries concerned the amount which should be paid for the use of the land and passages underground in wrongfully taking the coal. This was a 'wayleave' inquiry that did not depend on any financial loss to the plaintiffs as a result of the use of their land. In modern terms it was an award of damages measured by value transferred – restitutionary damages. On appeal to the Lord Chancellor, the inquiries were upheld with a small variation immaterial to this inquiry.[169] Although subsequent litigation resulted in the quashing of these inquiries, this was for entirely separate reasons. The subsequent litigation was brought after the partners had died and depended upon the rule *actio personalis moritur cum persona*: an action for a wrong does not survive the death of the wrongdoer. This rule was only applicable to torts[170] and no longer exists.[171]

Another example of restitutionary damages for equitable wrongs can be seen in the decision of Nicholls VC in *Universal Thermosensors Ltd v Hibben*.[172] Referring to the equitable wrong of breach of confidence, Nicholls VC approved a measure of damages based upon the reasonable value of the *use* of confidential information wrongfully obtained stating:

> [A]n award of damages in such circumstances would not be a novelty. There are several fields where the courts have awarded damages to a plaintiff whose property is wrongfully used by another even though the plaintiff has not suffered any pecuniary loss by such user. The cases concerning this principle [are] sometimes called the 'user principle'.

A final example is the case of *Tang Man Sit v Capacious Investments Ltd*.[173] Mr Tang committed a breach of trust by secretly letting, as homes for the elderly, 16 houses which were to be assigned to Capacious Investments. When the time came for execution of the assignment the homes were therefore incumbered with the leases. In the Privy Council the central question was one of election between the awards which had been made. This issue need not distract for present purposes. The Court of Appeal in Hong Kong had held that 'damages' were available under two different heads for this breach of trust.

Head A was damages for 'the wrongful use and occupation' and Head B was damages for the financial loss from the decreased value of the property because it was incumbered with leases.[174] Lord Nicholls, in giving the advice of the Board, went out of his way to affirm that:[175]

---

169 *Phillips v Homfray* (1871) LR 6 Ch App 770.

170 *Sollars v Lawrence* (1743) Willes 413, 421 (Willes CJ).

171 This rule was abolished by the Law Reform (Miscellaneous Provisions) Act 1934.

172 [1992] 1 WLR 840, 856; see Edelman, J, 'Assessing Damages for a Breach of Confidence' [2000] Restitution LR 230.

173 [1996] AC 514.

174 *Ibid*, 519.

175 *Ibid*, 520.

> In the present case nothing turns on the historic distinction between damages, awarded by common law courts, and compensation, a monetary remedy awarded by the Court of Chancery for breach of equitable obligations. It will be convenient therefore to use the nomenclature of damages which has been adopted throughout this case.

Examined closely however, although Head B of the damages are compensatory damages, Head A of the damages, damages for the wrongful use and occupation, are best seen as restitutionary damages. On the evidence, had Mr Tang not secretly let out the houses, Capacious Investments would not have done so and thus Capacious Investments suffered no financial loss from the use and occupation.[176] Such an award of damages is not concerned with loss but reverses the transfer of objective value. It should be qualified by the epithet 'restitutionary'. In *Ex Parte James*,[177] Lord Eldon referred to the same award as 'an occupation rent' for the possession of land in breach of fiduciary duty. This award corresponds precisely with the common law awards of *mesne* profits or wayleaves for trespass; awards that are now commonly recognised as restitutionary damages.

Exemplary damages

It follows from everything that has been said above that exemplary damages should also be available, where required, to punish equitable wrongdoing in the same way as they are available to punish common law wrongdoing. Indeed, as observed by Lord Diplock in one of the seminal cases on common law exemplary damages, equity has a long history of punishing deliberate wrongdoers by denying allowances when an account of profits is sought, thereby stripping more than the actual profit made.[178] This has been accepted in New Zealand, where it has been acknowledged that exemplary damages are available for the equitable wrongs of breach of confidence[179] and breach of fiduciary duty.[180] In Canada it has also been accepted that exemplary damages can be awarded for breach of fiduciary duty.[181] In its report, *Aggravated, Exemplary and Restitutionary Damages*,[182] the Law Commission recommended that English law also accept that exemplary damages are available for equitable wrongs, which it defined as breach of fiduciary duty (which includes breach of trust), breach of confidence and knowing assistance in a breach of fiduciary duty.[183]

---

176 It was noted that before Mr Tang's breach of trust, 'the houses stood empty. There were complications over Mr Kung's [the owner of Capacious Investments Ltd] estate': *ibid*, 518.

177 (1803) 8 Ves 337, 351; 32 ER 385, 390.

178 *Broome v Cassell & Co* [1972] AC 1027 (HL), 1129–30. See also *Phipps v Boardman* [1965] Ch 992, 1030 (Pearson LJ), cited by Mason P in *Harris v Digital Pulse* [2003] NSWCA 10, [166].

179 *Aquaculture Corp v New Zealand Green Mussel Co Ltd* [1990] 3 NZLR 299 (CANZ).

180 *Cook v Evatt (No 2)* [1992] 1 NZLR 676 (HCNZ).

181 *Whiten v Pilot Insurance Co* (2002) 209 DLR (4th) 257, 287; *Norberg v Wynrib* (1992) 92 DLR (4th) 440 (SCC), 505–07; *McDonald Estate v Martin* [1995] CCL 1142 (Man CA); *Gerula v Flores* [1995] CCL 8583 (OCA).

182 Law Commission, above n 18, 5.54, 5.55.

183 *Ibid*, Appendix A, Draft Bill. Exemplary damages for breach of fiduciary duty were also supported by Brett LJ in *Smith v Day* (1882) 21 Ch D 421, 428.

The New South Wales Court of Appeal, in *Harris v Digital Pulse*,[184] was recently sharply divided on this issue of whether exemplary damages should be available for a breach of fiduciary duty. Mason P approved the judgment of Palmer J at first instance, quoting from Professor Maitland, his 'dream', that 'the day will come when lawyers will cease to inquire whether a given rule be a rule of equity or a rule of common law: suffice it that it is a well-established rule administered by the High Court of Justice'.[185] Mason P said:[186]

> ... the availability of exemplary damages should be co-extensive with the rationale of the remedy. That rationale is the composite goal of punishing, deterring and vindicating a person who is the victim of wrongdoing clearly proscribed. In that context, it is, as Palmer J observed, absurd to think that a plaintiff whose life savings were stolen by a solicitor would have any different sense of outrage depending upon whether the defendant was sued at common law for deceit or in equity for breach of fiduciary duty.

Unfortunately, Mason P was in dissent and the majority of the New South Wales Court of Appeal was of the opinion that exemplary damages could not be awarded for a breach of fiduciary duty.[187] Until this matter comes before the High Court, in Australia exemplary damages will be treated differently at common law and in equity.

Professor Tilbury's fears

Professor Tilbury, in his chapter in this volume,[188] raises the fear that standardisation of the nomenclature of damages 'runs the risk of ignoring the nature of the rights in issue and of failing to achieve the optimal "fit" of obligation and remedy'. The example he gives is that the use of the label 'damages' in equity will invite the application of the same rules of causation and remoteness of damage as apply for common law 'damages'. But there is no single set of causation or remoteness rules at common law. Indeed, it is because common law, with its use of the label 'damages', has never ignored the nature of the underlying wrong that we have different rules of remoteness of damage for intentional torts as opposed to negligence[189] and for torts as opposed to breach of contract.[190] Rather than obscure, the nomenclature of 'damages' directs attention to these important questions of remoteness and causation.

Professor Tilbury considers that a danger of standardising the language of damages is that it will require a determination of whether (and, presumably, which) current rules of damages are to apply to the equitable monetary remedies

---

184 [2003] NSWCA 10.

185 *Ibid*, [149].

186 *Ibid*, [195].

187 For a discussion of the decision, see Edelman, J, 'A Fusion *Fallacy*' (2003) 119 LQR 375.

188 Tilbury, M, 'Remedies and the Classification of Obligations', Chapter 2 of this volume.

189 *Palmer Bruyn & Parker Pty Ltd v Parsons* (2001) 208 CLR 388.

190 For a detailed discussion comparing remoteness rules for torts and breach of contract, see Burrows, A, 'Limitations on Compensation', in Burrows, A and Peel, E (eds), *Commercial Remedies*, Oxford: OUP, 2003, 27.

within the category of 'wrongs'. Far from being a danger, surely this is a goal that should be applauded. Consider a fiduciary that acts in good faith but in breach of fiduciary duty and purchases shares with knowledge acquired from his fiduciary position. He sells the shares for a large profit. He invests the profit in real estate. The real estate doubles in value. He sells the real estate, realises this value and invests it in the stock market making a fortune. Is the principal entitled to an award of disgorgement of the fortune (perhaps subject to an allowance for the skill of the fiduciary)? When is such profit too remote? Such questions can only be addressed if rules of remoteness are developed for all monetary awards for wrongdoing:[191]

> The question of whether specific profits were made from an infringement is similar to that of proximate cause in the tort context: just as there comes a point beyond which effects cannot legally be attributed to an initial tortious action, so too there comes a point beyond which an infringer's profits from its enterprises as a whole, cannot legally be attributed to a particular act of infringement.

Rather than obscure, a standardised language of 'damages' will direct attention to these important questions by directing inquiry into these areas.

CONCLUSION

This chapter has sought to demonstrate that the only coherent meaning that can be given to the word 'damages' is a money award given for a wrong. Compensation for loss is not and should not be the exclusive concern of common law damages. The common law has clearly accepted the existence of non-compensatory damages in the form of nominal damages, restitutionary damages, disgorgement damages and, perhaps best known, exemplary damages.[192] None of these damages awards, including the one to which most objections are made – exemplary damages – is an anomaly that should be abolished. There are powerful and compelling reasons for them in particular cases. They have a coherent role and their recognition and acceptance in the common law is legitimated by history and utility.

With this definition, there is no logical reason why equity cannot also recognise that the money awards it gives for equitable wrongs are 'damages'. Equity gives precisely the same damages awards (compensatory, restitutionary, disgorgement and, in jurisdictions apart from Australia, exemplary damages) as the common law. Much utility can be gained from rationalising the methods by which the two systems make the same awards where the awards are being made for the same purposes. This classification has the potential to bring great clarity to the law by treating like responses alike.

Although there are promising signs in England, Canada and New Zealand, in Australia such coherence in equity's nomenclature is unlikely in the immediate future. But even in Australia it would still be a step forward to recognise the

---

191 *Frank Music Corp v Metro-Goldwyn Mayer Inc*, 886 F 2d 1545 (9th Cir CA, 1989), 1553.

192 *Redrow Homes Ltd v Betts Bros plc* [1999] 1 AC 197 (HL), 207 (Lord Jauncey), 209 (Lord Clyde).

commonality of the goal of awards at common law and in equity when given as a response to wrongdoing, the goal being compensation, restitution, disgorgement or punishment.

4

RESCISSION, RESTITUTION AND CONTRACTUAL ORDERING: THE ROLE OF PLAINTIFF ELECTION

*Michael Bryan**

INTRODUCTION

The purpose of this chapter is to examine the rationale for requiring a plaintiff to elect to rescind a contract as a precondition to claiming the restitution of money paid under the contract. It is well known that the term 'rescission' is one of the most ambiguous in the law.[1] One type, known variously as 'classical' rescission, rescission *'ab initio'* or retrospective rescission, sets aside a contract or gift which has been procured by some wrongdoing, such as mistake, misrepresentation, equitable fraud, breach of fiduciary duty, undue influence or unconscionable conduct.[2] The purpose of this type of rescission is to restore both parties to their precontractual financial position. No question of restoring property will of course arise if the contract is wholly executory. Under a partially or wholly executed contract the process of returning property, and of making allowances for depreciation of property or for services performed, must be effected either by the parties themselves exercising a form of 'mutual self-help' or by court order. If it is a contract that is being rescinded, equitable orthodoxy, at least in Anglo-Australian jurisdictions, requires a plaintiff to elect to rescind the contract as a prerequisite to the return of money paid or property transferred under the contract.[3] The orthodoxy was applied by the Full Court of the Supreme Court of Western Australia in the recent decision of *Hancock Family Memorial Foundation v Porteous*.[4] The judgment of the Full Court conveniently summarises the various justifications put forward at different times for the election requirement, and therefore provides an opportunity for reassessing their cogency.

---

* I am grateful to participants at the Melbourne Obligations Conference 2002 for their comments on a draft of this chapter. Thanks also to Rosemary Parsons for her research assistance. I am of course responsible for all errors.

1 Meagher, RP, Gummow, WMC and Lehane, JRF, *Equity Doctrines and Remedies*, London: Butterworths, 3rd edn, 1992, [2401], identifies five senses in which the term 'rescission' is used.

2 A contract can also be voidable at law for fraudulent misrepresentation or duress. A plaintiff may elect to rescind the contract and invoke equity's adjustive powers exercisable in its concurrent jurisdiction: *Alati v Kruger* (1955) 94 CLR 216, 223–24. Restitution at common law of money paid under the contract can be separately claimed: *Hill v Perrott* (1810) 3 Taunt 274; 128 ER 109.

3 *Daly v Sydney Stock Exchange* (1986) 160 CLR 371; *Guinness plc v Saunders* [1990] 2 AC 663; *Lonrho plc v Fayed (No 2)* [1992] 1 WLR 1; *Greater Pacific Investments Pty Ltd (In Liq) v Australian National Industries Ltd* (1996) 39 NSWLR 143.

4 (2000) 22 WAR 198 (*'Hancock'*). Application for special leave to appeal to the High Court was refused: (2000) 74 ALJR 1536.

A second type of rescission, also known as repudiation or termination for breach, operates prospectively so as to entitle a party to a contract upon breach of condition, or upon the occurrence of such other event as entitles a party under the contract to 'rescind', to treat the contract as no longer binding. Rescission in this sense operates prospectively, discharging both parties from further performance, though accrued rights and causes of action continue to be enforceable.[5] Orthodoxy – here common law, not equitable – requires the contract to be rescinded, or terminated, as a precondition to restitution of benefits conferred under the contract, unless the contract is discharged by operation of law, by reason of frustration, supervening illegality, under statute, or, more rarely, where the contract provides for automatic discharge.[6]

The recent decision of the High Court in *Roxborough v Rothmans of Pall Mall Australia Ltd*[7] invites a reconsideration of the termination requirement. A majority of the High Court ordered restitution of money paid under a valid contract which the payer had not elected to terminate. The facts of *Roxborough* raise a variety of issues, as complex as they are controversial, concerning restitution of money for failure of consideration where the payer has shifted the risk of failure to a third party. If the judgments are any guide, the termination requirement does not seem to have been forensically significant to the parties arguing the appeal. Nevertheless, as Kirby J recognised in his dissenting judgment, to permit restitution of benefits conferred under an unterminated contract has disturbing implications for upholding the security of contractual bargains. The aim of the second part of the chapter is to tease out some of these implications.

Both types of rescission have attracted recent judicial and academic analysis.[8] While the focus of most academic writing has been on the principles governing the adjustive process consequent upon rescission, some attention has also been paid to the rationale for plaintiff election. Many of the critiques apply insights derived from restitution scholarship. The recovery of money in an action for money had and received upon termination of a valid contract on the ground of failure of consideration is well established. The restoration of property upon the making of an order of rescission *'ab initio'* can also effect restitution. In *Portman BS v Hamlyn Taylor and Neck* Millett LJ analysed rescission in these terms:

> The obligation to make restitution must flow from the ineffectiveness of the transaction under which the money was paid and not from a mistake or misrepresentation which induced it ... If the payer exercises his right of rescission in time and before the recipient deals with the money in accordance with his instructions, the obligation to make restitution may follow.[9]

---

5 *McDonald v Dennys Lascelles* (1933) 48 CLR 457; *Johnson v Agnew* [1980] AC 367.

6 Mason, K and Carter, JW, *Restitution Law in Australia*, Sydney: Butterworths, 1995, [1102], [1208].

7 (2001) 185 ALR 335 (*'Roxborough'*).

8 In addition to the cases cited see *Vadasz v Pioneer Concrete (SA) Pty Ltd* (1995) 184 CLR 102; *Maguire v Makaronis* (1998) 188 CLR 449; *Smith New Court Securities v Scrimgeour Vickers (Asset Management) Ltd* [1997] AC 254. Academic analysis, in addition to the articles cited in this chapter, includes Proksch, L, 'Rescission', in Parkinson, P (ed), *The Principles of Equity*, Sydney: Law Book Co, 2nd edn, 2003, Chapter 25.

9 [1998] 4 All ER 202, 208.

The modal auxiliary, 'may', in the final sentence introduces an important qualification. There is no suggestion in this passage that rescission is *inherently* restitutionary. Some analyses have suggested that rescission invariably reverses unjust enrichment. For example, it has been argued that rescission of a wholly executory contract is restitutionary since the defendant is, by the exercise of rescission, compelled to restore to the plaintiff a chose in action, namely the right to sue the plaintiff under the rescinded contract.[10] The argument is logical but there is no evidence, either in the passage cited or elsewhere in the authorities on rescission, that the expansive definition of enrichment on which it is based has been judicially accepted. Another reason for rejecting the argument that rescission is necessarily restitutionary is that in some cases an order of rescission may recreate a contract on new terms instead of setting aside the contract and ordering restitution of benefits conferred.[11] These are important limitations on a restitutionary analysis of rescission, justifying Millett LJ's tentative recognition of its validity. Nevertheless, the premise of this chapter is that the restoration of property under a rescinded contract effects restitution (or counter-restitution where property is returned to the plaintiff), and that the objective of a court order in such a case is to reverse unjust enrichment.

Although the consequences of exercising 'retrospective' rescission and 'prospective' termination are significantly different, both are conditioned upon the plaintiff's election of the remedy. Election determines, or is taken to determine,[12] the moment when the parties' legal obligations are no longer governed exclusively by the contract but by other legal regimes, including the law of unjust enrichment.[13] On the face of it the exercise of election fulfils the important function of defining the frontier between contract law and an award of restitution for unjust enrichment. But if this is correct, case law sheds a surprisingly faint light on the question as to what acts or words constitute a valid election for this purpose.

The stimulus for writing this chapter is the following passage in the judgment of Callinan J:

> I would reject the respondent's submission that it is only in cases in which contracts have been frustrated, discharged for breach, or held to be unenforceable, or otherwise avoided, that a party may obtain restitution. Gyles J answered that submission, correctly, in my opinion, in this way:
>
> > The contract [here] has been executed in all respects save for payment of the licence fee by the respondent. The licence fee is no longer payable. It cannot and will not be paid by the respondent. That is the end of the matter.

---

10 Nahan, N, 'Rescission: A Case for Rejecting the Classical Model?' (1997) 27 UWA L Rev 66, 72.

11 *Solle v Butcher* [1950] 1 KB 671; *Grist v Bailey* [1967] Ch 532. The power to 'reform' a rescinded contract is unaffected by the disavowal of an equitable doctrine of common mistake by the English Court of Appeal in *Great Peace Shipping Ltd v Tsavliris Salvage (International Ltd)* ('*The Great Peace*') [2002] 4 All ER 689.

12 See text at nn 25–28.

13 Arbitration and choice of law clauses will continue to apply following termination: *Heyman v Darwins Ltd* [1942] AC 365; *State Rail Authority of New South Wales v Codelfa Construction Pty Ltd* (1982) 150 CLR 29.

> Performance is no longer possible. If formal termination by the appellants is necessary, then bringing these proceedings is sufficient.[14]

This is the only analysis of the termination requirement to be found in *Roxborough*, and it raises more questions than it answers. Is termination of a contract a 'formal' requirement? If not, what is its substantial justification? And most critically of all, if the bringing of legal proceedings for restitution of money paid under a contract can amount to an election to terminate, why do contract and restitution textbooks continue to insist that termination is a distinct precondition to establishing a claim for restitution? In the course of answering these questions it will be suggested that the arguments for retaining the election requirement are in fact weak, and that the law needs to develop other methods to ensure that the security of contractual bargains is not undermined. An alternative scheme for determining the availability of restitution of benefits conferred under voidable and valid contracts will be sketched out.

RESTITUTION FOLLOWING RESCISSION OF A VOIDABLE CONTRACT

The plaintiffs in *Hancock Family Memorial Foundation v Porteous* were companies created and controlled by the mining entrepreneur, Mr Lang Hancock, for the purpose of receiving royalties from his mining operations. Late in life Hancock married the defendant and arranged for his companies to buy houses and a Bentley car in the defendant's name. After his death his daughter acquired control of the family companies. She alleged that Hancock had acted in breach of his fiduciary obligations as managing director in causing the companies to acquire these properties for Mrs Porteous (as the defendant had become upon remarriage after Hancock's death). The relief sought was for the properties to be held on constructive trust for the companies whose money had been used to buy them. At trial Anderson J dismissed the claim, holding that the payments had in fact discharged legitimate loans made to the companies by Hancock and other parties. Alternatively, even if the purchase of the properties had amounted to a breach of fiduciary duty, the contracts to buy the houses and the car had not been validly rescinded by the companies. Upon appeal the second ground was relied upon by the Full Court as the principal reason for denying relief. The Hancock companies 'cannot leave the contracts on foot and at the same time deny the borrowers title to the money which the contracts confer'.[15]

In refusing proprietary relief to the Hancock companies the Full Court applied a strong line of authority holding that rescission of a contract for equitable wrongdoing is a precondition to the imposition of a constructive (or resulting) trust over property which has been acquired by the wrongdoer under the contract.[16] On the present state of the authorities it would clearly be imprudent for any court below the highest appellate level to hold otherwise. Nevertheless, the

---

14 *Roxborough* (2001) 185 ALR 335, 390–91, citing Gyles J, dissenting [1999] 95 FCR 185, 214 (Full Court of the Federal Court of Australia).

15 (2000) 22 WAR 198, 220 (Full Court).

16 See the authorities listed, above n 3.

principle applied by the Full Court is not so firmly entrenched as to be beyond challenge. Few cases decided prior to *Hancock* have denied relief solely on the ground that the plaintiff had failed to rescind the contract of loan.[17] Moreover, the strictness of the requirement has been doubted. Dr Glover considers that the election requirement 'has a formalism which seems inappropriate beside many conceptions of the constructive trust'.[18] And in the recent decision of *Robins v Incentive Dynamics Pty Ltd (In Liq)*[19] Mason P, for the majority of the New South Wales Court of Appeal, characterised the election to rescind as 'at least a practical necessity'[20] rather than an immutable rule, while Giles JA went as far as to reject the necessity for an election where no policy justification for the requirement could be found.[21] If the election to rescind is indeed the gatekeeper to proprietary relief some convincing explanation as to why it is necessary to employ this janitor still seems to be called for.

Three justifications for the election requirement can be extracted from the case law. They need to be taken seriously because they are directed to ensuring that legitimate interests protected by contract and property law are not overridden by a mechanical application of the unjust enrichment principle. But, it will be suggested, these interests can be protected by the application of techniques which are well established elsewhere in private law, and that they do not, taken individually or in combination, justify retention of the election requirement.

The avoidance of double recovery

It is sometimes argued that, in the absence of an election to rescind a voidable contract, a lender might be able to recover the amount of the loan as a debt under the contract from the borrower, as well as by way of a constructive trust from a third party recipient of the money. This rationale was identified by the Full Court in *Hancock*:

> It stands to reason that a party who lends money to another under a voidable contract of loan must avoid the contract before asserting equitable title to the money lent and before seeking relief against third parties by way of tracing. Were that not to be so, the lender would notionally be able to claim repayment of the moneys due as a debt under the contract, and at the same time recover, by equitable remedies, from the borrower, or third parties with knowledge or volunteers, property acquired through the moneys lent.[22]

The prevention of excessive recovery is the cornerstone of any system of corrective justice. Unjust enrichment by subtraction is essentially a 'zero sum

17 Of the authorities cited by the Full Court only *Greater Pacific Investments Pty Ltd (In Liq) v Australian National Industries Ltd* (1996) 39 NSWLR 143 can be said to have been decided solely on this ground.

18 Glover, J, *Commercial Equity: Fiduciary Relationships*, Sydney: Butterworths, 1995, [6.37].

19 [2003] NSWCA 71 (9 April).

20 *Ibid*, [73].

21 *Ibid*, [82]. The rationales identified, namely 'a way of ensuring that account is taken of the rights of third parties before equity grants a proprietary remedy, and of guarding against recovery under the contract of loan as well as having the proprietary remedy', will be considered below.

22 (2000) 22 WAR 198, 214.

game', restoring an enrichment, or its monetary value, to a plaintiff who has been wrongfully deprived of the enrichment by the defendant or by a third party. No plaintiff should be entitled to recover more than the amount of which she has been deprived.[23] But election is a crude antidote to the malady of over-compensation. Failure to exercise a timely election may, as in the *Hancock* case, prevent *any* recovery even where equitable wrongdoing has been established. Post-judgment supervision of relief awarded to a plaintiff, including the enforcement of rights of contribution,[24] is a more precisely calibrated technique for preventing excessive compensation than the somewhat erratic justice achieved by adherence to the election requirement.

Preventing the divesting of vested property rights: the priority argument

The election requirement is often justified on the ground that it distinguishes between property recoverable under an order of rescission and property which cannot be restored because a third party has acquired in good faith a valid title under the voidable contract. The undesirability of disturbing settled title to property transferred under such a contract is the principal reason put forward by Brennan J in *Daly v Sydney Stock Exchange Ltd* for requiring proof of plaintiff election:

> But where property has been sold or conveyed, the purchaser's beneficial title must be ascertained by reference to the sale so long as it stands; the vendor cannot insist on an equitable interest in the property if he does not choose to enforce his equity to avoid the sale: see *per* Kitto J in *Latec Investment Ltd v Hotel Terrigal Pty Ltd (In Liq)* (1965) 113 CLR 265 at 277–278; *Re Sherman dec'd* [1954] 1 Ch 653 at 658. Similarly, until the lender elects to avoid the contract of loan he cannot assert an equitable title to the money lent. He cannot at once leave the contract on foot and deny the borrower the title to the money which the title confers.[25]

Lord Goff gave the same reason in *Guinness plc v Saunders* for declining to impose a constructive trust over contractual remuneration paid to a director, Ward, under a voidable contract:

> [T]he insuperable difficulty in the way of this proposition is again that the money was on this approach paid not under a void, but under a voidable, contract. Under such a contract, the property in the money would have vested in Mr Ward (who, I repeat, was *ex hypothesi* acting in good faith) and Guinness cannot short circuit an unrescinded contract simply by alleging a constructive trust.[26]

---

23 Disgorgement of the profits of wrongdoing raises different considerations, being distinct from unjust enrichment by subtraction: Edelman, J, *Gain-Based Damages*, Oxford: Hart, 2002; Edelman, J, 'The Meaning of "Damages": Common Law and Equity', Chapter 3 of this volume.

24 *Burke v LFOT Pty Ltd* (2002) 187 ALR (HCA).

25 (1986) 160 CLR 371, 388 ('*Daly*').

26 [1990] 2 AC 663, 698. In the event it was held that Guinness could recover the payments since the contract under which they had been made was void as being beyond the powers of the directors. See also *ibid*, 698–99.

It is beyond argument that rescission must not become a means for unsettling titles to property acquired by parties in good faith and without knowledge of, or responsibility for, the equitable ground for setting aside the contract. The reference to *Latec Investments Ltd v Hotel Terrigal Pty Ltd (In Liq)* by Brennan J reminds us that, where property has been transferred under a voidable contract, a claim to restitution is in effect a priority dispute between the transferor, on the one hand, and the immediate recipient (the other party to the contract) or later recipient (any party claiming title through the immediate party) on the other.[27] The transferor has an 'equity' to rescind which a timely election converts to an equitable interest. On this analysis, the 'equity' will prevail against the immediate recipient, unless barred by laches or some other equitable ground, but will only defeat the claim of the later recipient, being a purchaser for value and without notice of the facts giving rise to the equity, if the plaintiff has elected to rescind before the later recipient acquired title to the property being claimed.

On the face of it, this analysis provides an important justification for the election to rescind. It serves to identify the moment at which the validity of the title of the later recipient will be determined. But the analysis is not in fact supported by judicial practice. In determining the proprietary consequences of rescission it is the date of the court hearing and not the date of election which is decisive. The critical case for the 'mere equity' analysis is that of property acquired by a good faith purchaser from the immediate recipient in the interval between election and the date of the judicial order giving effect to rescission. If the purpose of an election is to prevent a valid title to property from being acquired subsequent to its exercise, then the 'mere equity' would enable the plaintiff to recover property acquired in this interval. But, whatever the theory may say, third parties are permitted to retain property acquired during this period, and there is no evidence of claims to property being 'backdated' to the date of the election.[28] The reason for this is that it is at the hearing that the court determines whether '*restitutio in integrum*' can be effected. The determination of title to property transferred under the contract constitutes part of the wider inquiry, undertaken by reference to the facts as they exist at the date of hearing, into restoring the parties to their precontractual position. *Alati v Kruger*[29] demonstrates the significance of this date in determining the availability of rescission. The purchaser of a fruit and vegetable business had closed down the business and assigned the lease back to the landlord between the date of commencement of proceedings and the date of judgment. In the opinion of the High Court these actions did not preclude relief since the 'validity of [the purchaser's] rescission depended only upon the question whether "*restitutio in integrum*" was possible *in the circumstances as they existed at the commencement of the action*'.[30] The discretionary nature of the remedy of rescission entitled the court to

27 Worthington, S, 'The Proprietary Consequences of Rescission' [2002] Restitution LR 28, 36–38. As Dr Worthington notes, other models of rescission have been proposed, but the 'mere equity' analysis is the generally accepted model, especially in Australia.

28 O'Sullivan, J, 'Rescission as a Self-Help Remedy: A Critical Analysis' (2000) 59 CLJ 509, 539–42, citing *Lagunas Nitrate Co v Lagunas Syndicate* [1899] 2 Ch 392.

29 (1955) 94 CLR 216.

30 *Ibid*, 223 (emphasis added). Query whether the date of judgment should not be taken as the appropriate date of assessment.

take into account the situation as it existed at the date of the hearing. As Janet O'Sullivan observes:

> ... it is simply inconceivable that the [election requirement] would ever operate inconsistently with the protection of bona fide third parties, and wherever the courts are required to determine whether rescission is barred, they test that issue at the only meaningful time: the date of the court order.[31]

Limiting the availability of proprietary restitution

This argument justifies the election requirement as a necessary curb on the indiscriminate award of proprietary remedies. Simple proof of the acquisition of property under a contract by the exercise of undue influence or unconscionable conduct, or by a breach of fiduciary obligation, should not by itself entitle the plaintiff to the benefit of a constructive trust or other proprietary remedy. Proprietary relief in such a case will withdraw from the wrongdoer's creditors an asset which would otherwise be available for distribution upon bankruptcy. This reason was emphasised by Gibbs CJ in *Daly v Sydney Stock Exchange*:

> [I]n the present case it was not necessary to find that a constructive trust existed in order to ensure that the firm was not unjustly enriched ... The benefit which the firm obtained in consequence of its breach of fiduciary duty was a loan of money, and the firm, as a debtor, was bound to repay the debt to the creditor, the appellant ... Further, the consequences of holding the money to be subject to a constructive trust and thereby transforming the creditor into a beneficiary suggest that it would be contrary to principle to recognise the existence of a constructive trust in a case such as the present. One consequence would be that the money, and any property acquired with it, would, on the firm's bankruptcy, be withdrawn from the general body of creditors; another would be that the appellant would require the firm to account for any profits made with the use of the money.[32]

The law is rightly astute to prevent simple contracts of loan from being transformed into security interests by operation of law. But insistence upon an election to rescind is not the most effective method of preventing proprietary overreach. Straightforward proprietary reasoning should entitle a plaintiff to the restoration of property from immediate and later recipients where, first, the plaintiff's property is traceably identifiable in the hands of the recipient, and secondly, a later recipient has not at the date of the claim purchased the property for good faith and for valuable consideration.[33]

The concluding words of this passage in the judgment of Gibbs CJ draw attention to some unfinished business in the law of rescission. Is a plaintiff who is

---

31 O'Sullivan, above n 28, 541.

32 (1980) 160 CLR 371, 377. Since Wilson and Dawson JJ agreed with Gibbs CJ, this reasoning, rather than the priority analysis of Brennan J, should be considered the *ratio* of the decision.

33 This is an application of the 'proprietary base' theory expounded in Birks, P, *An Introduction to the Law of Restitution*, Oxford: Clarendon, 1989, 378–85. A more sophisticated version, incorporating an element of risk analysis, is proposed by Burrows, A, 'Proprietary Restitution: Unmasking Unjust Enrichment' (2001) 117 LQR 412. Either version could be applied in this context. The fear of proprietary overreach against which Gibbs CJ cautioned in *Daly v Sydney Stock Exchange* would be realised by the adoption of other, more 'remedial' criteria for the award of a constructive trust.

entitled to the restoration of property under a rescinded contract also entitled to profits which have accrued to the recipient from use of that property? The model of rescission adopted by Australian courts has assumed that an affirmative answer should be given to this question without any real canvassing of the relevant policy arguments. Upon the exercise of rescission the recipient holds the property received under the impugned transaction upon constructive trust for the plaintiff, subject to such adjustments as the court chooses to make in order to achieve 'practical justice' between the parties.[34] Since (so the argument runs) a constructive trust entitles the beneficiary to the appreciated value of the trust property, or to profits derived from the property, these must also be handed over to the plaintiff. But it is not wholly obvious why the constructive trust, which is in this context simply a proprietary remedy for subtractive unjust enrichment, should automatically entitle the plaintiff, rather than the defendant's unsecured creditors, to any profits derived from the utilisation of the property. Recent English authority suggests that a right to the return of property carries the right to the profits, regardless of whether the plaintiff's entitlement is characterised as deriving from property law or from the law of unjust enrichment.[35] But different answers could be given depending on whether the profit is inherent from the use of the property, or part of its 'natural fruits', or again whether it has been derived from a profitable resale of the asset. It may also be relevant to establish whether the ground of rescission is the type of 'equitable wrong' such as a breach of fiduciary duty, which has traditionally been held to attract the application of profit disgorgement remedies.[36] This is not the place to explore these alternatives, but there seems no reason in principle for assuming that an entitlement to the return of property under an order of rescission includes a right to the restoration of profits made by the wrongdoer under the rescinded transaction.

None of the three reasons advanced for requiring an election to rescind as a precondition for the award of a proprietary remedy is conclusive, though all shed light on aspects of the operation of a judicial order of rescission to which attention would have to be paid if the precondition were to be abolished. More positively, there are two arguments for abolishing the election requirement.

The first is that it is no easy matter to determine what precisely constitutes an election for this purpose. In the *Hancock* decision the initiation of legal proceedings to avoid the contracts was held not to constitute an election.[37] A communication to the other contracting party of an intention to rescind is usually required.[38] But the need for communication will be waived where that party has made it impossible for the plaintiff to give notice of her intention to rescind.[39] This

---

34 *Greater Pacific Investments Pty Ltd (In Liq) v Australia National Industries Ltd* (1996) 39 NSWLR 143.

35 *FC Jones & Sons (Trustee in Bankruptcy) v Jones* [1997] Ch 159; *Foskett v McKeown* [2001] 1 AC 102.

36 See Worthington, above n 27, for a full discussion of these alternatives.

37 (2000) 22 WAR 198, 215.

38 Beale, HG (ed), *Chitty on Contracts*, London: Sweet & Maxwell, 1999, vol 1, [6]–[108]; *Sargent v ASL Developments Ltd* (1974) 131 CLR 634, 655–56 (Mason J).

39 *Car and Universal Finance Co Ltd v Caldwell* [1965] 1 QB 525.

will typically be the case where the wrongdoer has absconded with the subject matter of the contract and resold it to the later recipient. The exception is pragmatic and sensible, but it does show that there is an important class of case in which the later recipient loses title to property in spite of being unaware that an election to rescind has been exercised.

Secondly, an aspect of rescission sometimes overlooked is that gifts, as well as contracts, can be rescinded on equitable grounds. *Louth v Diprose*[40] is a well known example, in which the High Court held that the plaintiff's gift of a house should be set aside on the ground that the defendant had taken advantage of the plaintiff's love for her in procuring the transfer. The trial judge's order that the house be held on constructive trust for the plaintiff was affirmed by the High Court. Where a gift is set aside there will be no question of the donor giving notice to the donee of an intention to rescind. This difference between contracts and gifts could be defended by reference to the special value accorded to sanctity of contract, which might be said to justify the application of the formality of an election as a prerequisite to rescission. But the law has an interest in security of transactions, extending more broadly than to security of contract; donees, as well as recipients of property under voidable contracts, have an interest in dealing with property they receive as their own. Moreover, some of the arguments for retaining the election requirement in contract law, for example that title acquired by a later recipient under a voidable transaction merits secure protection, apply equally to a recipient who takes the gifted property from the donee. That the courts in the gift cases have been able to protect the security of title of later recipients without recourse to the election requirement must cast some doubt over the utility of that requirement in the contract cases.

The difficulty in formulating a convincing justification for the election requirement is a symptom of a deeper confusion. Insistence upon plaintiff election to rescind in *Daly*, *Guinness v Saunders*, *Hancock* and other decisions has resulted in the conflation of two distinct issues. The first is the right of the plaintiff to elect to affirm or avoid a voidable contract, the contract being valid unless and until the election to rescind has been exercised. In this primary sense the requirement fulfils the important function of establishing whether the plaintiff proposes to continue performance of the contract in spite of the existence of the ground of rescission.[41] The objection to allowing a plaintiff who has affirmed a contract to claim restitution of benefits conferred under the contract is obvious; to do so would be to permit the plaintiff both to recover property transferred under the contract, and to enjoy the benefit of the defendant's full performance.

Assuming that the plaintiff has not affirmed the voidable contract, a wholly distinct question is whether the plaintiff has established a basis for a proprietary claim in unjust enrichment. Plaintiff election is irrelevant to the determination of this issue. A court must adjudicate the proprietary entitlements of the plaintiff, the immediate recipient and any later recipients, respectively, in accordance with the recognised priority rules for determining title to property, as they apply at the

40 (1992) 175 CLR 621.

41 *White and Carter (Councils) Ltd v McGregor* [1962] AC 413.

5

'UNJUST ENRICHMENT': THE SAME OLD MISTAKE?

*Steve Hedley**

One of the most puzzling aspects of 'unjust enrichment' has always been its cunning disguise as an established and traditional common law subject. It is all tricked out with fancy Latin phrases; it has its own history. It is easy to discern differences of approach at different periods of history, and to convince ourselves that the modern approach is better than what preceded it. It all seems very respectable, and very well rooted in the fabric of the common law.

This is all the more surprising because, as everyone knows, this is all make-believe. The subject was virtually unheard-of 30 years ago. The ancient and respectable cases which are supposed to lend antiquity to the subject do not, in fact, mention it, nor is there any reason to suppose that the judges who decided them would approve of modern developments.[1] And the detail of the theory of unjust enrichment was elaborated less than 20 years ago! What is going on?

The standard explanation accuses our predecessors of a century or so ago of an extraordinary blunder. Apparently, they spotted 'tort' and 'contract' and ran them to ground, but wholly failed to notice 'unjust enrichment', even though it was in many respects very similar. So, the story runs, unjust enrichment fits so well into the traditional scheme for private law because its niche was always there, even if we have only recently filled it. It stands alongside contract and tort and is in many respects very similar to them.

And, indeed, the theory of 'unjust enrichment' is modelled on contract and tort. Unfortunately, it is based on very old-fashioned versions of those topics. Far from providing an antidote to outmoded versions of contract and tort, the supposedly novel 'unjust enrichment' entrenches them further. We are simply making again the same mistake that earlier scholars made – we are trying to fit the modern law into the same sort of over-simplified conception that we would now reject in other areas.

---

* I would like to thank Andrew Robertson for organising the splendid conference in Melbourne at which I gave this paper, and the marvellous audience for their various reactions to it. For subsequent work leading to the book, my thanks to Andrew Robertson in chief, and also to Joachim Dietrich and James Edelman for useful comments on a draft.

1 On the 'classic' cases of *Moses v Macferlan* (1760) 2 Burr 1005, 97 ER 676, *United Australia v Barclays Bank* [1941] AC 1, and *Fibrosa Spolka Akcyjna v Fairbairn Lawson Combe Barbour* [1943] AC 32, see Hedley, S, *Restitution: Its Division and Ordering*, London: Sweet & Maxwell, 2001, 208–10.

THE BATTLEFIELD THAT IS RESTITUTION

My starting point is to draw together various criticisms that have been made of particular portions of unjust enrichment. The object is to show that the controversies here now extend to cover the whole field. More precisely, there is no liability or set of liabilities which is uncontroversially based on unjust enrichment, or which has no other plausible explanation.

Necessarily I must be selective. Different claims have been made at different times for just what 'unjust enrichment' covers; I cannot hope to cover every liability which has at some point been claimed for 'unjust enrichment'. Looking at the matter historically, it was Goff and Jones who made the greatest territorial claims for unjust enrichment, in the mid-1960s.[2] In the first edition of their *Law of Restitution* there are all manner of strange and wonderful legal liabilities, including marine salvage, what happens to the estates of murder victims where the murderer seems about to inherit, and attornment in respect of money. Yet there was surprisingly little theory used in the course of the book. At that point restitution was rather formless, albeit that many argued that there was something definite hiding within that formlessness.

Then the empire of restitution began to shrink, starting a remorseless decline which has continued to this day. Some topics simply vanished out of later editions of Goff and Jones, never to be seen again. Others were more openly abandoned. Then, in 1985, we have the canonical statement of the theory of unjust enrichment, in Birks' *An Introduction to the Law of Restitution*.[3] Restitution is then no longer an amorphous blob: it has a clear structure. And just as the descent of Moses from the mountain, bearing the tablets of stone, is usually regarded as a significant event in Jewish history, so equally Oxford University Press's publication of the *Introduction* is usually regarded as a significant event for restitution lawyers. Yet the *Introduction* did not stop the retreat of the subject. Birks took a distinctly narrower view of restitution than did Goff and Jones. And the debate which followed it has inexorably generated more and more scepticism about unjust enrichment as the basis of the subject. So the retreat continues.

Stated in more detail, the cases Birks was trying to explain as examples of 'unjust enrichment' can be divided into four rough categories. Once so divided, the retreat is pretty evident.

First, there are the cases of restitution by wrong. Birks' *Introduction* had seemed to claim these as part of 'unjust enrichment'.[4] But 12 years later the author announced that he had changed his mind. He now asserted that they could not be so explained, that these cases were not part of unjust enrichment properly so called.[5] And this view is now almost universally held: the structure of ideas which tries to

2 Goff, R and Jones, G, *The Law of Restitution*, London: Sweet & Maxwell, 1966. At the time of writing, the current edition is the 6th, 2002.

3 Oxford: OUP, 1985.

4 See especially *ibid*, 83–98.

5 Birks, P, 'Misnomer', in Cornish, W *et al* (eds), *Restitution: Past Present and Future*, Oxford: Hart, 1998, 1.

hold the other areas of the subject together simply cannot be stretched to include restitution for wrongs. Not everyone accepts this, to be sure. Andrew Burrows has put in a rear-guard defence of the broader view of unjust enrichment, the so called 'quadrationist' point of view, albeit on the rather minimal basis that 'one should think very carefully before abandoning a strongly declared position in favour of another marginally preferable position'.[6] Oxford always was, by tradition, the home of lost causes. And we in the younger universities can only admire the way they have managed to carry this noble tradition over into a new century. But, despite that, Burrows' arguments seem to most commentators to lack force.[7]

Secondly, there are cases where the plaintiff claims some item of property. This is treated by Birks as an example of 'unjust enrichment' – to say that someone else has your property is to say that they are unjustly enriched at your expense?[8] Yet surely the protection of property is a fundamental idea to private lawyers. It does not need to be 'explained' by reference to some other notion. While no doubt we can dig deeper into any legal notion, it is hard to see how a simple and obvious notion can be 'explained' by an abstruse, controversial and difficult one. The 'unjust enrichment' theory provides an involved and theoretically dubious explanation for something that has no need of an explanation in the first place. That said, to accept that these cases are a matter of property law, rather than unjust enrichment, is not in itself a magic key to them. But it avoids unnecessary and complex talk of unjust enrichment, and lays a good foundation for fruitful investigation. Put at its lowest, it is not an area which cries out for a theory of unjust enrichment.[9]

Thirdly, there is the area of subrogation, recoupment and contribution – roughly, questions of what happens when the plaintiff pays off a debt which the defendant should have paid. There is no space for a detailed consideration of this here; suffice it to say that most writers in practice treat this as distinct from the rest of restitution. Indeed, this area of law has subsisted happily for several centuries without any suggestion that it has anything to do with unjust enrichment, and I'm not convinced that unjust enrichment has anything useful to add. This is despite Charles Mitchell's elaborate and learned advocacy of an unjust enrichment explanation.[10] Mitchell's analysis is ingenious, but ultimately it does little to further an analytical understanding of the law. It explains nothing that needs explanation, it makes few predictions in unsettled areas, and makes too many predictions that are flatly wrong, contradicting clear rules laid down in the cases.[11] For these and other reasons, its merits are in doubt.[12]

---

6 'Quadrating Restitution and Unjust Enrichment: A Matter of Principle?' [2000] Restitution LR 257, 258.

7 See, eg, Wright, D, 'Wrong and Remedy: A Sticky Relationship' [2001] Singapore Jnl Leg Stud 300, 303–04.

8 See, especially, Birks, P, 'Property and Unjust Enrichment: Categorical Truths' [1997] NZULR 623.

9 See generally Grantham, RB and Rickett, CEF, 'Property and Unjust Enrichment: Categorical Truths or Unnecessary Complexity?' [1997] NZULR 668.

10 Mitchell, C, *The Law of Subrogation*, Oxford: OUP, 1993.

11 Eg, his prediction that the availability of subrogation is controlled by the presence or absence of 'unjust factors': see Hedley, above n 1, 135–40.

12 See in more detail Hedley, above n 1, Chapter 5.

With the fourth and final group of cases, we come to the main topic of this chapter.

DIRECT RESTITUTION

Once those other cases are set on one side, we are left with the cases of direct restitution, where the plaintiff has directly conferred a benefit on the defendant, and claims restitution for it. These include the most basic examples of restitution, such as restitution for mistake or failure of consideration – the actions we still tend to call by their 18th century names, the action for money had and received, the *quantum meruit* and the *quantum valebat*. What is the correct way of dealing with these cases? This seems to me to be the key question, for now, in the structure of private law. If Birks is right, and these cases are best seen as examples of unjust enrichment, then there *is* a category of claims based on unjust enrichment, and the only question is how large it is. If however, as I suggest, these liabilities are better seen as part of contract law, then the entire structure of unjust enrichment begins to creak. If *these* cases can't be treated as uncontroversial examples of unjust enrichment, then it is hard to point to anything else that is. The alleged 'principle of unjust enrichment' is then in some difficulty, because there is nothing substantial left for it to explain.

Yet the idea that these liabilities are part of the law of contract is usually dismissed today as an antiquarian fiction, suitable perhaps for the 17th or 18th centuries, but not for the modern world. Even writers with no love of unjust enrichment take it for granted that to base liability on an implied contract instead is not a sensible alternative. But I suggest that the idea has not been taken as seriously as it deserves. At one time, no doubt, it seemed sensible to draw a sharp line between contractual liabilities, based on the intentions of the parties to the contract, and other liabilities, imposed by the law irrespective of intent. But that line has been steadily breaking down over the last half-century or more. The distinction is simply not so sharp as it once was, and it is time to re-think it.

The starting point is to ask how cases of direct restitution are normally dealt with. If you directly benefit me by doing work for me, or supplying goods, or whatever, what law do we normally expect to apply? The obvious answer is, the law of contract. This is the legal vehicle through which nearly all economic exchange takes place. From a legal technical point of view, direct conferment of benefit is usually either by way of contract or by way of free gift; and it is the law of contract that tells us how to distinguish those two situations. And as is elementary, the crucial question is whether the recipient contracted to pay or not. We look for: the presence or absence of agreement; the presence or absence of consideration; the presence or absence of intent to create legal relations; and so on.

This is all simple and uncontroversial. But note the significance for restitution. It shows that we clearly do have a body of rules on which benefits should be paid for, and indeed which it is unjust not to pay for. And this body of rules is called 'the law of contract'. I do not contend that this is *all* the law of contract does – that law is too vast and complicated for such generalisations. But it is the main thing it does. When there is action in court over a contract, it is usually to enforce payment for benefits conferred.

Now what happens if the facts *almost* establish a contract, but just fall short? Usually, that is the end of the matter – no contract, no liability to pay. Yet there are some marginal situations (*very* few) where there cannot be a contract, but the facts reveal a substantial reason why the defendant nonetheless should pay. So in these cases there is no contract, but it is nonetheless fair to act as if there were one. Routine examples are that the benefits were plainly meant to be paid for, but one or both of the parties was acting under a mistake; or was being unfairly pressured by the other; or lacked capacity to enter into binding obligations. Another case is where the precise amount to be paid was never settled, or some legal formality was not complied with. In those instances, there cannot be a 'contract' strictly so called. But if in fact the benefits were transferred, then very often the fair result is the same as in contract. If an arrangement is too vague to form a contract, benefits conferred under it nonetheless earn remuneration much as if there was a contract. If an arrangement for benefits lacks legal formality, then partly performing that arrangement often creates rights similar to contractual ones.

So in my view the pattern of liability does not support a simple distinction between cases of contract (leading to full liability) and cases of no contract (with no liability). There is in fact a middle case: where there is no complete agreement, but nonetheless the case is sufficiently close to contract to merit contractual remedies *in favour of someone who has performed their side*. I happily concede that these cases do not involve 'contract' in the normal sense. But I insist on the similarity with contract, which is too great to be ignored. Some might wish to call them examples of 'quasi-contract' – but that term carries too much historical baggage already, and gratuitously uses Latin where English seems adequate to the task. So let us call this phenomenon *near-contract*, or *almost-contract*, or *not-quite-contract*. Or perhaps, with a nod to the brave new world of cyber-space, we should call it *virtual contract*. Any one of these phrases is adequate to convey the central concept – that while falling outside the standard definition of contract, nonetheless these cases fall to be treated in much the same way as contracts.

'VIRTUAL CONTRACT' OR 'UNJUST ENRICHMENT'?

So this is the issue. We have these cases of direct restitution, which I here call near-contract or virtual contract, but which Birks calls unjust enrichment. What, if anything, is wrong with my contractual way of putting it? It is very hard to find a statement of reasons in the literature. Those who support a radically distinct 'unjust enrichment' have tended to assume its distinctiveness, rather than demonstrating it. And the analogy with contract has been summarily dismissed as unworthy of serious attention, rather than explicitly argued against. But I will try to sketch out (what I take to be) the more principled objections to a contractual approach.

First, actual transfer of benefit might be said to be the key to the matter. It might be argued that for these cases there is only a remedy if a benefit is *actually* transferred, whereas it is elementary in mainstream contract law that rights are created simply on proof of agreement. Now in theory this is correct. But in practice, plaintiffs who have not performed their side of the bargain have a rough time of it in contract law. The courts simply do not apply the same criteria to purely executory arrangements as they do to arrangements where one side has performed. In most situations, a plaintiff who has not performed is in a pretty weak position to complain of the other side's breach: the exceptions, while justifiable, are rare. And indeed this is how it should be in any rational law of contract.[13]

A second objection to treating these restitution cases as contractual is that it involves a fiction. Actual contracts should not be confused with fictitious contracts or quasi-contracts, some will say. Whatever principle is at work in these restitutionary cases, it cannot be the same as that behind the law of contract, because there is, by definition, no contract. Actual promises to pay must be kept distinct from fictitious ones.

My answer to that is to ask who, precisely, is engaging in fictions here. The idea that contract is 'based on promises' is drilled into law students at an early and impressionable age. But those who have progressed further than that elementary stage know that this has elements of fiction in it. No doubt it is true that the law of contract aims to reflect party intent, where it can do so. But it is quite another matter to say that each and every aspect of the law of contract in some esoteric way 'represents' the will of the parties; that is a quite unwarranted descent into mysticism. In most matters, contract lawyers have no clear evidence as to what the parties intended. They get by with the application of default rules. These rules may or may not have been intended by the parties; their whole object is to avoid ascertaining whether that is so or not. So long as parties who may have wanted to specify a different set of rules had a fair chance to do so, the courts are happy simply imposing the default rules. They do not know whether either or both parties intended those rules, and by and large they do not care either. And discerning what role party intent, or likely intent, plays in framing the rules in the first place is a complicated matter, not easily resolved.[14]

So I suggest that a claim for benefits directly conferred on the defendant must either be contractual, or be so closely analogous that it must be treated in the same category.

One consequence of my argument is that the reasoning in the famous *Pavey & Matthews* case badly needs to be re-thought today.[15] In this case, builders did work on the defendant's cottage. When the work was finished, however, the defendant pointed out that the contract for the work was never put into the form that statute

---

13 See, eg, Atiyah, PS, *An Introduction to the Law of Contract*, Oxford: OUP, 4th edn, 1989, 50–58.

14 See, eg, discussion in Riley, CA, 'Designing Default Rules in Contract Law: Consent, Conventionalism, and Efficiency' (2000) 20 OJLS 367.

15 *Pavey & Matthews Pty Ltd v Paul* (1987) 162 CLR 221.

required. She therefore declined to pay for it. The High Court agreed that the statute prevented the builders from suing in contract. The statute clearly stated that contracts of that sort had to be in writing, and so a builder who had failed to secure a written agreement could not sue in contract. However, said a majority, it was undeniable that the builders had conferred a valuable benefit on the defendant, unjustly enriching her. Did the statute forbid actions in respect of unjust enrichment? It made no mention of them. So the action succeeded.

Now this is the sort of approach I have great difficulty with and, on the way the issues were framed in that case, I would have to side with Brennan J, who dissented. In fact, his argument can be stated more starkly than it was. The majority argument is simple pedantry. It boils down to an assertion that the builders' action was not an action in contract, but rather an action for remuneration for the benefit the builders have conferred. But that is a distinction without a difference. The contract action was also an action for remuneration for the benefit conferred. To test this, ask how far someone gets by suing in contract if they have not conferred the benefit they agreed to confer. No one can expect to be paid for work they have not done, and the law of contract almost invariably manages to avoid that result. And surely if the statute bars a contractual action for remuneration, then it should equally bar that same action dressed up in another way, a restitutionary way. So *on the issues as actually framed in the case*, the majority judgments seemed to me to be flawed. The builders had simply dressed up a contractual claim in the language of unjust enrichment, without altering the substance. If the contractual claim was barred by statute, then so should the restitutionary claim be barred. The statutory ban on 'contracts' must also apply to causes of action practically indistinguishable from contracts.[16]

(As a side-issue, however, note that the *result* in *Pavey & Matthews* is not necessarily wrong. Perhaps the builders deserved their money. My point is that the contractual claim and the 'unjust enrichment' claim must go the same way – there is no practical difference between the two, and so the law must treat them in the same way. It is another question which way they should both go. And where Parliament has simply declared a certain type of contract unenforceable, without any attempt to provide a remedial scheme for parties who have acted as if it were valid, I do not think it should lightly be assumed that each and every possible contractual action is unavailable. So, in my view, what the High Court should have done is to look at *why* the statute required writing – what policy this requirement served. It may be that the court feels able to remunerate builders for work actually done, without undermining that policy. The court might, in other words, be saying that the policy of the act is sufficiently served by holding executory contracts caught by the ban, without denying remuneration to builders who have actually performed the contract. But my main point here is a simpler one: whatever answer is reached on that question, it cannot vary depending on whether the action is dressed up in 'contractual' or 'restitutionary' clothes.)

---

16 This point is made at greater length in Dietrich, J, *Restitution – A New Perspective*, Leichhardt: Federation, 1998, 111–13 and 119–22.

There is nothing irrational or fictitious about viewing these cases in near-contractual terms. If it is said that it is a fiction to base any remedy on the intentions of the parties to the transaction, then certainly I agree. But this is equally true of contract generally. How many parties *intend* a remedy of damages, or a right to specific performance? How many parties *intend* to be subject to the rule in *Hadley v Baxendale*?[17] None that I'm aware of. Party intention just isn't relevant in that way.

The real problem, then, is that the concept of a law of unjust enrichment, distinct from contract law, is built on a rather old-fashioned idea of contract. The notion of unjust enrichment would have slotted neatly into the law if it had been developed in (say) 1880. With the simple distinction the academics of that time accepted between rights created by the parties and rights created by the law, a dichotomy between contract and restitution might have found acceptance without too much difficulty. Fully negotiated contracts were then taken as the paradigm for all contracts, which encouraged academics to draw a simplistic distinction between what was contractual and what was not. As of today, however, no one should attempt to build their theories on such a shaky foundation. Surely no reasonably well informed writer supposes that the average contract is freely negotiated, or indeed negotiated at all. Contract is now inescapably tied up with other notions – no simple distinction can be drawn between what was intended by the parties and what the law imposes on them. There now is a considerable overlap with tort. Misleading behaviour inducing someone to make a contract is a wrong for which compensation is available, without any pretence that the remedy was 'intended' by anyone. Promises are enforced not merely by contract but also by reliance-based doctrines. Equitable notions of consent and wrongs are not as dead as were supposed a while ago, but very much alive and capable of generating new rights, and so forth. A theory which assumes a neat distinction between contract and the rest of the law may have been fit for the century before last, but it should be looked at with some suspicion today.

THE VARIETIES OF UNJUST ENRICHMENT

Having focused the argument on the particular area of direct restitution, what are the implications for the more general idea of unjust enrichment?

We need to draw a sharp distinction between vague references to 'unjust enrichment' on the one hand, and more precise references that invoke a clear concept of what it is on the other. This is, I think, the same distinction that Gummow J was making recently when he distinguished between 'unjust enrichment ... seen as a concept' and unjust enrichment seen as a 'definitive legal principle'.[18] Of course, there is a continuum of usages between these, but it is, I think, useful to consider these endpoints.[19]

---

17 (1854) 9 Exch 341; 156 ER 145.

18 *Roxburgh v Rothmans of Pall Mall Australia Ltd* [2001] HCA 68, [74].

19 Cf Virgo's rather similar distinction between unjust enrichment's 'descriptive' and 'substantive' meanings: Virgo, G, *The Principles of the Law of Restitution*, Oxford: OUP, 1999, 8–9.

Suppose the reference to unjust enrichment is vague, so that we are dealing with Gummow J's 'unjust enrichment as a mere concept'. Then the reference is unobjectionable, but it is also quite close to meaningless. *Any* claim for money can be described as a claim for unjust enrichment by someone who is so inclined: any plaintiff can sum up their case by saying that the defendant will be unjustly enriched unless the court orders payment of a certain sum. Absent some theory to confine it, 'unjust enrichment' can describe any money claim whatever. Indeed, it is worse than this, for 'unjust enrichment' can also be used to describe any *defence* to a money claim as well – the defendant argues that the plaintiff will be unjustly enriched if the claim is allowed. My learned colleague, Mr O'Dell, recently seemed to claim this as a distinctively Irish usage[20] – but while the Irish deserve some of the credit for it,[21] the English seem to be at least as bad.[22] I do not know whether this particular virus has made it to Australia yet. I do know that there is nothing in the logic of 'unjust enrichment' to stop it.

I think that the prevalence of this vague usage must also be borne in mind when considering the argument from European law. It is often said that, as the UK is progressively absorbed into 'ever closer union' with the other nations of Europe, it is inevitable that unjust enrichment will more and more become a feature of its various legal systems. If 'unjust enrichment' is being used in the vague sense, I think this is probably right; but, given the impalpable nature of the vague usage, it is not very important either. If it is being used in a more precise sense, the answer is that there is no reason to suppose that Europe will force the UK into a pattern of liability which the other Member States scarcely accept themselves. And whatever is to be said for the precise formalism of the German approach to restitution, it has evidently not over-influenced the French or the Italians, whose approach is much more laid-back.[23]

What then of the more precise conceptions of unjust enrichment, which Gummow J calls 'unjust enrichment as a definitive legal principle'? I will concentrate here on the conception of unjust enrichment promoted by Birks, as it is the most widely accepted one.

I think it is vital to remember the basis on which Birks' scheme for unjust enrichment was originally defended. Birks never claimed that his doctrine of unjust enrichment had any very great practical consequence, or involved any principle of morality. Indeed, he went out of his way to suggest that this was at best an irrelevant consideration, and that at worst we would imperil the entire legal system by asking questions about what was just and what was not.[24] The

20 'Unjust Enrichment, Irish Style' (message to the Restitution Discussion Group, 24 January 2002, archived at www.ucc.ie/law/restitution/rdg/kk0201009.htm).

21 Eg, Consumer Credit Act 1995, s 55: 'Where a creditor or an owner is compensated or recovers possession of goods in any action by virtue of this Act the court shall ensure that the compensation or repossession does not entail any unjustified enrichment of the creditor or the owner, as the case may be.'

22 Eg, Value Added Tax Act 1994, s 80(3): 'It shall be a defence, in relation to a claim under this section, that repayment of an amount would unjustly enrich the claimant.'

23 For a general survey, see Schlechtriem, P, Coen, C and Hornung, R, 'Restitution and Unjust Enrichment in Europe' [2001] European Rev of Private Law 377.

24 Most famously in *An Introduction to the Law of Restitution*, Oxford: Clarendon, 1985, 19–20.

struggle between different conceptions of justice was, in his view, to be left to the politicians. The role of the jurist was simply to produce workable classifications of actions and results.

I think that much too little attention has been paid to this point. Much academic writing on unjust enrichment seems to assume that there is a principle here with strong and established moral credentials, that while there may be little dispute over precisely when and how it applies, nonetheless it makes sense to refer to 'the principle against unjust enrichment'. Yet these credentials are hard to discern.[25] Taken at its highest, Birks' argument was no more than that the law's internal consistency, in the context of restitutionary claims, required the recognition of unjust enrichment. He did not claim that it was a moral principle or an aim of public policy. It is not surprising that the area has ended up as a moral and policy wasteland – that was always the intention. There is much loose talk here of how a principle against unjust enrichment is 'intuitively satisfying'. Maybe so, but it would be surprising if this translated into any legal principle. Enriching yourself is not, after all, intrinsically objectionable in modern Western societies. It is not an obvious concern for the legal system in the way that failing to pay your debts or inflicting harm on others is.

The only virtue claimed for unjust enrichment theory being its consistency, it follows that it must stand or fall with that supposed consistency. It is therefore very much to the point that the theory of unjust enrichment is currently in a mess, that every academic who investigates the matter has a different theory, and that the divergence of opinion seems to getting worse rather than better. Considered as a job-creation scheme for legal academics, this is all quite splendid. From what other point of view it is to be considered an asset to the law, I do not know.

As to the definition of 'enrichment', there is no unanimity. All the different theories start from the point that money is an unproblematic example of enrichment, and then try, in their various ways, to apply the analogy of money to other benefits. The result (since liability to refund money is traditionally rather wider than liability to refund other types of asset) is a steady broadening of the law, as academics seek to extend the rules for money to other assets. Speaking for myself, I think the premise is entirely wrong. For other legal purposes, we have no problem in distinguishing different types of assets, nor in accepting that money is quite different from other types. No one expects the legal rights arising from a loan of a car to be much like those for the loan of a house, and neither is remotely like the rights created by a loan of money. Why should the law of restitution be any different?

As to the definition of 'injustice', again there is no unanimity. I have read many textbooks on unjust enrichment; I have yet to find any two which agree with one another on the list of 'unjust factors' which supposedly establish injustice for this purpose. Specialists in this area will be familiar with the controversies: over how much can be explained by a factor of 'mistake' and how it should be defined;

---

25 On the difficulties in defining any supposed moral principle of 'unjust enrichment', see Hedley, above n 1, 218–19.

whether cases with a public law element need different treatment, and if so how; whether 'failure of consideration' is properly to be regarded as an unjust factor; and so forth. And this is before we get on to those who wish to emulate the Canadians and the Germans, by abandoning the idea of 'unjust factors' altogether, talking rather of enrichments for which there is no good 'legal ground'.

I need not labour the point, I think. If the purpose of the systematic theory of unjust enrichment is to clarify the law, then it has so far failed, and there is no reason to expect success in the future. If the theory has some other object, this object has yet to be articulated.

CONCLUSION

The concept of 'unjust enrichment' is just an instrument – a tool for doing certain types of legal work. It seems to be something of a legal perennial. It is certainly very hard to keep the notion out of lawyers' heads altogether, in this century or any other. So we have to decide what job of work we want it to do. But it should not lightly be assumed that a very precise concept of unjust enrichment will necessarily produce desirable results. On the contrary, it may be best to keep the theory as vague and unconstraining as possible, lest (as Gummow J has put it) substance and dynamism in the law are restricted by dogma.[26]

---

26 *Roxburgh v Rothmans of Pall Mall Australia Ltd* [2001] HCA 68, [74].

6

ON THE DISTINCTION BETWEEN CONTRACT AND TORT

*Andrew Robertson**

The classical understanding of the law of obligations was founded on the idea that a sharp distinction could be drawn between contract and tort. Contractual rights and obligations were seen to be shaped by the parties and adopted by consent. The law of contract was regarded as the realm of voluntary obligations; a contract was seen as a manifestation of the will of the parties.[1] Hugh Collins has noted that during the classical age the perceived role of the law of contract was to facilitate voluntary choices.[2] The idea that a contract could be imposed, or that a contractual obligation could be involuntary or non-consensual, was untenable.[3] A clear boundary was thought to exist between contract and tort.[4] As Jay Feinman has observed: 'Classical theorists saw real, objective differences between contract law, in which liability was imposed only through the consent of the parties, and other private law fields, in which liability was imposed for causing injury to another (tort) or for violating another's entitlement (property).'[5] While duties in contract were thought to be 'fixed by the parties themselves', duties in tort were 'primarily fixed by the law'.[6] Sir William Anson wrote in 1879 that the wrongdoer's obligation in delict to make good his breach of duty 'is not created by the free-will of the parties, but springs up immediately on the occurrence of the wrongful act'.[7]

The classical distinction between contract and tort continues to exert great influence on the courts and legal scholars. The validity of the distinction is routinely assumed in contract judgments and contract scholarship. Although

---

* This chapter is the first part of a broader research project on voluntariness, autonomy and contract law. I would like to thank Patrick Doyle for the valuable research assistance he provided in the early stages of this research project and David Campbell, Ralph Cunnington, Joachim Dietrich, Fred Ellinghaus, David McLauchlan, Anne Orford, Jeannie Paterson and Megan Richardson for their helpful comments on an earlier draft of this chapter.

1 See Atiyah, PS, *The Rise and Fall of Freedom of Contract*, Oxford: Clarendon, 1979, especially at 405–08.

2 Collins, H, *The Law of Contract*, London: Butterworths, 3rd edn, 1997, 6.

3 *Ibid*, 7. Thus in some cases non-consensual contractual obligations were rationalised on the basis of estoppel: *Smith v Hughes* (1871) LR 6 QB 597, 607, 609; *Harris v The Great Western Railway Co* (1876) 1 QBD 515, 530.

4 Gilmore, G, *The Death of Contract*, Columbus, OH: Ohio State UP, 1974, 95 noted the 'insistence of the classical theorists on the sharp differentiation between contract and tort'.

5 Feinman, JM, 'Critical Approaches to Contract Law' (1983) 30 UCLA L Rev 829, 832.

6 Winfield, PH, *The Province of Tort*, Cambridge: CUP, 1931, 40.

7 Anson, WR, *Principles of the English Law of Contract*, Oxford: Clarendon, 1893: Pt 1, § 2(2).

defects in the classical model are often pointed out,[8] decisions continue to be made on the basis of a perception of the distinction between contract and tort that is little different from that prevailing in the 19th century. PS Atiyah noted in 1978 that, despite increasing criticism, 'the conceptual apparatus which still dominates legal thinking on these issues is the apparatus of the nineteenth century'.[9] Atiyah's own criticism of the tendency to 'draw far too sharp a line between contract and tort'[10] has been surprisingly little heeded.

The purpose of this chapter is to elaborate and advance Atiyah's argument that a sharp distinction cannot be drawn between contract and tort. This is not to suggest that the liability and damages rules of contract are the same as those of tort. Nor is it to argue, as Grant Gilmore did, that contract and tort 'are gradually merging and becoming one'.[11] Rather, it is to question the idea that contract is a distinctive, voluntary species of obligation that can be seen as a kind of private law, and to question the distinctiveness of tort as a category of imposed obligation that enforces conformity with community standards of behaviour. This chapter suggests that contract law is to a significant extent informed by values and standards routinely attributed to the law of tort. The focus of the chapter is on the extent to which the distinction between contract and tort is undermined by the principles of contract law. This chapter views the boundary from the point of view of contract: its primary focus is on contract cases; its principal claim is that it is necessary to mis-state the basis of contractual obligation in order to draw a sharp distinction between contract and tort; its main concern is with the consequences for contract law of the drawing of an inaccurate distinction.

Many judges and legal scholars would accept the critique of a rigid distinction between contract and tort presented in this chapter. Nonetheless, the classical view continues to be repeated without qualification in authoritative legal texts. These texts assume that contract is about what people intend, while the law of torts is concerned with what people do.[12] The legal community is divided on its willingness to acknowledge the defects in the classical model. At times this division is reflected in inconsistent statements within the one text. To take one example, Richard Craswell suggests that 'a common belief holds that tort law imposes duties without regard to a party's consent, while contract law enforces only those duties that a party has voluntarily assumed'.[13] He almost immediately contradicts this assertion, however, by suggesting that a more enlightened view is widespread: 'By now, it is well understood that the distinction between contract and tort is not that simple, and that it does not line up neatly with any distinction

8 On the US literature, see Feinman, above n 5, 829–33. The leading Australian example is Swanton, J, 'The Convergence of Tort and Contract' (1989) 12 Syd LR 40, 41: 'the traditional suggested distinctions between contract and tort were never wholly convincing.' In England, of course, the dominant voice has been that of PS Atiyah, discussed below.

9 Atiyah, PS, 'Contracts, Promises and the Law of Obligations' (1978) 94 LQR 193, 194; *Essays on Contract*, Oxford: Clarendon, 1986, 11.

10 *Ibid*, 'Contracts, Promises', 221; *Essays on Contract*, 41.

11 Gilmore, above n 4, 96.

12 Atiyah, above n 9, *Essays on Contract*, 13.

13 Craswell, R, 'Against Fuller and Perdue' (2000) 67 U Chic LR 99, 129.

between voluntary and involuntary obligation.'[14] How is it that these two beliefs can be held simultaneously? Some of those who know that there are significant flaws in the distinction between contract and tort still insist that at some fundamental level they can be distinguished.[15] This chapter is the first step in an attempt to understand that paradox. My goal here is to demonstrate the persistence of the 'common belief' in the sharp distinction between contract and tort and to provide a detailed account of the reasons why the distinction is 'not that simple'.

MARKING THE BOUNDARY

Both the House of Lords and the High Court of Australia have in recent cases drawn sharp distinctions between the basis of obligation in contract and that in tort. In each case the distinction influenced the outcome, affecting the determination of liability in one case and remedy in the other. The first case is the 1995 decision of the House of Lords in *Henderson v Merrett Syndicates Ltd*.[16] The House of Lords was concerned in that case with the question, amongst others, whether an obligation in tort could exist concurrently with a co-extensive obligation in contract. The issue was whether the agent for a Lloyds insurance syndicate was liable in tort as well as in contract for a failure to take care to protect the interests of the Lloyds Names (that is, those ultimately responsible for the underwriting). The House of Lords held that the agent was liable in tort as well as contract, allowing the plaintiffs to claim alternative remedies in contract and tort. In a speech with which the other members of the House of Lords concurred, Lord Goff justified the conclusion that liability in tort could exist concurrently with liability in contract on the basis that 'the tortious duty is imposed by the general law, and the contractual duty is attributable to the will of the parties'.[17]

The distinction drawn by Lord Goff was adopted by the High Court of Australia in its 1999 decision in *Astley v Austrust Ltd*.[18] The plaintiff in that case was a trustee company that sought legal advice before accepting the role of trustee of an existing trading trust. The company's solicitors failed to advise the company that it should not accept the office of trustee without excluding personal liability for trading losses. The solicitors breached a duty of care in tort, but also breached

---

14 *Ibid*, 130.

15 Eg, Knapp, C, 'Rescuing Reliance: The Perils of Promissory Estoppel' (1998) 49 Hastings LJ 1191, 1333 criticises 'Gilmore, McNeil and others' for:

> ... blurring the line between commitments which have been voluntarily assumed and those that are socially imposed. One may concede that the line between the two is wavering, illogical and marked by needlessly confusing overlaps, and yet feel that there is a fundamental difference between the two types of obligations, a difference worth preserving in the structure of the law. *While tort law deals with conduct that flouts general notions of behaviour in society, contract law addresses injuries occasioned by the breaking of commitments voluntarily expressed.*
>
> (Emphasis added, footnote reference omitted.)

16 [1995] 2 AC 145.

17 *Ibid*, 194.

18 (1999) 197 CLR 1.

an implied contractual duty to take reasonable care. The company was guilty of contributory negligence in taking on the office of trustee and borrowing large sums of money without making proper inquiries as to the viability of the business or the sufficiency of the trust assets. One issue before the court was whether legislation requiring the apportionment of damages in the event of contributory negligence required the reduction of an award of contract damages as well as tort damages. By a majority of 4:1, the court held that the statute in question did not apply to a contract claim, even where liability in contract and tort was concurrent.

In a joint judgment, Gleeson CJ, McHugh, Gummow and Hayne JJ held that it was clear from the 'history, text and purpose' of the contributory negligence legislation that it was not intended to apply to contract claims.[19] Under the heading 'policy considerations' they said that this result was not anomalous or unfair because the theoretical foundations of tort and contract are fundamentally different. 'Tort obligations are imposed on the parties; contractual obligations are voluntarily assumed.'[20] Gleeson CJ, McHugh, Gummow and Hayne JJ cited Lord Goff's emphasis in *Henderson v Merrett Syndicates Ltd* on the will of the parties as the factor that supported different results in contract and tort.

This perpetuation of the classical distinction between contract and tort is not confined to the courts, as the following examples demonstrate. The first two examples are drawn from the English literature, the second two from the United States. In his book of essays on the law of obligations, Andrew Burrows justifies doctrinal differences between contract and tort on the basis of a 'root distinction between voluntary and purely imposed obligations'.[21] Contract, he says, is 'based on a voluntary undertaking' while in tort 'the liability is purely imposed'.[22] The practitioner treatise *Chitty on Contracts* tells us that 'contractual obligations are voluntary and particular to the parties, whereas liability in tort is imposed by law as a matter of policy and affects persons generally'.[23] In an article on promissory estoppel, Charles Knapp claims that: 'While tort law deals with conduct that flouts general notions of behaviour in society, contract law addresses injuries occasioned by the breaking of commitments voluntarily expressed.'[24] Charles Fried has provided a book-length argument that contract law is based on 'the promise principle', that is, 'that principle by which persons may impose on themselves obligations where none existed before'.[25] Fried notes that tort law 'typically deals with involuntary transactions'.[26] Since contract is concerned with obligations the parties have assumed, Fried suggests, the focus of the inquiry is on

---

19 *Ibid*, 6.

20 *Ibid*, 36.

21 Burrows, A, *Understanding the Law of Obligations*, Oxford: Hart, 1998, 13.

22 *Ibid*. In an earlier footnote (*ibid*, fn 29, 10), Burrows seems to accept that contractual obligations are not in fact voluntary, but constitute 'what a reasonable man regards the promisor as having accepted an obligation to do'.

23 Beale, HG (ed), *Chitty on Contracts*, London: Sweet & Maxwell, 1999, vol 1, 31. The proposition is later qualified: *ibid*, 34–35.

24 Above n 15.

25 Fried, C, *Contract as Promise*, Cambridge, MA: Harvard UP, 1981, 1.

26 *Ibid*, 4.

the will of the parties. The focus in tort, on the other hand, is on 'the injury suffered by the plaintiff and the fairness of saddling the defendant with some or all of it'.[27] Fried opposes the assimilation of contract to tort through the principle of reliance on the basis that it would subordinate 'a quintessentially individualist ground of obligation and form of social control, one that refers to the will of the parties, to a set of standards that are ineluctably collective in origin and thus readily turned to collective ends'.[28]

This chapter questions the extent to which contract can be seen as an 'individualist ground of obligation', or 'one that refers to the will of the parties'. In both contract and tort, rights and obligations are to some extent shaped by the deliberate actions of the parties. Both contract and tort, however, also involve the application of community standards that are 'collective in origin'. Both contract and tort are concerned with what people do, as well as what they intend. Both draw heavily on the notion of reasonableness. Lord Steyn has observed that reasonableness in contract law 'postulates community values', is 'concerned with contemporary standards' and is evidenced by 'usages and practices of dealings' in the relevant field.[29] This echoes Atiyah's conception of reasonableness as a 'basic community judgment' that draws on 'collective moral ideas and even customary practices', 'rather than private autonomy'.[30] Lord Denning has said in the context of tort that:

> In determining responsibility, the law eliminates the personal equation. It takes no notice of the views of the particular individual or of others like him. It requires everyone to exercise all such precautions as a man of ordinary prudence would observe ...[31]

In many respects, as we will see, the law of contract also 'eliminates the personal equation' and requires everyone to act as the courts imagine a reasonable person would act.

BLURRING THE BOUNDARY

The objective approach to contract formation

Offer and acceptance

The theory that contract rests on voluntary obligation is not easily reconciled with the objective approach to contract formation.[32] The principles relating to contract

---

27 *Ibid*, 4.

28 *Ibid*, 5.

29 Steyn, J, 'Contract Law: Fulfilling the Reasonable Expectations of Honest Men' (1997) 113 LQR 433, 434.

30 Atiyah, above n 9, *Essays on Contract*, 87.

31 *Froom v Butcher* [1976] QB 286, 294, quoted with approval in *Astley v Austrust Ltd* (1999) 197 CLR 1, 16.

32 Atiyah, above n 9, *Essays on Contract*, 21.

formation and related principles of mistake tell us that contractual obligation arises not from consent to legal obligation, but from the appearance of consent. Conduct amounts to an offer if a reasonable person would construe it as such, regardless of the intentions of the offeror.[33] Acceptance is also determined objectively: 'The objective theory of contract requires an external manifestation of assent to an offer.'[34] Where there is no clear offer and acceptance, the court does not ask whether there was mutual assent, but whether mutual assent has been manifested.[35] The fundamental question is whether a reasonable person in the position of each of the parties would think there was a concluded bargain.[36]

Under an objective approach to contract formation it is possible for a party to incur a contractual obligation against his or her will. More commonly, a party will contract on terms to which he or she has not subjectively consented. In *Empirnal Holdings Pty Ltd v Machon Paull Partners Pty Ltd*,[37] the parties were found to have contracted on the basis of unsigned written terms sent by one party (architects) to the other (a developer). The developer refused to sign the document because its managing director did not sign contracts. The developer nevertheless went ahead and took the benefit of work done by the architects. The 'ultimate issue' for the New South Wales Court of Appeal was whether a 'reasonable bystander' would conclude that the developer had signalled acceptance of the terms.[38] The question was not whether the developer intended to assume the obligations set out in the contract, or whether the developer consented to those obligations, but whether the developer had behaved in a way that justified the imposition of these obligations according to norms of reasonable behaviour. McHugh JA described the case as 'not so much one of acceptance by silence as one of taking the benefit of an offer with knowledge of its terms and knowledge of the offeror's reliance on payment being made in return for his work'.[39]

That a contract can arise without a consensus, and that it may not reflect the will of one of the parties, is most clearly illustrated by a unilateral mistake as to terms. Consider a situation where one of the parties is, unbeknown to the other, and unbeknown to the hypothetical objective bystander, mistaken as to a fundamental term of the contract. If A signs a contract to sell land to B for $15,000 thinking the price was in fact $150,000 then, in the absence of unconscionable conduct by B, A is bound. This is so whether one adopts the objective theory of

---

33 *Carlill v Carbolic Smoke Ball Co* [1893] 1 QB 256.

34 *Empirnal Holdings Pty Ltd v Machon Paull Partners Pty Ltd* (1988) 14 NSWLR 523, 534.

35 *Brambles Holdings Ltd v Bathurst City Council* (2001) 53 NSWLR 153, 179.

36 *Ibid.*

37 (1988) 14 NSWLR 523 ('*Empirnal*').

38 *Ibid*, 535.

39 *Ibid*, 536. The fine distinction between contract and promissory estoppel is illustrated by comparing this case with *Waltons Stores (Interstate) Ltd v Maher* (1988) 164 CLR 387, which also involved a failure by one party to sign a contractual document followed by detrimental reliance by the other. In *Waltons* the failure to sign or renounce the document was held to amount, not to a contractual promise to perform in accordance with that document, but to an implied non-contractual promise to sign or the inducement of an assumption that the document had been or would be signed. Kirby P noted in *Empirnal* (1988) 14 NSWLR 523, 528 and 531 that the result reached in that case might also have been reached by way of estoppel had it been pleaded.

contract formation (which is concerned only with the outward manifestations of the parties' intentions and not the intentions themselves) or a subjective approach (which requires a consensus between the parties), coupled with the principle of estoppel recognised in *Smith v Hughes*.[40] Under the principle in *Smith v Hughes*, A is estopped from denying the existence of a contract if A led B to enter into the contract on the assumption that A was assenting to B's terms. It now seems clear that the approach articulated in *Smith v Hughes* has given way to the more transparent objective approach to contract formation. In *Taylor v Johnson*,[41] Mason ACJ, Murphy and Deane JJ observed that in the UK the speech of Lord Atkin in *Bell v Lever Bros Ltd*[42] has led to 'the near eclipse of the subjective theory' and suggested that 'the clear trend in decided cases and academic writings has been to leave the objective theory in command of the field'.[43] The objective approach is now adopted without question in the contemporary cases, textbooks and other literature.[44]

Intention to create legal relations

Like offer and acceptance, the intention to create legal relations principle requires only that the parties manifest such an intention, not that they actually hold such an intention at the time the contract is made. In *Ermogenous v Greek Orthodox Community of SA Inc*, the High Court of Australia noted that the word 'intention' is used in the context of an intention to create legal relations, as in other contractual contexts, to describe that which would 'objectively be conveyed by what is said and done, having regard to the circumstances in which those statements and actions happened. It is not a search for the uncommunicated subjective motives or intentions of the parties'.[45] Similarly, in England it has been said that: 'The judicial task is not to discover the actual intentions of each party; it is to decide what each was reasonably entitled to conclude from the attitude of the other.'[46]

---

40 (1871) LR 6 QB 597. See also *Harris v The Great Western Railway Co* (1876) 1 QBD 515, 530. As Dalton, C, 'An Essay in the Deconstruction of Contract Doctrine' (1985) 94 Yale LJ 997, 1039–45 has explained, it is not possible to draw a clear distinction between the subjective and objective approaches to contract formation. If one adopts a subjective approach, objective considerations must inevitably play a role, as *Smith v Hughes* shows. Similarly, as evidenced by *The Crown v Clarke* (1927) 40 CLR 227, subjective considerations inevitably affect the implementation of an objective approach: see Heffey, P, Patterson, J and Robertson, A, *Principles of Contract Law*, Sydney: Law Book Co, 2002, 78–79.

41 (1982) 151 CLR 422.

42 [1932] AC 161, 217–27.

43 (1982) 151 CLR 422, 429.

44 See, eg, *Cambridge Nutrition Ltd v British Broadcasting Corp* [1990] 3 All ER 523, 542; *Brambles Holdings Ltd v Bathurst City Council* (2001) 53 NSWLR 153, 170–79; Treitel, GH, *The Law of Contract*, 10th edn, London: Sweet & Maxwell, 1999, 1 and 8 and the literature cited therein, 1, fn 2.

45 (2002) 209 CLR 95, 105–06.

46 *Gloag on Contracts*, 2nd edn, 7, quoted with approval by Lord Reid in *McCutcheon v David Macbrayne Ltd* [1964] 1 WLR 125, 128.

Consideration

The bargain theory of consideration requires the court to determine whether something has been given 'in return for' a promise.[47] Consideration is the price for which the promise is bought.[48] In most cases, however, the bargain element is a matter of objective determination, since the parties rarely spell out explicitly that 'X is being given in return for Y'. The question the courts ask is whether what is claimed to constitute consideration *appears* to have been given in return for the promise.[49] In cases at the margins, we simply do not know whether the parties saw themselves as being involved in an exchange of this in return for that. In *Beaton v McDivitt*,[50] for example, it was not at all clear whether Beaton undertook cultivation work *in exchange for* McDivitt's promise to transfer land or simply *in reliance* on it. The distinction between bargain and reliance, between contract and estoppel, depended on the court's interpretation of the parties' behaviour.

In some cases the requirement of consideration is taken to be satisfied without any reference to the bargain question, even from an objective standpoint. Some judgments reveal no consideration of the question whether a reasonable person in the position of each of the parties would view the alleged consideration as having been given in return for the promise. In these cases the courts ask only whether the promisor has received *a benefit* or incurred *a detriment* from the agreement in question, not whether the parties *appeared to regard* that benefit or detriment as something being given or undertaken in return for the promise, much less whether the parties themselves *actually regarded* the benefit or detriment as a *quid pro quo*.[51]

Contractual obligation arising from behaviour

In order to make a contract, then, the courts do not require that the parties have *actually* reached a consensus, that they *actually* intended to be legally bound or that they *actually* intended to exchange one thing for another. Under the objective approach to contract formation, it is enough that the parties appeared to reach a

---

47 *Australian Woollen Mills Pty Ltd v The Commonwealth* (1954) 92 CLR 424; *Beaton v McDivitt* (1987) 13 NSWLR 162.

48 *Dunlop Pneumatic Tyre Co Ltd v Selfridge and Co Ltd* [1915] AC 847, 855; *'R' v Attorney General for England and Wales* (unreported, Privy Council on appeal from the New Zealand Court of Appeal, 17 March 2003, [30]–[32]). There remains some doubt as to whether the bargain theory represents the law in England. While Atiyah, above n 9, *Essays on Contract*, 69 has argued that the bargain theory 'never took root in England', Beatson J, *Anson's Law of Contract*, Oxford: OUP, 28th edn, 2002, 90 states that: 'A benefit conferred or a detriment suffered otherwise than in return for the promise of the other party cannot constitute consideration.'

49 *Australian Woollen Mills Pty Ltd v The Commonwealth* (1954) 92 CLR 424, 456.

50 (1987) 13 NSWLR 162.

51 See, eg, *Brambles Holdings Ltd v Bathurst City Council* (2001) 53 NSWLR 153, 182, 197; *Musumeci v Winadell Pty Ltd* (1994) 34 NSWLR 723, 748–49. The characterisation of non-bargain detriment as consideration in *Musumeci v Winadell Pty Ltd* completely obliterates the distinction between consideration and detrimental reliance and thus undermines the distinction between contract and equitable estoppel. Cf *Williams v Roffey Bros & Nicholls (Contractors) Ltd* [1991] 1 QB 1, 16 where Glidewell LJ said the practical benefit received by a promisor was 'capable of being consideration' for the promise.

consensus, appeared to intend to be bound and appeared to strike a bargain involving an exchange. As to the last element, the cases referred to in the above paragraph suggest that it may be sufficient that each party received a benefit or incurred a detriment from the transaction.

As Judge Learned Hand pointed out in 1911, contract is an obligation that attaches by the force of law to certain conduct. That conduct ordinarily represents the actual intentions of the parties, but need not necessarily do so.[52] Contractual obligation is not, then, ultimately based on consent, but on an objective manifestation of consent. It arises from behaviour that appears consensual.[53] Contract cannot then be seen as a system of voluntarily assumed obligations. If you behave in a particular way, you will incur a contractual obligation irrespective of your intentions, just as you may incur an obligation in tort by behaving in a certain way, irrespective of your intentions. Ultimately contractual obligations, like those in tort, are imposed on the basis of norms of reasonable behaviour. Contract must therefore be seen as a system of obligation that is at least to some extent public.[54] If a person conducts herself in a particular way, she can incur contractual obligations without her consent and against her will. These non-consensual contractual obligations are clearly based on enforced conformity to community standards of behaviour.

Objectivity in interpretation

External standards are also imposed on contracting parties through the principles and process of interpretation. When a dispute as to the meaning of a contract arises, that dispute is resolved by reference to what a reasonable person would believe the parties meant by the provision in question. The court gives effect to the intention of the parties 'objectively determined'. The interpretation of a contract, Lord Hoffmann said in *Investors Compensation Scheme Ltd v West Bromwich Building Society*, 'is the ascertainment of the meaning which the document would convey to a reasonable person having all the background knowledge which would reasonably have been available to the parties in the situation in which they were at the time of the contract'.[55] In *Reardon Smith Line Ltd v Hansen-Tangen* Lord Wilberforce famously said that: 'When one speaks of the intention of the parties to the contract, one is speaking objectively – the parties cannot themselves give direct evidence of what their intention was – and what must be ascertained is *what*

52 *Hotchkiss v National City Bank of New York*, 200 F 287, 293 (1911). See Dalton, above n 40, 1042–45.

53 Seavey, WA, 'Review of "The Province of the Law of Tort"' (1932) 45 Harv LR 209, 209 observed that a person is not liable in contract because he has agreed to be, but because 'he has made a manifestation to which the law attaches, with or without his intent, certain consequences'.

54 Dalton, above n 40, 1011.

55 [1998] 1 All ER 98, 114. This passage was quoted with approval by Gleeson CJ, Gummow and Hayne JJ in *Maggbury Pty Ltd v Hafele Australia Ltd* (2001) 210 CLR 181. See also *Bank of Credit and Commerce International SA v Ali* [2001] 1 All ER 961.

is to be taken as the intention which reasonable people would have had if placed in the situation of the parties.'[56]

The most striking feature of the objective approach is that, in combination with the parol evidence rule, it excludes extrinsic evidence of the parties' intentions from the process of interpretation.[57] When the courts interpret a contract, it is 'impermissible to receive contextual material or extrinsic evidence to indicate what the *subjective* intentions, beliefs or expectations of the makers were'.[58] The tendency of this rule to separate intentions from obligations is exemplified by the decision in *Brambles Holdings Ltd v Bathurst City Council*.[59] That case concerned the interpretation of a series of contracts under which Brambles managed a waste disposal depot on behalf of the council. One of the questions for the court was whether liquid waste fell within the expression 'general commercial waste' used in a contract made on 12 July 1990. Both the trial judge and the New South Wales Court of Appeal held that, on an objective interpretation, 'general commercial waste' did include liquid waste. Evidence of a mutual belief that the contract did not regulate the charging of fees for liquid waste was held to be irrelevant and inadmissible. That evidence included correspondence in January and February 1990 in which the parties made an arrangement relating to liquid waste that was inconsistent with the July 1990 contract. It included post-contractual conduct relating to liquid waste that was consistent with the January/February arrangement and inconsistent with the fee structure set up by the July contract. Finally, it included testimony from the relevant officers of each of the contracting parties indicating that they believed the July contract did not relate to liquid waste.[60]

Heydon JA said: 'the construction of a contract is an objective question for the court, and the subjective beliefs of the parties are generally irrelevant in the absence of any argument that a decree of rectification should be ordered or an estoppel by convention found.'[61] Perhaps the most striking illustration of the way in which the objective approach to interpretation can undermine the will of the parties is the statement of Ipp AJA that the parties were 'wrong' in their understanding of the meaning of the agreement. Ipp AJA observed that 'the parties (wrongly in my view) believed that the July 1990 contract ... did not regulate the charging of fees for liquid wastes'.[62] He said: 'The parties did not believe that the July 1990 contract applied to liquid waste and they did not intend to invoke any clause of that contract on the basis that it governed the determination of fees for liquid waste.'[63] Referring to the trial judge's

---

56 [1976] 3 All ER 570, 574 (emphasis added).

57 'The law excludes from the admissible background the previous negotiations of the parties and their declarations of subjective intent': *Investors Compensation Scheme Ltd v West Bromwich Building Society* [1998] 1 All ER 98, 114. Cf UNIDROIT Principles of International Commercial Contracts 1994, Art 4.

58 *Royal Botanic Gardens and Domain Trust v South Sydney City Council* (2002) 186 ALR 289, 316.

59 (2001) 53 NSWLR 153.

60 *Ibid*, 191.

61 *Ibid*, 164.

62 *Ibid*, 193.

63 *Ibid*, 194.

interpretation of the July 1990 contract, Heydon JA noted that 'there is some evidence that in 1990 and 1991 both the Council and the defendant did not share his conclusions, but in the absence of any argument for a decree of rectification or for an estoppel by convention the actual opinions of the parties are irrelevant'.[64]

Brambles Holdings Ltd v Bathurst City Council may be seen as proof of Oliver Wendell Holmes' claim that 'nothing is more certain than that parties may be bound by a contract to things which neither of them intended'.[65] It certainly shows that the objective approach to the interpretation of terms has a tendency to separate contractual obligations from the will of the parties.[66] We may accept that in most cases the actual intentions of the parties will coincide with the intentions that a reasonable person would attribute to them. But in making a contract the parties necessarily subject themselves to the court's interpretation of their rights and obligations. That interpretation will not always correspond to the rights each party thinks she is acquiring or the obligations each thinks he is undertaking. Whether or not the exclusion of extrinsic evidence of the parties' intentions is justified by pragmatic considerations, it cannot be denied that this practice ensures that there will be cases in which the parties' intentions do not correspond to their rights and obligations.

Gap-filling and default rules

It is now well accepted that contractual obligations do not spring fully-formed from the will of the parties. Contract law is itself a significant source of contractual rights and obligations. Parties inevitably leave gaps in their agreement, which differ in scope depending on the extent of negotiation. Even the most detailed contract will not be free of gaps. At the other end of the spectrum, some contracts consist of nothing but gaps.[67] The courts must deal with those gaps. It is therefore well recognised that a major part of contract law consists of default rules or gap-filling devices that operate to shape the parties' primary obligations. Less well recognised, but probably more pervasive, is the gap-filling role of contract law at the secondary or remedial level.[68]

Primary obligations

At the primary level the courts shape the parties' obligations in several ways. First, as we have seen, the courts shape the parties' contractual obligations

64 *Ibid*, 168.

65 Holmes, OW, 'The Path of the Law' (1897) 10 Harv LR 457, 463.

66 For criticism of this approach, see McLauchlan, D, 'A Contract Contradiction' (1999) 30 VUWLR 175; McLauchlan, D, 'The New Law of Contract Interpretation' [2000] NZ Univ LR 147, 166–67.

67 Eg, certain contracts are made between specialist medical practitioners and their patients in which nothing is the subject of express agreement. In some cases, at least in Australia, neither the obligations of the medical specialist nor the fees to be paid by the patient are agreed in advance of treatment. There may be no advance discussion of these issues whatsoever, and therefore no express terms of the contract.

68 On the Austinian distinction between primary and secondary obligations, see Tilbury, M, 'Remedies and the Classification of Obligations', Chapter 2 of this volume, 15–17.

through the objective approach to interpretation of the language used by the parties. Secondly, the courts shape the parties' contractual obligations through the application of objective tests to determine what constitute the terms of the contract. A statement made during negotiations constitutes a contractual promise if a reasonable person would regard the statement as promissory and would infer that the parties intended the promise to form part of the contract. Lord Denning said in *Oscar Chess Ltd v Williams* that:

> The question whether a warranty was intended *depends on the conduct of the parties, on their words and behaviour, rather than on their thoughts.* If an intelligent bystander would reasonably infer that a warranty was intended, that will suffice.[69]

A person making a statement may therefore find that it constitutes a contractual promise, even if that is not what the speaker intended. Similarly, a person signing a contractual document will be bound by its terms, regardless of his or her intentions and regardless of his or her knowledge of those terms.[70] Whether liability under a signed contractual document can be avoided by a plea of *non est factum* depends in part on whether the signer has been negligent or careless.[71] A party seeking to incorporate unsigned written terms need only do what is reasonable to bring these terms to the notice of the other party.[72] The non-drafting party may have no knowledge of the terms and no intention that they should form part of the contract.

Thirdly, the parties' rights and obligations are shaped by the doctrine of frustration.[73] In applying the doctrine of frustration, the courts relieve the parties of their obligations where a change of circumstances renders performance impossible or something radically different from what the parties intended.[74] The application of the doctrine of frustration requires the courts to make an objective determination as to the scope of the parties' obligations and whether the risk that the supervening event might occur should be taken to have been assumed by one of the parties. The conclusion in frustration cases that one party has or has not assumed the risk in question is necessarily a matter of imputed intention or fictitious consent.

The fourth and most pervasive gap-filling device at the level of primary obligation is the implied term. The courts routinely deny fashioning contracts for

---

69 *Oscar Chess Ltd v Williams* [1957] 1 All ER 325, 328 (emphasis added), adopted by Gibbs CJ in *Hospital Products Ltd v United States Surgical Corp* (1984) 156 CLR 41, 61–62.

70 *L'Estrange v F Graucob Ltd* [1934] 2 KB 394.

71 *Saunders v Anglia Building Society* [1971] AC 1004; *Petelin v Cullen* (1975) 132 CLR 355. Atiyah, above n 1, 732–33 argues that the focus on external conduct and even negligence in the courts' approach to signed documents suggests a movement 'away from consent as the basis of liability'. He suggests that the finding of contractual liability in *United Dominions Trust Ltd v Western* [1975] 3 All ER 1017 on a document carelessly signed in blank almost amounts to a merger of this part of the law of contract with the law of tort.

72 Eg, *Oceanic Sun Line Shipping Co Inc v Fay* (1988) 165 CLR 197, 229; *McCutcheon v David MacBrayne Ltd* [1964] 1 All ER 430, 433.

73 A similar point could be made about the power (conferred by the courts) to terminate for breach: see Craswell, R, 'Contract Law, Default Rules, and the Philosophy of Promising' (1989) 88 Michigan LR 489, 520–21.

74 *Codelfa Construction Pty Ltd v State Rail Authority of NSW* (1982) 149 CLR 337; *Davis Contractors v Fareham Urban District Council* [1956] AC 696.

the parties, and prefer to rationalise implied terms on the basis that they represent the 'presumed intention' of the parties.[75] It is clear, however, that the obligations of contracting parties are to a significant extent determined by the implication of terms by the courts. The courts impose obligations on the parties by implying terms 'by law' (in all contracts, or all contracts of a particular type) and 'in fact' (in particular contracts). Both types of implication draw on external policy considerations and involve the imposition of standards that are fixed by the law, not by the parties. The most strikingly tort-like of implied terms are those requiring parties to act in conformity with community standards such as good faith and reasonableness. These include the implied duty to co-operate in doing all that is necessary for performance of the contract and to ensure that the other party receives the benefits for which he or she has contracted.[76] They also include implied obligations to exercise powers and discretions conferred by a contract in good faith,[77] reasonably[78] and not 'dishonestly, for an improper purpose, capriciously or arbitrarily'.[79]

We may consider first the implication of terms 'as a matter of law' in contracts of a particular type. A term may be implied by law on the basis of custom or trade usage,[80] on the basis that it is necessary to ensure the enjoyment of contractual rights,[81] or on the basis that it is 'so much a part of the common understanding as to be imported into all transactions of the particular description'.[82] Those criteria do not, however, 'provide a complete account' of the basis for implication of a term in law.[83] The courts impose such terms on a similar basis to the imposition of duties in tort, taking into account a wide range of considerations. Samuels JA observed in *Simonius Vischer & Co v Holt & Thompson* that a term implied by law is 'imported by operation of law whether the parties intended to include it or not'.[84] He went on to observe that: 'The imposition of terms as a matter of law amounts to no more than the imposition of legal duties in cases where the law thinks that policy requires it.'[85]

In *Hughes Aircraft System International v Airservices Australia*,[86] Finn J explored at some length the role played by 'considerations of public policy' which he said 'can and do have an overt part to play in some instances in determining whether it is necessary that an obligation should be implied as a matter of law in a

---

75 Eg, *Codelfa Construction Pty Ltd v State Rail Authority of NSW* (1982) 149 CLR 337, 353.

76 *Secured Income Real Estate (Australia) Ltd v St Martin's Investments Pty Ltd* (1979) 144 CLR 596.

77 *Burger King Corp v Hungry Jack's Pty Ltd* [2001] NSWCA 187.

78 *Paragon Insurance plc v Staunton* [2002] 2 All ER 248, 263; *Renard Constructions (ME) Pty Ltd v Minister for Public Works* (1992) 26 NSWLR 234, 263.

79 *Paragon Insurance plc v Staunton* [2002] 2 All ER 248, 262. Similarly, *Secured Income Real Estate (Australia) Ltd v St Martin's Investments Pty Ltd* (1979) 144 CLR 596.

80 *Con-Stan Industries of Australia Pty Ltd v Norwich Winterthur Insurance (Aust) Ltd* (1986) 160 CLR 515.

81 *Byrne v Australian Airlines Ltd* (1995) 185 CLR 410, 450.

82 *Ibid*, 449.

83 *Hughes Aircraft System International v Airservices Australia* (1997) 146 ALR 1, 39.

84 [1979] 2 NSWLR 322, 348.

85 *Ibid*.

86 (1997) 146 ALR 1 ('*Hughes*').

contract'.[87] This, Finn J suggested, was illustrated by the obligation of secrecy imposed on professionals.[88] The most tort-like formulation of contractual duties implied by law is that of Viscount Simonds in *Lister v Romford Ice & Cold Storage Ltd*.[89] In deciding whether a term relating to insurance should be implied in a contract between driver and employer, Viscount Simonds suggested that the court was required to:

> ... take a wider view, for we are concerned with a general question, which, if not correctly described as a question of status, yet can only be answered by considering the relation in which the drivers of motor-vehicles and their employers generally stand to each other. Just as the duty of care, rightly regarded as a contractual obligation, is imposed on the servant ... just so the question must be asked and answered *whether in the world in which we live today it is a necessary condition of the relation of master and man* that the master should, to use a broad colloquialism, look after the whole matter of insurance.[90]

As Finn J noted in *Hughes*,[91] Viscount Simonds went on to consider the 'more general considerations' including the 'social consequences' that might flow from the implication of the term in question in contracts of the relevant type.[92] More recently, in *Wong Mee Wan v Kwan Kin Travel Services*,[93] the Privy Council took into account a range of such considerations in deciding whether a particular term should be implied in a package holiday contract. The term in question was an implied promise by the package tour operator that services supplied by the operator (including those performed by sub-contractors) would be carried out with care and skill. The considerations taken into account by the Privy Council included the question whether the obligation would impose an intolerable burden on tour operators. The Privy Council found that it would not, since the operator could protect itself by negotiating suitable terms with sub-contractors or obtaining insurance cover.[94] The Privy Council also considered whether it was reasonable that an injured passenger should be obliged to undertake the difficult task of pursuing a claim in a foreign country.[95] The term was implied.

As Charles Fried has observed, the implication of a term involves the imposition of an external standard on the parties.[96] Public standards such as fairness are applied to regulate the implication of terms by law.[97] It is said that 'a

---

87 *Ibid*, 39. See further Peden, E, 'Policy Concerns Behind the Implication of Terms in Law' (2001) 117 LQR 459.

88 *Ibid*, citing *Tournier v National Provincial & Union Bank of England* [1924] 1 KB 461, 474 and *Parry-Jones v Law Society* [1969] 1 Ch 1, 7 and 9.

89 [1957] AC 555.

90 *Ibid*, 576 (emphasis added).

91 (1997) 146 ALR 1, 39–40.

92 [1957] AC 555, 579.

93 [1996] 1 WLR 38.

94 *Ibid*, 46.

95 *Ibid*, 47.

96 Fried, above n 25, 61.

97 This is not to suggest that reasonableness or fairness of itself provides a basis for implication: in each case it is one of two or more requirements that must be met before a term will be implied.

term implied in law in a particular type of contract must be reasonable with a just regard given to the interests of both parties'.[98] Similarly, terms are implied on the basis of custom or trade usage only if the custom is 'fair and proper and such as reasonable, honest, and fair minded men would adopt'.[99] Terms implied in fact are also regulated by community standards of fairness. One of the requirements that must be met for implication of a term required to give business efficacy to a contract is that the term must be 'reasonable and equitable'.[100] This requirement was found not to have been satisfied in *Byrne v Australian Airlines Ltd*.[101] In that case, a term sought to be implied in an employment contract was rejected on the basis, *inter alia*, that it would 'operate in a partisan fashion. It would favour the interests of the employee at the expense of those of the employer'.[102]

Secondary obligations

At the secondary or remedial level of obligation the gap-filling role of contract law is even more fundamental. A defining feature of a contract is its enforceability. A contract is enforceable only in the sense that the court will grant remedies if the primary obligations are breached or a breach is threatened. Contracts rarely make comprehensive provision for the remedial consequences of a breach. Even sophisticated agreements that make some provision for remedial consequences typically leave much to be decided by the courts in the event of breach. The courts often point out that a contracting party can negotiate for protection against a particular risk, such as the loss of unusual profits or distress and disappointment caused by a breach.[103] Contracting parties rarely avail themselves of this opportunity. In all but the most sophisticated commercial contracts the level of damages is left entirely for the court to determine according to standards external to the agreement. If the parties do make a contractual stipulation as the quantum of damages, the fairness of the stipulation is closely scrutinised. The availability of non-monetary remedies is entirely a matter for the court: parties cannot stipulate that an injunction or specific performance will be available. The same goes for an account of profits in jurisdictions in which it is available.[104] The entire remedial regime can, therefore, be seen as a gap-filling device.[105] Remedial obligations are

98 *Young & Marten Ltd v McManus Childs Ltd* [1969] 1 AC 454, 465–66.

99 *Produce Brokers Co Ltd v Olympia Oil and Cake Co Ltd* [1916] 2 KB 296, 298. Cf *Con-Stan Industries of Australia Pty Ltd v Norwich Winterthur Insurance (Aust) Ltd* (1986) 160 CLR 515, 237 (insistence that this type of implication is based on the presumed intentions of the parties, rather than 'broader considerations').

100 *BP Refinery (Westernport) Pty Ltd v Shire of Hastings* (1977) 180 CLR 266, 283.

101 (1995) 185 CLR 410.

102 *Ibid*, 442–43.

103 Eg, *Koufos v C Czarnikow Ltd* [1969] 1 AC 350, 386; *Baltic Shipping Co v Dillon* (1993) 176 CLR 344, 369.

104 *Attorney-General v Blake* [2001] 1 AC 268; cf *Hospitality Group Pty Ltd v Australian Rugby Union Ltd* [2001] 110 FCR 157.

105 *Contra* Burrows, above n 21, 11–14 (see especially 14, fn 43), who argues that secondary obligations in contract are (like primary obligations in contract) voluntary and can be distinguished from obligations stemming from wrongs or unjust enrichment, which are purely imposed.

almost always imposed, rather than assumed, and they are shaped by community standards, rather than standards fixed by the parties.[106]

When considering the role of the courts in shaping remedial obligations, it is important to remember the famous lesson taught by Fuller and Perdue: that 'damages awards depend on judicial policy choices, rather than the parties' own intentions'.[107] In fashioning the principles relating to the assessment of damages, the courts 'establish a normative order'.[108] The most basic principle of contract damages is that they should protect the innocent party's expectation interest, by placing the innocent party in the position he or she would have occupied if the contract had been performed.[109] As Fuller and Perdue pointed out, the innocent party's entitlement to expectation damages is not fixed by nature or the intentions of the parties, but determined by the courts.[110] 'If a contract represents a kind of private law, it is a law which usually says nothing at all about what shall be done when it is violated.'[111] Atiyah has observed that contract law intervenes to deal with the situation of a breach of contract 'in the nature of an accident, much in the way that tort law deals with accidents'.[112]

Three other damages principles illustrate further the role of community standards in determining contract damages awards. First, the mitigation principle prevents the recovery of damages in respect of loss the plaintiff could have avoided by taking reasonable steps. This fundamental determinant of contract damages is based on the idea that the contract breaker 'is not to be exposed to additional cost by reason of the plaintiffs not doing what they ought to have done as reasonable men'.[113] A second clear example of the imposition of community values is where a contracting party seeks as damages the cost of rectifying defective building work. Such damages are recoverable only if it would be reasonable to rectify the defect.[114] Contract damages protect the plaintiff's expectations only if those expectations accord with community norms determined by the courts. The significance of the defect to the plaintiff and the importance of the rectification work to the plaintiff are simply left out of account.

---

106 Charles Fried has asserted that 'to the extent that contract is grounded in promise, it seems natural to measure relief by the expectation, that is, by the promise itself'. But as Craswell, above n 73, 517–20, has pointed out, there is no clear connection between the promise and the expectation damages principle. A promise by A to do x says nothing about what should happen if A should fail to do x. Randy Barnett, 'Contract Remedies and Inalienable Rights' (1986) 4 Soc Phil and Policy 179 has argued that a presumptive rule in favour of specific performance is more compatible with a consent theory of contract.

107 Atiyah, above n 9, *Essays on Contract*, 77.

108 Fuller, LL and Perdue, W, 'The Reliance Interest in Contract Damages: I' (1933) 46 Yale LJ 52, 52–53.

109 *Commonwealth v Amann Aviation Pty Ltd* (1991) 174 CLR 64; *Robinson v Harman* (1848) 1 Ex 850, 855; 154 ER 363, 365.

110 Fuller and Perdue, above n 108.

111 *Ibid*, 58.

112 Atiyah, above n 9, *Essays on Contract*, 77.

113 *British Westinghouse Electric and Manufacturing Co Ltd v Underground Electric Railways Co of London Ltd* [1912] AC 673, 689.

114 *Ruxley Electronics & Constructions Ltd v Forsyth* [1996] 1 AC 344; *Bellgrove v Eldridge* (1954) 90 CLR 613.

The most obvious way in which the law of damages limits party autonomy is through the rule against penalties. If the parties make express provision for the quantum of damages to be paid in the event of breach, the courts will enforce such a promise only if it is regarded as fair, according to external standards imposed by the courts. A promise by one party to pay a particular sum to another in the event of breach will be struck down as a penalty 'if the sum stipulated for is extravagant and unconscionable in amount in comparison with the greatest loss that could conceivably be proved to have followed from the breach'.[115]

Implied terms, default rules and consent

It is clear from the above discussion that the courts are required to do a great deal of gap-filling in order to define both primary and secondary contractual obligations. An interesting question is whether 'gap-fillers' such as implied terms can be said to represent the will of the parties. In other words, can the parties be said to have implicitly 'consented' to the obligations (including remedial obligations) and restrictions on their contractual rights implied by the courts? In many cases the courts treat implied terms as consensual. Lord Millett said in *Agnew v Länsförsäkringsbolagens AB* that:

> All contractual obligations are voluntary, whether they are contained expressly in the contract or imposed on the contracting parties by law. No-one is compelled to undertake contractual obligations. If parties voluntarily enter into a contract, they seldom express all the contractual terms in the contract. It is often necessary for the law to imply terms into the contract.[116]

The High Court in *Astley v Austrust Ltd* also appeared to regard implied contractual obligations as having been consented to by the parties. The contractual obligation under consideration in that case was the implied duty of a solicitor to take reasonable care in the discharge of his professional duties. That duty arose out of the same circumstances and was 'co-extensive in content'[117] with the obligation imposed by the law of tort.[118] Moreover, the court accepted that '[t]he implied term of reasonable care in a contract of professional services arises by operation of law'.[119] Nevertheless, the High Court in *Astley v Austrust Ltd* insisted, as the House of Lords did in *Henderson v Merrett Syndicates Ltd*, that 'the contractual duty is attributable to the will of the parties'.[120] The Supreme Court of Canada, on the other hand, has accepted that a distinction cannot be drawn

115 *Dunlop Pneumatic Tyre Co Ltd v New Garage and Motor Co Ltd* [1915] AC 79, 87.

116 [2001] 1 AC 223, 264.

117 *Hawkins v Clayton* (1988) 164 CLR 539, 585. As the High Court noted in *Astley v Austrust Ltd* (1999) 197 CLR 1, 23, however, there are important practical differences between the two causes of action: they 'have different elements, different limitation periods, different tests for remoteness of damage and, as will appear, different apportionment rules'.

118 As has been observed by Davis, G and Knowler, J, 'Down but not Out: Contributory Negligence, Contract, Statute and Common Law' (1999) 23 Melb ULR 795, 816.

119 (1999) 197 CLR 1, 22.

120 *Henderson v Merrett Syndicates Ltd* [1995] 2 AC 145, 194, quoted in *Astley v Austrust Ltd* (1999) 197 CLR 1, 36.

between implied contractual obligations and obligations in tort.[121] The source of the action, they said, 'whether styled in contract or tort', 'is an objective expectation, defined by the courts, of the appropriate obligation and the correlative right'. There is, therefore, 'no issue of private ordering as opposed to publicly imposed liability'.[122]

Randy Barnett argues that non-mandatory implied terms can be justified on the basis of consent.[123] He suggests that when parties manifest an intention to be legally bound they indirectly consent to the background rules of contract law that fill the gaps in their agreement. The failure of the parties to contract around a default rule that they 'might have changed by speaking up'[124] has a significance for Barnett, as the dog that did not bark in the night did for Sherlock Holmes. For Barnett, the failure of parties to contract around such default rules signifies their consent to them, in the same way that, for Sherlock Holmes, the failure of the dog to bark indicated that 'the midnight visitor was someone whom the dog knew well'.[125]

Whether or not we are prepared to accept Barnett's notion of tacit consent, it does not provide a basis for distinguishing contract from tort, because obligations in tort can be justified on a tacit consent basis just as well or just as badly as those arising by way of contract default rules.[126] If persons engaging in contractual behaviour indirectly consent to the legal consequences of that behaviour, then persons engaging in other activities might equally be said to consent to the legal consequences of their behaviour. Duties in tort can, in some circumstances, be avoided by the use of contract terms excluding liability or notices disclaiming liability.[127] But even beyond those situations, there is an extent to which obligations in tort can be avoided, and can thus be treated as consensual (in Barnett's sense) when not avoided.[128] A person who drives on the road tacitly consents to a duty of care to other road users in the same way that a person entering into a contract tacitly consents to an obligation to exercise his contractual

---

121 *British Columbia Hydro and Power Authority v BG Checo International Ltd* (1993) 99 DLR (4th) 577, 585–86.

122 *Ibid.*

123 Barnett, RE, 'The Sound of Silence: Default Rules and Contractual Consent' (1992) 78 Virginia LR 821.

124 *Ibid*, 865.

125 Doyle, Arthur Conan, 'Silver Blaze', in Baring-Gould, W (ed), *The Annotated Sherlock Holmes*, 1967, 261 at 280, quoted by Barnett, above n 123, 821.

126 Coleman, J, *Risks and Wrongs*, Cambridge: CUP, 1992, 184 has argued that 'tort law is simply contract law by default provision writ large, and is analytically indistinguishable from it'.

127 A defendant can exclude or limit an obligation in tort by notice (subject, in the UK, to the Unfair Contract Terms Act 1977), provided the defendant has taken reasonable steps to bring the notice to the attention of the plaintiff: *Ashdown v Samuel Williams & Sons Ltd* [1957] 1 QB 409; *White v Blackmore* [1972] 2 QB 651. In *Ashdown v Samuel Williams & Sons Ltd*, Jenkins LJ drew the principle justifying the imputation of knowledge of a notice from *Parker v South Eastern Railway Co* (1877) 2 CPD 416, a contract case concerned with the incorporation of terms by notice. In both contract and tort the notice is effective because the party displaying it has acted reasonably, not because the other party has acted voluntarily.

128 Seavey, above n 53, 210 suggests that since 'tort liability is ordinarily the consequence of voluntary action' we can say that, except in rare cases, 'tort obligations are assumed in the same sense that contractual obligations are assumed'.

rights in good faith.[129] The contractor signifies his consent by his failure to contract out of the good faith obligation, while the driver signifies his consent by his failure to catch a taxi or bus, walk or stay at home.[130] The driver is in fact far more likely to be aware of his duty of care, so his consent is more likely to be real. To paraphrase Lord Millett,[131] we might say that, just as no one is compelled to undertake contractual obligations, no one is compelled to engage in conduct giving rise to a duty of care.

It is often pointed out that an implied term is one that the parties to a contract 'can, and often do, bargain away or limit as they choose'.[132] It might be argued that obligations in tort can be distinguished from implied contractual obligations on the basis that tort obligations cannot easily be avoided: a person's freedom of behaviour would be severely constrained if he or she did not wish to accept the obligations imposed by the law of tort. Contractual duties, though, are also difficult to avoid. It is no more feasible to avoid undesirable contractual obligations than it is to avoid undesirable obligations in tort. As Robert Hale and others have pointed out, we must all contract in order to live.[133] Inequalities of bargaining power, the use of non-negotiable standard form contracts and disproportionate transaction costs prevent contracting parties from routinely choosing contract terms in the quotidian practice of contracting. Even in a situation involving no standard form, where the bargaining power is roughly equal and negotiation is feasible, a contracting party cannot simply choose the terms on which he or she wishes to contract. For example, we can only speculate on the outcome if the solicitors in *Astley v Austrust Ltd* were bold enough to suggest to a commercial client that they were not prepared to accept an implied contractual duty to take reasonable care in discharging their professional duties.

The consent of a contracting party to a particular default rule is genuine only if the party had a real choice as to whether to accept that rule. Such a choice depends on the contracting party having some knowledge of the applicable default rules, having an inclination to contract around them[134] and having the practical ability to contract around them. In relation to knowledge, Barnett

---

129 As Atiyah has observed, above n 9, 'Contract, Promises', 221; *Essays on Contract*, 41: 'it remains true that nearly all tort liabilities arise in the course of the performance of voluntary actions. A person who negligently injures another while driving his car is voluntarily on the road, voluntarily driving his car, and may be said to submit himself to the requirements of the law *with as much or as little truth as the seller of goods.*' (Emphasis added.)

130 The road user is clearly unable to avoid obligations to other road users other than by refraining from driving. Kerr LJ said in *Harris v Wyre Forest District Council* [1988] QB 835, 853 that: 'it would obviously be irrelevant for a driver sued in negligence to say that he had displayed a sign on the top of his car, "No liability accepted for any collision – keep out of the way." The reason is that anyone driving a car is *ipso facto* subjected to an inescapable duty of care towards other users of the highway which he necessarily assumes by driving.'

131 *Agnew v Länsförsäkringsbolagens AB* [2001] 1 AC 223, 264.

132 *Astley v Austrust Ltd* (1999) 197 CLR 1, 22.

133 Hale, RL, 'Coercion and Distribution in a Supposedly Non-coercive State' (1923) 38 *Pol Sci Quar* 470; Hale, RL, 'Bargaining, Duress and Economic Liberty' (1943) 43 Col LR 603; Dalzel, J, 'Duress by Economic Pressure I' (1942) 20 North Carolina LR 237, 239; Radin, M, 'Contract Obligation and the Human Will' (1943) 43 Col LR 575, 578–81.

134 As to why parties are unlikely to be so inclined, see Eisenberg, MA, 'The Theory of Contracts', in Benson, P (ed), *The Theory of Contract Law*, Cambridge: CUP, 2001, 206, 247–56.

suggests that it is not necessary for parties to know what the default rules are: consent can be presumed provided the default rules reflect commonsense or conventional expectations.[135] But are there commonsense or conventional expectations relating to default rules, even amongst lawyers? We can point to substantial disagreements amongst judges and contract scholars as to whether particular community standards (such as good faith, reasonableness and unconscionability) should be imposed in particular contexts and what those standards mean in a particular case.[136] But it may be easier to learn of the default rules of contract law than to avoid them. A party will only, of course, have the practical ability to contract around a particular rule where that party's bargaining power is sufficiently high and the transaction costs are proportionate to the value of the transaction or the risk involved. It may not be possible to contract out of all duties imposed by the law of tort, but in some situations it may be easier to avoid the behaviour that gives rise to a tort obligation than to contract around a default rule. It may, for example, be easier to catch a bus or taxi to avoid a driver's duty to other road users than to learn about all of the default rules applicable to a particular contract, draft an agreement excluding those one does not want and then to impose one's wishes on the other contracting party.

CONCLUSIONS

This chapter has shown that it is not possible to identify a single source of contractual obligation, such as promise, consent or will. Rights and obligations in contract are to some extent shaped by consensus reached between the parties, to some extent imposed by one party on another and to some extent imposed on both parties by law. Similarly, obligations in tort are to some extent shaped by voluntary arrangements between the parties,[137] to some extent shaped by the unilateral actions of one party[138] and to some extent imposed by law. It is, therefore, a misconception to suggest that a sharp distinction can be drawn between contractual obligations and obligations in tort on the basis that the former are voluntarily assumed while the latter are imposed. The source of obligation in each case is far more complex.

This conclusion has significant implications for our understanding of the law of obligations. Andrew Burrows has suggested that 'the distinction between voluntary obligations and purely imposed obligations – and hence between liability for breach of a binding promise and liability for all other wrongs – is of

135 Barnett, above n 123.

136 For examples of such disagreement between judges, see *Renard Constructions (ME) Pty Ltd v Minister for Public Works* (1992) 26 NSWLR 234 (reasonableness) and *Stern v McArthur* (1988) 165 CLR 489 (unconscionability) and contrast *Service Station Association v Berg Bennett* [1993] 45 FCR 84 with *Hughes Aircraft Systems International v Airservices Australia* (1997) 146 ALR 1 (good faith).

137 See *Hedley Byrne & Co Ltd v Heller & Partners Ltd* [1964] AC 465, 483, 486, 494, 497, 528–29; *Henderson v Merrett Syndicates Ltd* [1995] 2 AC 145, 181; *Williams v Natural Life Health Foods Ltd* [1998] 1 WLR 830 and the discussion in Whittaker, S, 'The Application of the "Broad Principle of *Hedley Byrne*" as Between Parties to a Contract' (1997) 19 LS 169.

138 See above n 127 and accompanying text.

fundamental importance in understanding the law of obligations'.[139] This chapter suggests the contrary. It shows that the boundary between contract and tort does not reflect a distinction between voluntary and imposed obligations. A model of the law of obligations that is based on such a distinction may be neat, but will not be accurate. This chapter suggests that in fact an understanding of the similarity between contract and tort is of fundamental importance in understanding the law of obligations. It is certainly of fundamental importance to an understanding of the nature and source of contractual obligation.

Two lessons for contract law may be drawn from this chapter. The first is that, as Clare Dalton has argued,[140] if contractual obligations are to a significant extent imposed by law, and are informed by values and standards determined by the courts, then the courts should be more explicit in articulating those values and standards and the principles involved in their development.[141] It is clear from the above discussion that the courts do this more frequently in some areas than others. The courts generally, and perhaps increasingly, articulate the considerations and values underlying the implication of terms as a matter of law in particular classes of contract. In other areas, such as the law of damages, the courts too frequently treat the relevant principles as a 'datum of nature'[142] or make unjustified appeals to the will or intentions of the parties.

Secondly, the way in which the courts formulate and apply the principles of contract law ought more consistently to take into account the limits of voluntariness in shaping contractual obligations. Atiyah has noted that judges can be constrained in contract cases by the misunderstanding that contract is 'based on one set of values'.[143] If one accepts that 'a very large part of modern contract law depends on the creation of obligations that do not arise from promises'[144] then standard-setting and gap-filling must be seen as a legitimate function of the court in contract cases.[145] While this chapter has shown that the courts play a significant role in filling gaps and setting standards in contract cases, some judges still deny that role, and decide cases on the basis that the role of the court is simply to give effect to the contract as an expression of the will of the parties.

A good example of the way in which a misconception of contract law can produce an unjust outcome is where one party has undertaken performance on the faith of a vague or incomplete promise and then seeks to enforce that promise. *Biotechnology Australia Pty Ltd v Pace*[146] was such a case. An offer of employment to a scientist provided that the employer would give the employee 'the option to participate in the company's senior staff equity sharing scheme'. The employee

139 Burrows, above n 21, 14.
140 Dalton, above n 40, 1030, 1066.
141 See also Steyn, above n 29, 433.
142 Fuller and Perdue, above n 108, 53.
143 Atiyah, above n 9, *Essays on Contract*, 49.
144 *Ibid*, 54.
145 See, eg, Steyn, above n 29, who argues that the courts should undertake this role in order to give effect to the reasonable expectations of the parties.
146 (1988) 15 NSWLR 130.

accepted the offer on the basis that equity sharing was to be part of his remuneration. There was no such scheme and none was brought into effect before he resigned four years later. The employee sought damages for breach of the term. The majority of the New South Wales Court of Appeal found the employer's promise unenforceable on the basis that it was illusory, incomplete and uncertain. Hope JA dissented, agreeing with the trial judge that the promise was enforceable. Hope JA took the view that the courts should 'strain to find criteria, at least for the minimum performance required of the promisor'.[147] He found that the employer was obliged to act honestly and reasonably in establishing a scheme in which the employee could participate. These standards would 'provide criteria to fix the amount of the minimum offer Biotech was required to make'.[148] Hope JA said that the law is not 'so removed from commercial and employment practice and exercise that expert evidence should not be admissible to establish what the minimum reasonable amount should be'.[149]

The majority judgments in *Biotechnology v Pace* posited a more limited role for the court in interpreting and giving content to the agreement. While McHugh JA was concerned that the court *could not* give effect to the promise, Kirby P took the view that the court *should not* do so. The court must, he said, 'draw back from filling the gaps which the parties themselves did not fill'.[150] That conclusion was justified on the basis that: 'Contracts are the agreements between parties. Generally, their terms must be those which reflect the will of the parties, objectively determined.'[151] The courts therefore have, Kirby P suggested, a 'limited capacity' to 'substitute their views of what is "fair" for the parties who have failed or neglected to do so'.[152] 'Well-meaning, paternalistic interference by courts in the marketplace' is inappropriate.[153] Kirby P noted that 'the willingness of the courts to fashion with precision a term which the parties have failed or neglected to clarify could be analysed in terms of differing fundamental attitudes concerning the role of the courts in disturbing the economic relations of contracting parties'.[154] It could also be rationalised in terms of differing judicial conceptions of the nature of contract law, and its relationship with the law of tort.

Underlying Kirby P's decision not to enforce the employer's promise in *Biotechnology v Pace* was a particular conception of contract law and its place within the law of obligations. This chapter has shown that this conception of contract law and its distinction from tort does not stand up to close scrutiny. The idea that contractual obligations represent the will of the parties and that the courts should refrain from 'paternalistic interference' is misconceived. The courts *do* fill the gaps that parties have failed to fill. Many primary and almost all secondary contractual obligations *are* determined by 'well-meaning, paternalistic

147 *Ibid*, 144.
148 *Ibid*, 147.
149 *Ibid*.
150 *Ibid*, 138.
151 *Ibid*, 132.
152 *Ibid*, 133.
153 *Ibid*.
154 *Ibid*, 136.

interference'. The existence of a contract, the content of a contract, the termination of a contract and the remedies available for breach are all shaped by the courts' view of what is fair. Contract cannot, therefore, be seen as a system of voluntary obligation that can be sharply differentiated from the law of tort.

7

THE 'OTHER' CATEGORY IN THE CLASSIFICATION OF OBLIGATIONS

*Joachim Dietrich**

INTRODUCTION

General

Much has been written recently about 'taxonomy' or, more specifically, about the classification of our law of obligations, particularly by Professor Birks.[1] Drawing comparisons with the science of Charles Darwin, Birks argues for greater awareness by lawyers of the importance of classification and for better taxonomy in our law. Leaving aside for now the doubts one may entertain about the merits of Birks' quasi-zoological approach to classification,[2] or about whether such

---

* Thanks are due to Rick Bigwood, Jim Davis, Pauline Ridge and Andrew Robertson for their helpful comments on earlier drafts of this chapter.

1 See, eg, Birks, P, 'Definition and Division: A Meditation on *Institutes* 3.13' ('*Institutes*') in Birks, P (ed), *The Classification of Obligations*, Oxford: Clarendon, 1997, 1–35, ('*Classification*'); 'Rights, Wrongs, and Remedies' (2000) 20 OJLS 1; 'Annual Miegunyah Lecture: Equity, Conscience, and Unjust Enrichment' (1999) 23 MULR 1; 'Equity in the Modern Law: An Exercise in Taxonomy' (1996) UWA L Rev 1 ('Taxonomy'). Many other commentators stress the importance of classification; see, eg, Mcbride, N, 'Classification and Legal Education', in Birks, *Classification*, Chapter 4. McKendrick, E, 'Work Done in Anticipation of a Contract which does not Materialise', in Cornish, WR *et al* (eds), *Restitution: Past, Present and Future*, Oxford: Hart, 1998, 163, 164 (and generally 164–67) ('Cornish *et al*'), in the context of precontractual liability, suggests that it matters 'a lot' into which categories we place such claims. See also Barker, K, 'Review' (1999) 19 LS 415, 417. Smith, L, 'Unjust Enrichment, Property, and the Structure of Trusts' (2000) 116 LQR 412, 444 states: 'good classification is the foundation of good doctrine, which in turn lets us be sure that we are treating like cases alike and different cases differently.' Much of this writing does not appear to question the underlying assumption of a classification system based on causes of action or causative *events* as the most appropriate starting point. For a different approach altogether, however, focusing on remedy as a basis for classification, see Stapleton, J, 'A New "Seascape" for Obligations: Reclassification on the Basis of Measure of Damages', in Birks (ed), *Classification*, 193.

2 See Samuel, G, 'Can Gaius Really Be Compared To Darwin?' (2000) 49 ICLQ 297, in which he tries to 'show that comparisons between legal and zoological taxonomy schemes are an epistemologically dangerous exercise' (329). At 298, he states:

> The legal model is incapable of being verified – if indeed it can be verified at all – in the same way that a zoological scheme of taxonomy can be verified … Apparent contradictions often result from misunderstanding about the nature of legal concepts and about the relationship between these concepts and the objects they are attempting to model. Thus there are dangers in thinking that legal rationality is necessarily the same as zoological taxonomy.

attention to taxonomy will ultimately result in improvement in our law,[3] the burden of his writing is in favour of a four-fold categorisation of the law of obligations. Starting with a classification of common law obligations into contract, tort, unjust enrichment/restitution, and other causative events, Birks incorporates equitable obligations, so that all obligations, *regardless of their jurisdictional and historical origins*, can be divided into the categories of consent, wrongs, unjust enrichment/restitution, and 'others'.[4] The category of consent thus includes, for example, both contracts and express trusts;[5] the category of wrongs thus includes, for example, both torts and equitable wrongs such as breaches of fiduciary duty.

There are obvious difficulties with this classification. For example, as has been argued in Chapter 6, above, it is not necessarily possible to equate contract law with 'consent'. *If* one accepts for now, however, this four-fold classification (and my own doubts about its utility will become evident below), very little attention has been paid to the obligations which might fall within the 'Other' category. The purpose of this chapter is to discuss some examples of legal obligations which would either clearly or at least arguably fall within the 'Other' category (for no other reason than that they clearly or arguably do not fall within the other three categories). Specifically, cases of precontractual liability will be considered. Such consideration shows that liability may arise which is best classified as lying between the established categories of consent and wrongs (more particularly, to the extent that they are the same, contract and torts respectively). This liability is established because some of the factors determinative of liability (or at least relevant to such determination) in each category are present, such that broader than usual 'contractual' liability may be justified by the presence of additional factors normally associated with establishing liability in tort, or broader than usual 'tort' liability may be established by the presence of additional factors normally associated with establishing liability in contract. This conclusion casts doubts upon the discreteness of the suggested categories and their content, and may shed light on the nature of legal obligations generally.

---

3 Campbell, D, 'Classification and the Crisis of the Common Law' (1999) 26 J Law & Soc 369, 377, reviewing the collection of essays in Birks, above n 1, *Classification*, concludes that 'though this collection is an attempt to deal with the failure of abstract doctrine, it is only with a cast of mind characterized by persistent confidence in such doctrine that the sophisticated filigree of classification advocated in it could be put forward as law reform'. Earlier, at 370, Campbell states: 'However powerful Birks's arguments, it is perfectly laughable to think that someone sitting in his study can produce a workable revision of the whole law of obligations.' Judges also may not be particularly concerned with the whole exercise: 'Lord Millett has said that judges are "profoundly uninterested" in schemes of classification, except where they aid analysis or affect the outcome of a dispute', to quote Smith, above n 1, 422 (citing Millett in 'The Law of Restitution: Taking Stock' (1999) 14 Amicus Curiae 4, 4). Smith immediately goes on to add: 'Good classification does both at different times.'

4 See Birks, above n 1, 'Taxonomy', 8–11; Birks, above n 1, 'Misnomer' in Cornish *et al*, 1; and Birks, P, 'The Law of Restitution at the End of an Epoch' (1999) 28 UWA L Rev 13.

5 But not, I would suggest contrary to Grantham, RB and Rickett, CEF, *Enrichment and Restitution in New Zealand*, Oxford: Hart, 2000, 48, fiduciary duties arising generally as an incidence of certain presumptive relationships.

Unjust enrichment/restitution

Before proceeding, I must say something about the unhappy label I have given the third category: unjust enrichment/restitution. The difficulty here is that there is debate amongst unjust enrichment theorists as to which label is the most preferable. Although the name 'restitution' has the pedigree of (recent) history, Birks argues that it is semantically unsound, resulting in a 'bent' classification. Birks argues that: '"[c]ontracts" and "torts" are events which trigger legal responses, while restitution, or more accurately the entitlement to restitution, is a response triggered by an event. Restitution belongs in the same series as compensation.'[6] Birks therefore prefers as more satisfactory the label 'unjust enrichment', since its reference is to the causative event rather than the remedial response. Other commentators continue to prefer the label 'restitution'.[7]

For those of us who are sceptical of the value of the 'unjust enrichment' principle as an explanation of much of what *historically*[8] lies within the subject-matter of restitution (because, historically, it originated in the 'quasi-contractual' common money counts), the choice of labels matters. I, for one, would reject the description of much of what is contained in restitution textbooks as being appropriately contained within textbooks on 'unjust enrichment'. Nonetheless, for the purposes of discussing the classificatory categories (without necessarily accepting their validity), if we accept that at least some topics within restitution are explicable in unjust enrichment terms, then such a category of causative events would have some content. An example may be the recovery of mistaken payments. But the consequence of this is *not* that the content of this category of unjust enrichment is the same as that contained within the subject of restitution. Indeed, I would suggest that if a four-fold categorisation were adopted, much of restitution could be said to fall within one of the other three categories, those of consent, wrongs, and 'others'. I do not propose to revisit in this chapter arguments as to how many of the various restitutionary-type claims in quasi-contract and equity[9] are not explicable in unjust enrichment terms.[10] As a general aside, however, it does cast some doubts on the value of Birks' logically driven scheme if recognisable, partly-historically defined or described subjects (perhaps in some

---

6 Birks, P, above n 1, 'Miegunyah Lecture', 10. See also Birks, above n 4, 'End of an Epoch'.

7 Cf Tettenborn, A, 'Misnomer: A Response', in Cornish *et al*, above n 1, 31, 36. Other commentators have also questioned Birks' view that restitution can be a response to causative events other than unjust enrichment: see McInnes, M, 'Restitution, Unjust Enrichment and the Perfect Quadration Thesis' [1999] 7 Restitution LR 118.

8 This is as opposed to some definitional or conceptual description of the subject.

9 If the attempted explanations of many of equity's liability rules in terms of unjust enrichment are unwarranted, then such rules would need to be explained and classified in other ways.

10 See further my attempts to do so in Dietrich, J, *Restitution: A New Perspective*, Sydney: Federation, 1998. As an aside, however, I agree with Samuel's observation, above n 2, 298, that '[t]he amount of intellectual energy spent on emancipating unjust enrichment from the categories of contract, tort and equity seems to bear little relation to the actual social benefits detectable in the restitution decisions themselves'. I am fortified in my scepticism about an all-embracing theory of unjust enrichment explaining the law of restitution by the statements of Gummow J in *Roxborough v Rothmans of Pall Mall Australia Ltd* (2001) 185 ALR 335, [70]–[75], as well as by the generally narrowly confined reasoning of all the judgments in that case.

cases even well understood subjects)[11] would need to be sacrificially dismembered on the altar of taxonomical purity.

Proprietary responses

A second preliminary point concerns the issue of proprietary remedies or responses, and the appropriate classification of their causative events. Birks has suggested, initially 'with some trepidation',[12] that all private law rights that people hold, whether *in personam* or *in rem*, derive from the four categories of causative events.[13] Other theorists, however, have questioned the relationship between property law and the law of obligations, and appear to treat 'proprietary' claims in ways that would require a considerable modification of Birks' four categories. Virgo, for example, has argued that the 'vindication of property rights' gives rise to both personal and proprietary remedies, but that 'unjust enrichment' can never give rise to proprietary remedies.[14] On this view, I assume, personal obligations would derive from five categories of events (if the 'vindication of property' event is excised from the 'Other' category), whereas proprietary rights would arise from four categories only, and not from unjust enrichment.[15] This debate is not central to the issues I want to explore in this chapter, but the difficulties must be noted.[16]

---

11 I would not suggest that restitution or quasi-contract can be so described.

12 Birks, above n 1, 'Taxonomy', 9. More recently, the element of trepidation appears to have dissipated: see Birks, P, 'Property and Unjust Enrichment: Categorical Truths' [1997] NZ Law Rev 623.

13 Birks, above n 1, 'Taxonomy', 8–9. Burrows is another commentator whose views appear largely to coincide with Birks'. See, eg, Burrows, A, 'Proprietary Restitution: Unmasking Unjust Enrichment' (2001) 117 LQR 412.

14 Virgo, G, *The Principles of the Law of Restitution*, Oxford: OUP, 1999, 11–16, 591–97. Support for Virgo's view comes from the House of Lords decision in *Foskett v McKeown* [2000] 2 WLR 1299. Tang Hang Wu suggests that the House of Lords decision appears 'incompatible' with Birks' analysis ('*Foskett v McKeown*' (2001) 25 Melb ULR 295, 299–300).

15 Virgo, above n 14, 15 acknowledges that property rights may arise by virtue of 'consent' or 'wrongs', but states that 'it is not clear that property rights can derive from the defendant's unjust enrichment'. For similar arguments in favour of 'property' as a causative event, though within a different classificatory scheme again, see Grantham and Rickett, above n 5, Chapters 3 and 4.

16 I have no concluded opinion as to the relative merits of these competing views. However, so far as a label of itself can ever be an explanation of obligations, I do lean towards the view that the notion of the 'vindication of property' may have more explanatory value than 'unjust enrichment'. This is not to suggest that there is any magic in the use of terms such as 'property' or 'ownership'. I accept the conclusions of Justice Finn ('Equitable Doctrine and Discretion in Remedies', in Cornish *et al*, above n 1, 251, 263) that property interests may be 'manufactured', and of Evans, S, 'Property, Proprietary Remedies and Insolvency' (2000) 5 Deakin LR 31, 33, that '"Property" can function as a lump-concept that distracts attention from substantive questions and distorts the process of resolving contested claims' and can be used to hide policy choices. What I am suggesting, however, is that there are identifiable policies underlying determinations of what is necessary for the protection of persons' property rights. By contrast, I suspect that unjust enrichment tells us little about the competing choices faced by the law, such as whether to extend that protection where property has been dealt with, modified in some way or 'substituted'. The point can be illustrated by Professor Burrows' discussion of *Foskett v McKeown* [2000] 2 WLR 1299, in 'Proprietary Restitution: Unmasking Unjust Enrichment' (2001) 117 LQR 412. (contd)

The 'Other' category

For now, then, let us accept as a starting point the four categories of obligations. I have already indicated briefly some of the content of the first three categories. I turn now to concentrate on the 'Other'. What might be contained within this inscrutably named category? The content of the 'other' category is determined by the defined composition of the first three categories as identified by the common grounds within each that justify the imposition of liability, namely, the consensual undertaking of an obligation, the commission of a wrong, or a defendant's unjust enrichment, respectively. But if this is accepted, as Birks points out, then anything that does not fit within the first three categories must be housed in a residual category, which is miscellaneous and 'of uncertain size'.[17] He states:

> The category 'others' is a sort of cheat. It virtually ensures the correctness of the classification, but perhaps only because a huge and various assortment of rights find their origin in that open-ended category.[18]

What are some examples of causes of action that might be placed within the 'Other' category, for no other reason than that they cannot be located anywhere else? Birks suggests examples such as the law of maritime salvage, 'rescue' cases forming the common law equivalent to the civilian *negotiorum gestio*,[19] liability for the payment of taxes, and judgment debts.[20] I do not attempt to list all of the possibilities, for as Birks notes, 'it would require remarkable learning to compile

---

(contd) In *Foskett v McKeown*, a fraudulent trustee used money taken from a trust fund in order to pay premiums on a life insurance policy. Upon the suicide of the fraudster, the (innocent) defendants received a £1 million pay-out on the policy. Importantly, the trust moneys used to pay the premiums were not necessary for the entitlement to the £1 million, since premiums paid earlier by the fraudulent trustee from his own money were sufficient to maintain the policy for the years before his death. The majority (Lord Browne-Wilkinson, Lord Hoffmann and Lord Millett) allowed the claimants to claim a proportionate share (according to the proportion of premiums paid with trust money) of the £1 million. The minority (Lord Steyn and Lord Hope of Craighead) considered that the claimants were only entitled to a lien over the pay-out for the trust moneys used as premiums. Despite the dramatically different conclusions of the majority and minority, Burrows says that unjust enrichment actually allows either of these possible outcomes. Burrows argues as follows:

> *Foskett* should be regarded as having answered the question, *within the law of unjust enrichment* (or at least within that part of the law of unjust enrichment concerned with tracing), of which of two possible approaches to the link between the defendant's enrichment and the subtraction from the claimant should be taken (422).

Given the radically different consequences, it seems unconvincing to me that both outcomes can be the result of the same causative event, namely the unjust enrichment of the defendants. Unjust enrichment appears to tell us little about whether the claim should succeed or not. In my view, the correct decision in *Foskett* should have been to refuse the plaintiffs' claim for a proportionate share, because it seems to take the policy of protecting persons' property to exceptional lengths where the property has been substituted and where there is no causal connection between the original property and its alleged 'product'.

17 Birks, above n 1, '*Institutes*', 19.

18 Birks, above n 1, 'Taxonomy', 9–10.

19 Liabilities arising as a result of justified rescue may themselves be considered under some common principle, such as 'unjust sacrifice' suggested by Sam Stoljar. In effect, despite the common law's supposed hostility to a concept equating to *negotiorum gestio*, there may be sufficient incidences of successful claims to justify such a category, imposing liability on broad policy grounds of encouraging rescue. See further, Dietrich, above n 10, Chapter 8.

20 Birks, above n 1, '*Institutes*', 19.

an exhaustive list'.[21] Instead, I consider here a few causes of action that *might* belong within this 'other' category (because there is some doubt at least as to where they sensibly fit), to see what questions they may raise about the four-fold classification scheme. (In doing so, I will undoubtedly raise more questions than I answer.) I shall briefly consider estoppel, and then consider the problem area of precontractual liability. The examples I shall consider cast doubt upon the utility of drawing strict boundaries, at least between the categories of consent and wrongs and, specifically, contract and tort.

OTHER CAUSATIVE EVENTS

Estoppel

I turn briefly to the doctrine or doctrines[22] of estoppel, on the assumption that estoppel by conduct is more than merely defensive, that is, that it can operate to create legal obligations and is thus a cause (or several causes) of action.[23] Broadly speaking, estoppel precludes an 'unconscientious' departure by a defendant from an assumption held by a plaintiff, knowingly encouraged or acquiesced in by the defendant, where such departure would prove detrimental to the plaintiff.[24] Despite such a general underlying rationale, however, estoppel has manifested itself (historically) in distinct doctrines that may operate in a diverse range of circumstances. Given this diversity, one could (untenably, in my view) seek to identify different 'types' of estoppel having different foundations, and thus place those types within consent, wrongs, or unjust enrichment.[25] But even if we were to do so, some types of estoppel would still be difficult to classify and would remain in the 'Other' events category. In any case, the preferable approach, in my view, is to regard estoppel as a sufficiently coherent concept. The unifying idea of preventing injurious departure from an assumption in unconscionable circumstances warrants treating estoppel as a single doctrine or group of

---

21 *Ibid.*

22 This depends on whether or not there is a unified, single 'concept of estoppel common to, or straddling, common law and equity': The Hon Sir Anthony Mason, 'The Place of Equity and Equitable Doctrines in the Common Law World: An Australian Perspective', in Waters, DM, *Equity, Fiduciaries and Trusts*, Toronto: Carswell, 1993, 19. See also *Commonwealth v Verwayen* (1990) 170 CLR 394.

23 The issue is not without controversy in Australia, but I suggest this is the case. At the very least, *Waltons Stores (Interstate) Ltd v Maher* (1988) 164 CLR 387 is authority for the proposition that estoppel can be used 'aggressively'. Although Deane J in *Commonwealth v Verwayen* (1990) 170 CLR 394, 445 denied that *Waltons* meant that estoppel is an 'independent cause of action', with respect, this reasoning seems artificial, and other judges have taken a different approach. See the discussion in Heffey, P, Paterson, J and Robertson, A, *Principles of Contract Law*, Sydney: Lawbook Co, 2002, 175–77.

24 See *Waltons Stores (Interstate) Ltd v Maher* (1988) 164 CLR 387; *Commonwealth v Verwayen* (1990) 170 CLR 394.

25 An example of such an attempt can be seen in Birks, P, *An Introduction to the Law of Restitution*, Oxford: Clarendon, 1985, 290–94, in which he seeks to divide proprietary estoppel cases into cases of active encouragement, giving rise to fulfilment of plaintiffs' expectations, and cases of acquiescence, which he considers to be restitutionary and based on unjust enrichment. For a criticism of this division, see Getzler, J, 'Unconscionable Conduct and Unjust Enrichment as Grounds for Judicial Review' (1990) 16 Mon ULR 283, and Dietrich, above n 10, 84–87.

doctrines. Into which category does that doctrine, or group of doctrines, fit? There has been considerable debate on this issue and a range of views expressed. Can estoppel be considered a wrong; or is it a consent-based, promissory doctrine akin to contract?[26] The very diversity of views which have been expressed indicates that there are difficulties.

The important thing to note is that estoppel does not operate in a doctrinal vacuum: it draws many of its ideas from the familiar categories of contract (consent) and tort (wrongs), as is evidenced by Dixon J's judgment in *Thompson v Palmer*.[27] Conduct that can give rise to a conclusion that a defendant's departure from an assumption is unjust ranges from that which has a strongly contractual flavour, such as where an assumption 'formed the conventional basis upon which the parties entered into contractual or other mutual relations', to tort-like conduct, such as where imprudence or carelessness is the proximate cause of the plaintiff's reliance on the assumption.[28] Importantly, other conduct may not be so readily classified as contract-like or tort-like, exhibiting elements of both.[29]

Classifying cases of estoppel therefore poses challenges for any taxonomy. One response to this difficulty might be simply to place estoppel in the 'too-hard' basket of 'other causative events'. I suggest, however, that this would seem unsatisfactory for at least two reasons: first, because the relevant 'Other' causative event (or events?) in such a case would still not readily be identifiable and, secondly, because of the close affinity of estoppel to both the categories of consent and wrongs. It is this idea – that causes of action may lie *between* two established categories and operate at the periphery of both – that I want to explore further in this chapter.

Precontractual liability

I shall explore this idea by reference to cases of precontractual liability, where plaintiffs seek to impose legal obligations upon defendants as a result of actions performed (usually work done) in anticipation of contracts that never eventuate. Although a final contract may have been anticipated by the parties, or they may even have believed that agreement has been reached, nonetheless the absence of

---

26 See Robertson, A, 'Situating Equitable Estoppel Within the Law of Obligations' (1997) 19 Syd LR 32, who considers the competing theories and concludes that estoppel is a wrong. See also Spence, M, *Protecting Reliance: The Emergent Doctrine of Equitable Estoppel*, Oxford: Hart, 1999, and Robertson, A, 'Reliance, Conscience and the New Equitable Estoppel' (2000) 24 Melb ULR 218.

27 (1933) 49 CLR 507.

28 *Ibid*, 547. Some cases of proprietary estoppel may provide examples, such as where representations are made as to a party's existing or future interest in land, but the maker of the representation has been careless in taking all necessary steps to ensure such interest has been or will be assigned.

29 The situation of where a party 'directly made representations upon which the other party founded the assumption' (*ibid*, 547) may encompass a wide range of circumstances and reasons justifying a conclusion that it is unconscionable for the maker of the representation to deny the assumption.

any objectively discernible, complete and reasonably certain agreement[30] precludes enforcement of any *contractual* obligations in relation to the plaintiff's actions.[31] The common law's response to problems of precontractual liability has been piecemeal: various doctrines and causes of action have been utilised by the courts to found precontractual liability. These include: resort to contract law itself, such as by enforcing an express or implied 'ancillary' contract in relation to work done in anticipation of an incomplete 'main' contract;[32] resort to equitable principles such as estoppel[33] and the constructive trust;[34] resort to rules within quasi-contract, restitution, or unjust enrichment; and, perhaps more rarely, resort to tort law.[35] Consequently, there has been debate over how best to classify or categorise claims for precontractual work, and as to the doctrines best suited to administering those particular claims.[36]

One's immediate assessment of such a *piecemeal* legal regime may be that it raises no difficult issues of classification at all, since each cause of action must be specifically classified and located within its own particular category. Two responses can be made to such an argument, however. First, relatively 'straightforward' classification may well be possible where (ancillary) 'contracts' or 'tort' are utilised to resolve 'precontractual' liability problems, but many cases resort to equitable doctrines or restitution or quasi-contract (in circumstances where unjust enrichment is *not* a satisfactory explanation of the cases),[37] and these are not causes of action that can so readily be classified as consent ('contract'), wrongs ('torts') or unjust enrichment. Secondly, I believe that all or at least most cases of precontractual liability can be explained in terms of elements or features *common* to the decided cases, even despite the very different causes of action utilised by courts to resolve the problem in this area. So if one of the purposes of classification is to identify like cases, and to classify them uniformly, while distinguishing unlike cases, then I suggest that most precontractual cases do

30 I am thus including both anticipated and incomplete contracts when considering precontractual liability.

31 See below, however, in relation to the enforcement of 'ancillary' contracts.

32 See, eg, *Brewer St Investments Ltd v Barclays Woollen Co Ltd* [1954] 1 QB 428 and generally Carter, JW and Furmston, MP, 'Good Faith and Fairness in the Negotiation of Contracts' Parts I & II (1994) 8 J Cont L 1 & 93, 106–17.

33 See, eg, *Waltons Stores (Interstate) Ltd v Maher* (1988) 164 CLR 387, *Metropolitan Transit Authority v Waverley Transit Pty Ltd* [1991] VR 176 and generally Carter and Furmston, above n 32, 100–03. Cases of proprietary estoppel are also relevant. Such cases involve either incomplete or defective contracts, often involving agreements which are less than fully formed because of the domestic context within which they are made. See, eg, *Giumelli v Giumelli* (1999) 196 CLR 101.

34 See, eg, *Banner Homes Group plc v Luff Developments Ltd* [2000] 2 All ER 117.

35 See, eg, *Box v Midland Bank* [1979] 2 Lloyd's Rep 391; *Esso Petroleum Co Ltd v Mardon* [1976] QB 801 and generally Carter and Furmston, above n 32, 94–98.

36 See, eg, the debate between McKendrick, E, 'Work Done in Anticipation of a Contract which does not Materialise', in Cornish *et al*, above n 1, 163 and Hedley, S, 'Work Done in Anticipation of a Contract which does not Materialise: A Response', in Cornish *et al*, above n 1, 195.

37 The point is conceded by a number of commentators, including ones who accept unjust enrichment as underlying much of restitution. See, eg, Beatson, J, 'Benefit, Reliance and the Structure of Unjust Enrichment' [1987] CLP 71. For detailed analysis, see Dietrich, above n 10, 64–66.

impose liability on *like* criteria. These criteria or elements are present regardless of the particular cause of action utilised by the courts. Essentially, and I do not want to repeat at length arguments I have made elsewhere,[38] the common elements are:

(1) a belief (at least on the part of the plaintiff) that a contract exists or will exist;

(2) a plaintiff has relied detrimentally on that belief or expectation;[39] and

(3) the defendant's conduct is such:

(a) that an obligation to bear the risk of a failure to contract, including, specifically, to pay for the plaintiff's work or make good his or her reliance loss, has been or will be assumed by the defendant; or

(b) that the risk of such failure (and usually of having to bear any reliance loss) is, in the circumstances, imposed upon the defendant.

These elements of liability suggest that questions of precontractual liability can be addressed by reference to a uniform and coherent set of requirements; indeed, some legal systems determine precontractual liability by reference to a unifying cause of action, such as *culpa in contrahendo* (breach of precontractual duty).[40] Regardless, however, of whether the solution lies in a single cause of action, or in several causes of action, I suggest that the crux of liability is found in the third element (provided that the first two are satisfied), which involves an assessment by the courts that the defendant has either accepted the risk of a failure to contract (and hence of the particular losses consequent thereon), or else is the more appropriate party to bear such a risk. Critically, this element suggests that the law draws on ideas from both contract and tort law in order to determine liability.

The point, note, is not that in a given case 'concurrent liability'[41] may arise in both contract and tort; this idea is trite at common law. Rather, the point is that liability may arise in a given case as a result of the operation of legal principles that cannot be classified as lying in either category (so that an action brought in either contract or tort *would fail*).[42] The liability principles in this context lie in between these categories and draw on principles of liability from both. Sometimes

---

38 See Dietrich, J, 'Classifying Precontractual Liability: A Comparative Analysis' (2001) 21 LS 153.

39 A plaintiff's detrimental reliance can take a variety of forms, such as by abandoning existing legal rights (eg, *Avondale Printers Stationers Ltd v Haggie* [1979] 2 NZLR 124) or otherwise forgoing opportunities (eg, *Banner Homes Group plc v Luff Developments Ltd* [2000] 2 All ER 117), or by carrying out work that is preliminary to the performance of the expected main contract (eg, *Brewer Street Investments Ltd v Barclays Woollen Co Ltd* [1954] 1 QB 428, 429; *Angelopoulos v Sabitino* (1995) 65 SASR 1). At times, the plaintiff may have begun or completed the very performance which forms the subject-matter of the incompletely negotiated contract (eg, *British Steel Corp v Cleveland Bridge & Engineering Co Ltd* [1984] 1 All ER 504).

40 For a comparative study, see Dietrich, above n 38.

41 Smith, SA, 'Concurrent Liability in Contract and Unjust Enrichment: The Fundamental Breach Requirement' (1999) 115 LQR 245, 248, points out that the term 'concurrent liability' is used in two different senses, namely, (1) that in respect of a particular set of facts, a plaintiff may satisfy the elements of two (or more) causes of action, and (2) that a breach of contract may also, as a possibility, 'support' or give rise to an action in tort, or vice versa.

42 It will be difficult to establish *all* the elements necessary for a claim in either category.

liability may be based more on principles fundamental to contract law (and can thus be described as more contract-like);[43] at other times, liability may be based more on principles at the heart of tort law (and can thus be described as more tort-like). Importantly, it is the existence of liability producing factors of *both* categories that *in combination* suffice to substantiate liability in some manner or form.[44] Note that the suggestion is not that there are two distinct sub-groups of liability. All I am suggesting is that in this area between tort and contract there are multiple intermediate stages of liability that ought not themselves be classified into rigid or conclusive sub-categories.[45] Hence, although I have stated the third element in terms of two types of conduct, this is a little simplistic and misleading. I am in fact suggesting a spectrum ranging from liability at the boundaries of contract, to liability *in between* contract and tort, to liability at the boundaries of tort.

That liability rules may draw upon principles from both contract and tort law is not a concept new to the common law, including (and especially) equity. As noted at the outset, estoppel appears to operate at the periphery of both contract and tort and covers a diverse range of subject matter.[46] Indeed, equity as a whole performs its well recognised ameliorative function by means of the metamorphosis and development of ideas already familiar to the common law. In part, such a function is necessary precisely because contract and tort are categories self-limited historically by their own internal conceptual criteria.

Perhaps the most significant insight to be gained from a conception of precontractual liability as lying between contract and tort is that it explains why, despite no cause of action in contract or in tort (or in unjust enrichment) being made out, liability may nonetheless arise. This liability is established because some of the factors determinative of liability (or at least relevant to such determination) in each category are present, such that broader than usual 'contractual' liability may be justified by the presence of additional factors normally associated with establishing liability in tort, or broader than usual 'tort' liability may be established by the presence of additional factors normally associated with establishing liability in contract.

---

43 At times, the circumstances are such as to justify an actual contract, ancillary to the incomplete main contract, realistically being implied. Unlike some unjust enrichment theorists, who consider that such findings of implied intention are often artificial and extend the boundaries of contract too far, I consider this an appropriate response in many cases. Nor does such an approach contradict my arguments in this chapter. In fact, in arguing for a spectrum of liability between contract and tort, this includes liability from the core of contract, to the (necessarily) 'hazy' edges of contract, through to liability in between contract and tort, to liability at the boundaries of tort law.

44 I have partly derived this idea from comparative study of German and Austrian law and, in particular, the work of Professor Koziol. See Koziol, H, '*Delikt, Verletzung von Schuldverhältnissen und Zwischenbereich*' [1994] JBL 209, and 'The Borderline Between Tort Liability and Contract', in Koziol, H (ed), *The Unification of Tort Law: Wrongfulness*, The Hague: Kluwer Law Int, 1998, 25. See Dietrich, above n 38.

45 Cf Koziol, above n 44, '*Delikt*', 217.

46 Note, however, Gilmore, G, *The Death of Contract*, Columbus, OH: Ohio State UP, 1974, Ch IV, 96, who suggests that the two fields 'are gradually merging and becoming one'.

The point can be illustrated by reference to two oft-cited cases, *William Lacey (Hounslow) Ltd v Davis*[47] and *Sabemo Pty Ltd v North Sydney MC*,[48] the facts of which are similar. In both cases, the plaintiffs were requested to do substantial preliminary planning work on the expectation that lucrative redevelopment contracts would be concluded. In both cases, the type and quantity of work requested went well beyond what a plaintiff may 'be expected to do without charge when tendering' for a contract,[49] so that expectations clearly arose that the work was not being performed gratuitously. In both cases, the respective courts considered that the risks of the expected 'main' contracts not being finalised (when the redevelopment projects were abandoned) rested with the defendants, for a variety of reasons. Importantly, the factors stressed by the courts in each case as justifying liability bear similarity to the preconditions of both contract and tort liability:

(1) the relationships were commercial, but they were conducted on an informal basis while negotiations for the main contract continued;

(2) the requests for the work to be performed were made in circumstances that implicitly created assumptions in both parties that remuneration in some form would occur, that is, that the work was not gratuitous;

(3) though not expressly stated in these terms in the judgments, it seems clear that the respective defendants were in a better position to safeguard against the losses, for example by clearly spelling out the terms upon which the precontractual work was being done;

(4) the negotiations were broken off by the defendants, not because of any failure to agree on a 'main' contract, but because of abandonment of their respective projects; and

(5) rather than seeking to enforce any expectations in relation to the abandoned 'main' contract, the respective plaintiffs sought to recover (and were awarded) their reliance losses.

In both cases, therefore, the courts in weighing up liability considered a combination of factors. Some of these were akin to the defining features of contract law – the assumption of obligations and risks, (implied) agreements, parties' (unstated) expectations and the like; others were akin to tenets of tort law (specifically negligence) – especially a concern for the compensation of foreseeable harms, and the imposition of liability on persons with the capacity through their actions to cause losses.[50] Significantly, after concluding that the case was not one of unjust enrichment, Sheppard J in *Sabemo* stated:

---

47 [1957] 2 All ER 712.

48 [1977] 2 NSWLR 880.

49 *William Lacey (Hounslow) Ltd v Davis* [1957] 2 All ER 712, 716.

50 In precontractual relationships, the closer, contract-like relationship existing between the parties gives rise to a corresponding increased vulnerability of each, in opening themselves up to the other in the course of negotiations. As has been pointed out, 'commercial transactions can only function smoothly ... if the increased risks [which contractual negotiations entail] are compensated with higher duties of care' than that owed to the ordinary person: Koziol, above n 44, '*Delikt*', 213, citing Welser, *Vertretung ohne Vollemacht*, 1970, 75 (my own translation).

> Plainly there are cases not founded on contract, nor in tort, nor upon the application of any equitable doctrine or principle, where there may be recovery.[51]

One way in which these taxonomical difficulties may be surmounted is to argue that, whatever the content of the precontractual duties established in the case law, breaches of such duties can be classified as 'wrongs'. On this argument, breaches of 'primary' precontractual duties can all be classified within the wrongs category. Birks has argued that the 'wrongs' category (including torts) is different from the other categories. Whereas the other categories define *primary* rights directly realised by the courts, wrongs involve *infringements* of primary rights.[52] He further argues that the primary duties that are infringed when a wrong is committed are themselves based in one of the other three categories of events.[53] The primary duty of care in negligence law, for example, is found in the 'Other' category. Even acceptance of these arguments, however,[54] does not alter the difficulty that the 'primary' precontractual duties are themselves of a 'hybrid' kind, sharing characteristics of both the consent category and of those in the 'Other' category that comprise the duties enforced through tort law. This, of itself, is significant. It challenges the drawing of strict boundaries between consent and

---

51 (1977) 2 NSWLR 880, 897. Davies, JD, 'What's In A Title' (1981) 1 OJLS 301, 304–05, referring to cases such as *Sabemo*, states: 'The facts of the cases have this in common, that the parties could not genuinely think themselves outside all legal liability but it is not easy to see how the facts fit any accepted category of liability. Such fact situations may not be all that rare and judges have proved themselves anxious not to let problems of classification constitute too great an obstacle to the provision of some remedy.'

52 'Taxonomy', above n 1, 16.

53 *Ibid*, 10.

54 I must confess to some considerable difficulty in understanding this aspect of Birks' categorisation. As I have noted, the primary duties, breach of which are wrongs, are categorised elsewhere in Birks' classification scheme. Thus, the duty to take reasonable care is found in the 'Other' category (*ibid*, 10). The corollary of this is that breaches of primary duties based on *consent* are also 'wrongs'. Hence, a breach of contract is classified as a wrong, giving rise to separate secondary remedies to relieve against the wrong. A 'breach of contract' is in fact a wrong (even though the reason why the contract is enforceable is said by Birks to rest on the consent of the parties and is not an imposed obligation) and the primary duties which are protected by tort law when breached are in fact found in the 'other' category (and thus founded on unspecified policy/moral concerns). If we accept this, then it does make the labels of consent and wrongs rather of limited utility. It means that the specific enforcement of (primary) contractual rights is said to be based on consent, whereas remedies for breach of contract are categorically different. Yet to the extent to which I perceive 'contract' is based on consent (and I share some of the doubts expressed by Robertson about this in Chapter 6, above) and categorically different to a tort, I similarly perceive 'breach of contract'. Under Birks' schema, however, it seems that the categories of 'contract' and 'tort' are no longer particularly relevant to allow us to classify causes of action. This is because the concerns of contract and tort which we assume are of relevance to each of those 'categories' are not, in fact, indicative or useful as starting points for telling us what the categories in Birks' four-fold classification are about. Perhaps my confusion stems from my perception of contract law as consisting of both the 'constitutive rules' establishing contractual rights and interests, as well as the 'protective rules' protecting those interests (to use the words of Cane, P, *The Anatomy of Tort Law*, Oxford: Hart, 1997, 10, 198–99. See also at 201–04, where Cane argues that breaches of contract should not be classified as torts (wrongs)). See also Grantham and Rickett, above n 5, 48–49, who put breach of contract within the consent category, but under a separate heading of 'indirectly' enforced obligations. They state that: 'such cases could just as well be placed in the category of wrongs. There may, however, be some justification for retaining them in the category consent, at least for the purposes of diagrammatic representation, in that the wrongs result from the breach of obligations assumed by the defendant party.'

'Others', and consent and wrongs. The challenge becomes all the greater if one accepts the view argued for in Chapter 6, above, that what are traditionally considered to form the core content of consent and wrongs, namely contract and torts, are not necessarily as distinct as has been suggested. As Robertson has argued, seeing contract essentially as a consent-based obligation ignores the fact that 'contract law is to a significant extent informed by values and standards routinely attributed to the law of tort'.[55]

Moreover, in the context of the precontractual liability cases, there is a complex interactive relationship between consent-based obligations and wrong-based obligations. It would be regrettable to ignore such a relationship, either by forcing causes of action (or a cause of action) of precontractual liability into contract, tort, (leaving aside the question of the extent to which they are indeed the same as consent and wrongs) or unjust enrichment, or simply by pretending that they have nothing to do with those categories and leaving them to languish in the 'Other'. Even if the last approach were taken, we would then face the difficulty of precisely identifying the relevant 'Other' causative event (or events). This would not be an easy task and, I suggest, would be one which invariably leads us back to contract and tort.

Another advantage that flows from recognition of precontractual liability as best classified as lying between contract and tort is that such classification may explain the range of remedial rights that follow from a finding of precontractual liability at common law. Further, such recognition may illuminate the question of what the appropriate remedy in a given case should be. If rigid categorisation of causative events is undesirable in this context, so it would seem is an inflexible approach to remedy. For example, if the reasons for liability in a given case lie closer to the conceptual core of contract, indeed such that there very nearly is a contract, then a remedy protecting a plaintiff's positive or 'contractual' expectations may be appropriate.[56] At the other end of the spectrum, where liability appears to be inspired by core tort concepts, such as a negligent infringement of a duty of care to warn against certain risks, then only compensation of (reliance) losses caused thereby would seem appropriate. If a given case falls somewhere in between these two extremes, then perhaps the most appropriate remedy is the protection of what a plaintiff may reasonably be entitled to expect, consistently with many of the cases themselves (awarding a quantum meruit for work performed, for example).

I have summarised my discussion in the form of the following diagram. Speculatively, I have included features that may be concerns of contract, tort, or the 'in-between' category.[57]

---

55 Robertson, A, 'On the Distinction between Contract and Tort', Chapter 6 of this volume.

56 *Banner Homes Group plc v Luff Developments Ltd* [2000] 2 All ER 117 and *Waltons Stores (Interstate) Ltd v Maher* (1988) 164 CLR 387 are good examples.

57 Note that the diagram does *not* represent situations of *concurrent* liability in contract and in tort. To accurately represent this, the two circles would need to overlap.

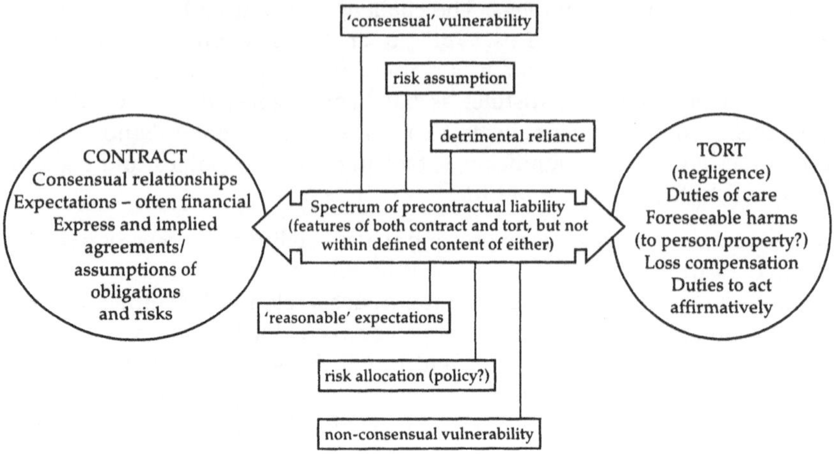

I am sure that there are many other situations in which 'causative events' giving rise to liability are, in fact, an amalgam of considerations normally associated with different categories,[58] such as contract and tort. This may be so even in relation to causative events categorised within one of the established categories. An example, I suggest, is the establishment of tort liability for purely economic loss. A finding of a duty of care to safeguard against purely economic loss does not involve a straightforward application of tort principles. Tort liability for (even foreseeable) purely economic losses is limited. One of the reasons underlying the law's reluctance to impose wide-ranging liability in tort for purely economic loss is the capacity for such liability to infringe excessively upon parties' freedom to engage in commercial activities which, of necessity, have economic consequences. This can be contrasted with the position under contract law, which protects against purely economic harms when a defendant has assumed an obligation in relation thereto. Hence, if the protection of purely economic loss is generally within the realm of contract law and not tort law, it is suggested that a duty in *tort* may arise if aspects of contract law are present, aspects which justify wider, more far-reaching obligations. For example, in *Perre v Apand*,[59] it was suggested by the High Court that if A owes a contractual obligation to B not to do a certain act in a way which harms B's economic interests, then there is no further infringement upon A's freedom of conduct if A does that something and is thereby held liable in tort

58 Other causes of action which are of uncertain classification and may draw on ideas from contract, tort and unjust enrichment may include: (1) situations of frustrated joint endeavours giving rise to obligations to share the burdens and benefits of such frustration (see Dietrich, above n 10, Chapter 7); and, perhaps (2) cases of subrogation. I am not convinced that all cases of non-contractual subrogation can be explained by reference to the principle of unjust enrichment, as Charles Mitchell argues in *The Law of Subrogation*, Oxford: Clarendon, 1994. For a persuasive rebuttal of this view, see Hedley, S, *Restitution: Its Division and Ordering*, London: Sweet & Maxwell, 2001, Chapter 5.

59 (1999) 198 CLR 180. See also *Hill v Van Erp* (1997) 188 CLR 159 (particularly at 231 (Gummow J): one of the functions 'of the law of tort, with respect to recovery of economic loss ... [is] the filling in of gaps left by the law of contract') and *White v Jones* [1995] 2 AC 207. See also Robertson, above n 55.

to C as well. Similarly, and referring again to precontractual liability, consensual relationships near contract may justify a finding of a duty of care greater than that ordinarily owed to one's neighbours.

CONCLUSION

Having considered one type of obligation that might be found within the 'Other' events category, we have seen that precontractual liability cases appear to draw on ideas already familiar to our law, suggesting that causes of action exist between contract and tort (and, to repeat the qualification above, *to the extent* that they are indeed the same thing, consent and wrongs). What do these conclusions say about the four-fold categorisation?

Perhaps we should bear in mind the words of Schlechtriem, Coen and Hornung, who, in the context of a comparative study of European restitution law (and, specifically, in the context of claims to recover property), point out:

> What is of interest in terms of comparative law is not how claims are characterised domestically but rather the fact that their object is the 'restitution' of possession. In comparative legal research, it is rather doubtful whether 'good classification is the foundation of good doctrine', to quote Lionel Smith[60] – in fact, 'good classification' in domestic terms may often be misleading on the wider comparative scene.[61]

In other words, in the comparative field, at least, classification is a hindrance rather than a help. This is precisely because different legal systems approach the identical problems from different categorical standpoints. Nonetheless, litigated disputes are often similarly resolved (or similarly confused and unresolved, as the case may be) albeit through very different legal tools. I raise the question as to whether classification may not, at times, also be a hindrance *within* a legal system. It may force us to attempt resolution of legal disputes within a straitjacket of established categories, rather than by reference to the specific factors courts consider and weigh up when determining liability.

The important thing about cases of precontractual liability is that we must not lose sight of the fact that the specifics of the problem need to be addressed and resolved. What are the critical relevant factors that support or detract from liability? This will involve close attention to the facts of the cases and to those considerations that the *judges* isolate as important – judges who are not necessarily concerned with the taxonomical 'integrity' of what they are doing. An example of excessive adherence to existing categories is McKendrick's attempt to classify cases of precontractual liability as either contract or unjust enrichment.[62] With respect, this leads to artificiality and poor law, even if many of the cases could be squeezed into those categories were we to desire it.[63] Insistence on the

60 Above n 1, 444.

61 Schlechtriem, P, Coen, C and Hornung, R, 'Restitution and Unjust Enrichment in Europe' (2001) 2 & 3 European Rev of Private Law 377, 400, fn 49.

62 McKendrick, above n 36.

63 See generally Dietrich, above n 38, and Hedley, above n 36.

existence of 'enrichment', for example, where the courts are not concerned with that issue, is a product of obsession with the established categories, despite their obvious and self-limiting boundaries.

Many of the arguments I have made in this chapter have been elegantly made by others. Peter Cane sums up the issue well:

> My argument is that the categories in themselves ought not to be given *dispositive* significance because they are no more than convenient *expository* devices for grouping together causes of action which share common features in terms of protected interests, sanctioned conduct and sanctions.[64]

The warning against giving categories dispositive significance becomes all the more critical where those categories are relatively new (such as unjust enrichment) or as yet unidentified. The latter would include categories of causative events yet to be articulated and identified within the presently uncertain content of the categories collectively labelled as 'Others'.

---

64 Cane, above n 54, 200. At 198 he states:

> Classifications, we might say, perform a useful 'expository' function, facilitating access to and understanding of the law. However, under the influence of the formulary way of thinking about law, classifications tend to take on a life of their own. We talk about causes of action 'in tort' or 'in contract'; and, more importantly, criteria of success and failure in legal actions may come to turn on such classifications. When this happens, classifications take on what we might call a 'dispositive' role ... It is very important that lawyers should remain the masters of their own categories and not become servants of such conceptualism.

8

INTEGRATING PROPERTY AND OBLIGATIONS

Robert Chambers

INTRODUCTION

Over the past 20 years, a great deal of progress has been made in what we now call the law of obligations. This includes contract, tort, unjust enrichment, and a variety of equitable obligations, such as fiduciary duties, duties of confidence, and duties created by estoppel. However, by definition, the law of obligations excludes the law of property. By obligations, we mean the obligations that correspond to personal rights. An obligation exists only because a particular person has a legal right to enforce it. The obligation and the personal right are two sides of a coin.

If, instead of calling this subject the law of obligations, we called it the law of personal rights, we would instantly be aware that it is incomplete: only part of a greater whole. The adjective 'personal' is used to distinguish those rights from one other kind: property rights. While personal rights correspond to obligations placed on specific persons, property rights correspond to obligations imposed generally on all members of society. In other words, if we flipped these coins over, from the obligation side to the personal right side, we would quickly see that many of them are similar to, and belong with, coins bearing property rights.

We would not exclude the law of property if we called the subject the law of personal and property rights or, more simply, the law of rights. However, we cannot do that. The term 'rights' is often used to refer to basic human rights, constitutional rights, civil liberties, and so on. That is a different subject. For the most part, the law of obligations is concerned, not with the obligations owed to, by, or between governments, but with the obligations owed by one private person to another. This subject already has a useful name: private law. Essentially, the law of obligations is the heart of private law, but with property removed.

This chapter is a call to unify private law by ending the separation of property law from the law of obligations. There are two main questions addressed in this chapter: first, why should we integrate property and obligations and, secondly, how do we do it?

WHY INTEGRATE PROPERTY AND OBLIGATIONS?

The short answer to the first question, why integrate property and obligations, is this: the isolation of those two subjects is harmful. It separates aspects of law that are alike and belong together. It makes it difficult for us to see important connections between different legal responses to similar problems, because those responses lie on different sides of the great property/obligations divide. This makes it more difficult to learn and apply the law, whether as students, teachers, practitioners, or judges.

If the integration of property and obligations makes our jobs easier, that is itself a strong argument in its favour. However, it is needed to prevent more serious harm. If we fail to see important connections between property and obligations, then we may fail to notice that the rules on one side of the divide are inconsistent with rules on the other side. People who ought to receive similar legal treatment are treated differently because of this inconsistency. Like cases are not treated alike and we loosen our grip on the fundamental principle of equality before the law. In other words, the law ceases to be just.

There are many instances of inconsistency caused by the division between the law of obligations and the law of property. Two examples are offered here. The first concerns restitution in a Torrens land titles registration system and the second concerns the division of family property.

Restitution in a Torrens system

The first example of inconsistency involves two Torrens mortgages. One was set aside and the other was enforced, even though the parties were similarly situated. In *Garcia v National Australia Bank Ltd*,[1] a woman was a director and shareholder of a corporation. She guaranteed the corporation's debt to its bank and granted a Torrens mortgage over her interest in the family home to secure that debt. The bank was not able to enforce the guarantee and the mortgage, because the woman's husband had pressured her to grant them and had misled her about the extent of the corporation's indebtedness and its solvency. The bank had notice of this risk, because it knew the woman was married to the other guarantor and, therefore, should have known that misrepresentations, pressure, or undue influence might be used to induce her to grant the guarantee and mortgage.

Compare *Garcia* with *Pyramid Building Society v Scorpion Hotels Pty Ltd*.[2] A corporation granted a Torrens mortgage to a bank to secure a loan. The mortgage was signed by one of the corporation's directors and his wife. However, she was not a director. The mortgage was a forgery and a portion of the loan was misappropriated by the director and his wife. The bank had notice of the forgery. If it had acted reasonably, it would have discovered that the mortgage was unauthorised. Nevertheless, the bank was entitled to enforce this mortgage and the debt it secured (including interest at 24.5%) because the mortgage was a Torrens mortgage. It was indefeasible unless the bank was guilty of fraud. Mere notice of forgery is not fraud for Torrens purposes.

These two cases cannot be reconciled. In both cases, someone granted a Torrens mortgage to an innocent bank, which loaned money in reliance on the

---

1 (1998) 194 CLR 395.

2 [1998] 1 VR 188 (Vic CA).

validity of the mortgage. In both cases, the mortgagor's intention to grant the mortgage was defective. In *Garcia*, the intention was vitiated by pressure and misunderstanding. In *Pyramid*, the intention was absent. In both cases, the bank had notice of the defective intention. In one case, the mortgage was set aside. In the other, it was indefeasible. These cases cannot stand together. We cannot say that notice of possible pressure invalidates a Torrens mortgage, while notice of forgery does not.

Why did this inconsistency happen? Probably because the lawyers and judges in one case approached the problem as belonging to the law of obligations, while those in the other case situated it in the law of property. The same problem was approached from two different perspectives, using different legal terminology. In *Garcia*, the problem was presented as one of unjust enrichment (dressed in the language of unconscionability). The woman's intention to benefit the bank was vitiated by pressure and mistake and the bank could not conscientiously enforce her obligations because it should have been aware of those risks and did nothing to alleviate them.

In *Pyramid*, the case was presented as a problem of indefeasibility of property rights. A registered property right to land is enforceable, regardless of defects in the underlying transaction, unless the right holder knows or suspects those defects when the right is registered.[3] In other words, the mortgage was indefeasible in the absence of actual fraud by the registered mortgagee.

If, in either case, the lawyers and judges had looked across the property/obligations divide, it is likely that they would have seen the problem and addressed it. There is a tension between the need to set aside defective transactions and the need for rights created by those transactions to be secure. This tension must be resolved one way or the other. Whatever solution is chosen, it must be applied consistently: like cases must be treated alike.

Family property

The second example of inconsistency concerns the division of family assets when a marriage or similar relationship comes to an end, one party owns most of the wealth acquired during the relationship, and the other party wants a share of it. In many cases, a court will compel an equitable division of that wealth by declaring that it is held on constructive or resulting trust for both parties.

For most Australians in this situation, the solution is now provided by statute. Under the Family Law Act 1975 (Cth), the court can divide family assets at the end of a marriage and order one spouse to support the other. There are State and territorial statutes giving courts the power to divide assets between de facto spouses and people in similar relationships.[4] However, these statutes do not provide a complete solution. Many cohabiting couples are not protected by them,

---

3 *Assets Co Ltd v Mere Roihi* [1905] AC 176 (PC).

4 Domestic Relationships Act 1994 (ACT); Property (Relationships) Act 1984 (NSW); De Facto Relationships Act 1996 (NT); Property Law Act 1974 (Qd), Part 19; De Facto Relationships Act 1996 (SA); Property Law Act 1958 (Vic), Part 9; Family Law Amendment Act 2002 (WA).

either because of where they live or because of the kind of relationship they have. Also, several statutes provide only for the redistribution of property rights and not for the payment of financial support.

The limitations of family property statutes mean that the courts' equitable jurisdiction is still needed. However, a declaration of trust can do only so much. Judges have consistently disclaimed any power to redistribute family wealth (apart from statute).[5] They merely declare the existence of equitable interests that can arise during a marriage or similar relationship. Perhaps more importantly, a trust can apply only to assets that are capable of being the subject of a trust.

Studies have shown that most couples earn more in one year than the total value of their combined assets.[6] In other words, the most important 'asset' each party has is the ability to earn income and, for many couples, the most important asset acquired during their relationship is the enhanced ability to earn income. Yet, the ability to earn income cannot be the subject matter of a trust.[7]

Suppose, for example, that I go to law school while my de facto spouse works two jobs to support us and makes many other sacrifices, such as moving interstate and forgoing educational, career, and family opportunities. I then qualify for practice, enhancing my earning potential by 500%, and leave her for a woman I met in law school. If, instead of my attaining a law degree, my de facto spouse and I had worked hard acquiring other forms of wealth in my name, such as a house, a car, and bank deposits, I would hold those on trust for both of us in proportion to our contributions to the relationship.[8] However, a massive earning potential cannot be the subject matter of a trust.

Naturally, many observers are frustrated with a system of law that can order the sharing of some assets but not others. As Claudia Wendrich said: 'If the most valuable asset is excluded from sharing, the purpose of the deferred community property regime, viz, the equal sharing of all assets acquired during the marriage, has not been achieved.'[9] She argues that earning potential 'should be considered property and thus shareable'.[10] There are several American States which treat professional qualifications, such as medical or law degrees, as property rights that can be shared by spouses.[11]

Why has so much energy been spent trying to classify professional qualifications and earning potential as property? A university degree or other qualification is not a property right. It is a recognition of the training, knowledge,

5 See, eg, *Windeler v Whitehall* [1990] 2 FLR 505, 506.

6 Weitzman, LJ, 'Marital Property: Its Transformation and Division in the United States', in Weitzman, LJ and Maclean, M (eds), *Economic Consequences of Divorce: The International Perspective*, Oxford: Clarendon, 1992, 85, 96–97; Wendrich, C, 'Who Should Profit from an Academic Degree Upon Marital Breakdown? Comparing Manitoba Common Law and the German Civil Code' (1997) 25 Manitoba LJ 267, 269.

7 *Caratun v Caratun* (1992) 96 DLR (4th) 404, 413 (Ont CA).

8 *Baumgartner v Baumgartner* (1987) 164 CLR 137.

9 Wendrich, above n 6, 269.

10 Wendrich, above n 6, 289; also see Weitzman, above n 6, 125.

11 See, eg, *O'Brien v O'Brien*, 452 NYS 2d 801 (1982); Weitzman, above n 6, 127–34.

and other attributes of its holder. Those attributes are an intrinsic part of the individual and cannot be shared or used by others. In a society where slavery is not permitted, one person cannot own any aspect of another living human being. One party to a marriage or similar relationship cannot be a beneficial part owner of the other party.

Why has this debate taken place solely on the property side of the property/obligations divide? Why have courts limited themselves to declaring the existence of property rights at the end of a relationship? In other situations, courts are happy to declare the existence of obligations. For example, if I injure you negligently, a court will declare that I am required to pay you a sum of money as compensation for your loss. The obligation to pay compensation is not created by the court. It arises when the loss is inflicted (but may be replaced by a judgment debt or a debt created by a contract of settlement). Similarly, if you pay me by mistake, a court will declare that I have an obligation to pay you a sum of money as restitution. Again, the court does not create that obligation. It arises when I am unjustly enriched at your expense.

The problem is that we began by asking the wrong question: how do we redistribute family property? This situates the whole inquiry within the law of property. We need to phrase that question in a way that does not ignore the law of obligations. Let us ask instead what rights are created during a marriage or similar relationship. If we take a wider view, we see that the problem is the same whether my de facto spouse makes sacrifices so I can buy a house or acquire a law degree. She has detrimentally relied upon her expectation of sharing the benefit of that house or that degree. I should have an obligation to share that benefit. The benefit of my house lies in my right to possess it. That is a property right I can share. The benefit of my law degree lies (in part) in my higher earning potential. That is a purely personal right that I cannot share. However, I can share its value. Even though I cannot transfer the right itself, I can pay my de facto spouse for her contribution to its acquisition. A court could declare the existence of an obligation to pay her a sum of money, based on the present value of my potential future earnings and the value of her contribution to my acquisition of that asset. That sum might be calculated by reference to my enrichment, her detriment, or her expectations.[12] However it is calculated, her right and my corresponding obligation should not depend on the existence of property.

When courts first started dealing with this problem of redistributing family assets at the end of a marriage or similar relationship, they looked for a solution within the law of trusts, thus limiting the distribution to rights capable of being the subject of a trust.[13] This would not have happened if courts had focused on the source of the rights rather than on the nature of the rights. In other words, rather than saying that this is a problem for the law of trusts, they should have said that this is a problem for the law of estoppel or the law of unjust enrichment. Rights

12 Chambers, R, 'Constructive Trusts in Canada' (1999) 37 Alberta L Rev 173, 203–07; reprinted (2002) 16 Trust LI 2, 7–10.

13 See Mee, J, *The Property Rights of Cohabitees*, Oxford: Hart, 1999, 18–22.

created by estoppel or unjust enrichment may be either personal or property.[14] As sources of rights, estoppel and unjust enrichment cross the property/obligations divide.

HOW DO WE INTEGRATE PROPERTY AND OBLIGATIONS?

The dominant method of dividing private legal rights into obligations and property has a long and useful history and should not be abandoned. However, there are other methods of organising those rights, which do not segregate obligations and property. We must be willing and able to use a different system of classifying rights when it serves our purpose to do so.

As Peter Birks points out in the introduction to *English Private Law*,[15] there are three main questions to ask concerning private legal rights: (1) against whom can the right be enforced; (2) what is the content of the right; and (3) how was the right created? The answers to these three questions identify the three essential characteristics of a right: its enforceability, its content, and its source. These are the characteristics we use most often to organise private legal rights. That organisation depends on the priority given to each characteristic during the sorting process. If we divide rights first according to their enforceability and then by content or source, we produce a very different picture than if we start with source and then move on to other characteristics. The integration or segregation of property and obligations depends on this choice.

Enforceability of rights

Normally, the enforceability of rights is the dominant characteristic by which private legal rights are organised. The first question we ask is whether the right is a personal right, that can be enforced only against specific persons, or is a property right, that can be enforced generally against other members of society. This produces two separate piles of private legal rights: obligations and property.

There is an important, but hidden, exception to this separation of obligations and property. The primary right to personal autonomy, held by all members of society, corresponds to obligations placed on all other members of society and not just on specific persons. Every member of society has a primary duty not to interfere with the persons and property of others. The right to autonomy of the person is, like a property right, enforceable generally against other members of society and not merely against specific persons. However, it is not a property right because it does not relate to anything apart from the right holder. All property rights are rights to things that are only contingently connected to us and not intrinsic aspects of ourselves.[16]

---

14 See, eg, *Black v S Freedman & Co* (1910) 12 CLR 105; *Ilich v The Queen* (1987) 162 CLR 110; *Giumelli v Giumelli* (1999) 196 CLR 101.

15 Birks, P (ed), *English Private Law*, Oxford: OUP, 2000, xxxviii.

16 Penner, JE, *The Idea of Property in Law*, Oxford: Clarendon, 1997, 112.

When private legal rights are divided according to their enforceability, our basic right to non-interference with the person belongs, not with other personal rights that are enforceable only against specific persons, but with property rights that are enforceable generally against other members of society. However, it lies hidden in that pile because it is enforced not directly as a primary right, but only indirectly against specific persons who wrongly interfere with that right. The torts against the person, such as battery, defamation, and negligent personal injury, are wrongful interferences with the primary right to personal autonomy. Those torts give rise to secondary rights (usually to be compensated for the loss caused by the interference) that are enforceable against specific wrongdoers and belong with other personal rights as part of the law of obligations.

If we set to one side the primary rights not directly enforced, the division of rights according to their enforceability produces two neat piles of property and obligations. Although it is common to organise private law in this manner, thus ignoring the primary right to autonomy of the person, we should never forget that this right is the greatest of all private rights. Along with the law of property, it protects our liberty by imposing on every other member of society a duty not to interfere with ourselves or our things. Disregarding those primary rights can produce a skewed view of private law that is focused on wrongdoing and the relationship between parties to litigation.[17] Most people do not litigate, but live their lives in accordance with their primary duties of non-interference with the persons and property of others.

Content of rights

The content of a right refers to the right holder's entitlement. What does it entitle the right holder to do or receive? For example, is it possession of a book, payment of a sum of money, or the loyal service of a trustee? We routinely organise property rights according to their content. We separate rights to land from rights to goods, rights to possession from non-possessory rights, beneficial ownership from security rights, and so forth.

We can also organise personal rights by content. For example, is the right holder entitled to receive payment of money, performance of a service, delivery of a quantity of goods, indemnity from a potential obligation, and so on? However, this does not dominate the law of obligations the way it does the law of property.

Source of rights

We usually organise obligations according to their third characteristic: the source of those obligations. This is how we begin our legal education, with the division between torts and contracts. We then go on to learn that obligations are also created by other events, such as unjust enrichment, estoppel, and statute. In contrast, this characteristic usually receives the lowest priority in the law of property. When we do divide property rights according to their source, we

17 See, eg, Weinrib, EJ, *The Idea of Private Law*, Cambridge, MA: Harvard UP, 1995.

normally make only one division. All property rights are created either by intention or by operation of law.

Trusts are a special case. They are almost always organised according to their source. The dominant classification of trusts divides them into express, implied, resulting, constructive, and statutory trusts. However, this does not match the standard division of obligations according to whether they are created by contracts, torts, unjust enrichment, or other events. Nor does it match the standard division of property rights into those created by consent and those created by operation of law.

Why do we classify trusts differently from both obligations and property rights? The division between law and equity may explain the difference. However, it may also be because a trust is a unique combination of personal and property rights. In other words, it crosses the property/obligations divide. Rights on one side of that divide are classified differently from rights on the other side. Rather than choose between them, trust lawyers and judges invented a third system used only to organise the law of trusts.

The problem

Our problem is caused by our almost constant reliance on the enforceability of rights as the dominant characteristic for classification. This means that property and obligations are almost always kept apart from each other. However, many legal problems do not confine themselves nicely to one side of the divide or the other. When we find a solution to a problem on one side of the divide, that solution needs to be applied or at least considered on the other side.

The current separation of property and obligations leads to a duplication of effort. Work, debates, and advances taking place in the law of obligations need to be repeated in the law of property and vice versa. Worse than this inefficiency is the risk of inconsistency. Rules developed on one side may be incompatible with rules on the other. A difference based on sound legal reasoning and policy can be defended. A difference caused by a lack of awareness of developments in other areas of law cannot be defended.

This problem is exacerbated by our normal choice of subsidiary methods of classification. While property rights are classified by content, personal rights are classified by source. This further obscures essential similarities between property and obligations. It can also produce nonsensical juxtapositions. For example, how do we make sense of the question, 'Is this contract or property?' We soon learn that the question really means, 'Is this a personal right or a property right?' It does not mean, 'Is this a right created by contract or a right created by some other event?' However, without this translation, the question is unintelligible, because it is attempting to compare two different characteristics of rights: source and enforceability. Since contracts can give rise to personal or property rights and property rights can be created by contracts or other events, there are four possible answers to the question, 'Is this contract or property?': contract, property, neither, or both.

If that is not problem enough, we then introduce trusts, which straddle the divide between property and obligations. They are classified according to their source, but with a system not found on either side of the divide. While it is clear how express and statutory trusts are created, there is a great deal of confusion and disagreement over the creation of implied, resulting, and constructive trusts and how that relates to the creation of other obligations and property rights.

The solution

The solution to this problem is fairly simple. We need the ability to reorganise rights in a way that brings personal and property rights together. Classification according to enforceability keeps them apart. Classification according to content does not help, since the content of most personal rights differs from the content of most property rights. However, a classification according to the sources of rights can bring similar personal and property rights together. Personal and property rights are created by contract, estoppel, unjust enrichment, breach of fiduciary duty, and many other events.

This is not a wholesale restructuring of private law. We need not abandon classifications based on enforceability or content. Those distinctions are essential and those methods of organising the law have served us well and will continue to do so. However, we need the ability to switch from one method to another whenever it would help us understand the law better. In other words, we need to be able to combine our two separate piles of personal and property rights and rearrange them into different piles according to the sources of those rights. We should be able to do this easily and without hesitation, whenever it suits our purpose to do so.

Classifying all private rights according to their source can have tremendous benefits. It can make it much easier to see essential similarities and differences in the law. However, to reap any of these benefits we must use the same method of classification for all rights. Do we organise all rights the way we organise obligations, depending on whether they are created by contracts, torts, unjust enrichment, or other events? Do we organise them like property rights, according to whether they are created by intention or by operation of law? Or do we sort them into express, implied, resulting, constructive, and statutory rights? We must choose one of those methods or invent another.[18]

There is no real choice. A two-fold division, of rights created by intention and rights created by operation of law, does not provide enough information: torts, unjust enrichment, estoppel, and so on, are thrown together into an unsorted heap. The method of organising trusts is not much better, because we do not yet agree on what is meant by the labels 'implied', 'resulting', and 'constructive'. We have to classify property rights and trusts the same way we classify obligations, but with two modifications. Contracts and torts are the two main sources of obligations, but not of property rights and trusts. While contracts are a significant

18 Birks, P, 'Equity, Conscience, and Unjust Enrichment' (1999) 23 Melb ULR 1, 24.

source of property rights and trusts, there are other significant ways to create those rights by consent. While wrongful interference with property is a tort, torts are not normally a source of property rights or trusts. However, there are other civil wrongs, such as breach of fiduciary duty, that do give rise to trusts. If all rights were classified as created by contracts, torts, unjust enrichment, or other events, many rights created by consent or wrongdoing would fall into the category of other events, greatly reducing the utility of a unified taxonomy. This problem is easily avoided by expanding the categories of contracts and torts, as Birks suggests, to include all rights created by consent and wrongs, respectively.[19] In this way, the sources of all private legal rights and duties can be organised into four categories: consent, wrongs, unjust enrichment, and other events. As discussed below, it is enlightening to sort them this way.

Consent

Contracts are the most common source of private legal rights. Most personal rights (such as rights to salaries, services, or bank accounts) are created by contract and so are many property rights (acquired through contracts of sale, lease, mortgage, and so on). However, contracts are only part (albeit the greatest part) of a larger category of rights created by consent. Personal rights can be created by other forms of consent, such as drawing or endorsing a cheque or declaring a trust. Property rights can be created by declaration of trust, delivery of possession, execution of a deed, or registration of a document.

Rights created by contract depend on some manifestation of the mutual consent of the parties to the contract. Rights can also be created by the consent of one person, such as the donor of a gift, testator of a will, or settlor of a trust. While donees of gifts and beneficiaries of trusts have opportunities to disclaim their interests, their consent is not required to complete the gift or constitute the trust.[20] The creation of rights by consent involves two basic steps: first, the intention to create the right and, secondly, the actions needed to give effect to that intention. Most rights can be created informally, with only some external manifestation of consent. For example, contracts can be formed by verbal or even unspoken indications of agreement. However, there are many situations in which intentions to create rights are not effective until certain formalities are observed. For example, the intentional creation of a legal property right to land usually requires the execution of a document followed by its delivery or registration.

The distinction between consent and other sources of rights is fundamental. All rights not created by consent arise by operation of law in response to some other event. Although this distinction is generally well understood, there are two potential errors that must be avoided. The first involves the use of implied consent. There are situations in which people make no express statements of consent, but it is clear from their actions and words that they do in fact consent to

---

19 Birks, P, *An Introduction to the Law of Restitution*, Oxford: Clarendon, rev edn, 1989, 39, 53.

20 *Standing v Bowring* (1885) 31 Ch D 282; *Rose v Rose* (1986) 7 NSWLR 679; see Crago, N, 'Principles of Disclaimer of Gifts' (1999) 28 UWA L Rev 65.

the creation of the right in question. This is how many contracts and gifts are made and why an express trust can be created even though the word 'trust' is never used. When consent is not expressed clearly, we may say that it was implied by a person's conduct. The right arises because the person did in fact consent and we call that consent implied to indicate only how it was manifested.

There is nothing wrong with using implied, but actual consent as a source of rights. The error occurs when consent does not exist, but is implied by law. Any right created by this form of implied consent does not belong in the category of rights created by consent. It arises by operation of law in response to some other event. The use of consent implied by law as a justification for the creation of rights obscures their real sources, thereby preventing meaningful comparisons and impeding development of the law. For example, rights to restitution of unjust enrichment were long regarded as quasi-contractual rights created by implied consent.[21] This helped delay the development of the modern law of unjust enrichment until the second half of the 20th century. The current debate over the source of resulting trusts involves this same issue: are they created by the presumed, but actual intention to create a trust or by operation of law to effect restitution of unjust enrichment?[22]

The second error is the assumption that intentions are relevant only for rights created by consent and not for rights created by operation of law. For example, it is often said that all constructive trusts arise regardless of intention, but this is false. As Gbolahan Elias demonstrated, many constructive trusts arise in response to specifically enforceable contracts, incomplete gifts, or detrimentally relied upon expectations.[23] In these situations, intention is not the direct source of the trust, but an important reason for imposing a trust. As Birks said: 'There is a fine but important distinction between intent conceived as creative of rights, as in an express trust or a contract, and intent conceived as a fact which, along with others, calls for the creation of rights by operation of law.'[24]

Intention is also important in cases of unjust enrichment. When an enrichment is unjust, it is usually because someone's intention to benefit another was vitiated or qualified in some way.[25] For example, that intention may be the product of mistake, undue influence, or duress. The right to restitution is not created directly by intention, but arises by operation of law as a response to relevant facts, including the intentions of the parties.

Wrongs

Wrongdoing follows consent as the second most important source of private rights. Torts are the most common form of civil wrongdoing, but there are others,

---

21 *Sinclair v Brougham* [1914] AC 398, 415; Birks, above n 19, 34–39.

22 See Swadling, W, 'A New Role for Resulting Trusts?' (1996) 16 LS 110; Chambers, R, *Resulting Trusts*, Oxford: Clarendon, 1997, 99–102.

23 Elias, G, *Explaining Constructive Trusts*, Oxford: Clarendon, 1990, 48–66.

24 Birks, above n 19, 65.

25 *Ibid*, 100.

such as breach of contract, breach of trust, breach of fiduciary duty, and breach of confidence. Wrongdoing does not have to involve malice or moral turpitude of any kind. Civil wrongs can be committed by honest, well meaning people who inadvertently trespass, buy goods that turn out to be stolen, or fail to take reasonable care while driving a car. A wrong is simply a breach of duty, regardless of the source of the duty or the nature of the breach.

Civil wrongs create rights for the victims of those wrongs and corresponding duties for the wrongdoers. Normally, the wrongdoer must pay the victim a sum of money. This sum can be measured in different ways to achieve at least three different purposes. First and foremost is compensation for loss caused by the wrong. The money paid provides a substitute for performance of the duty breached. The calculation of loss depends on the duty breached. For example, compensation for loss caused by a tort is measured by the position the victim would have been in if the tort had not been committed, while compensation for loss caused by a breach of contract or trust is measured by the position that would have been obtained if the contract or trust had been properly performed.

Secondly, if wrongdoers profit from their wrongs, they may have to pay their victims a sum equal to the value of those profits. This is restitution of wrongful enrichment (sometimes called 'disgorgement'),[26] which is measured not by the victim's loss, but by the wrongdoer's gain. Thirdly, a wrongdoer who intentionally violates a victim's rights may be compelled to pay exemplary or punitive damages to the victim as a form of punishment. This sum is not measured by the victim's loss or the wrongdoer's gain, but is designed to deter intentional wrongdoing.[27]

Wrongdoing can also give rise to property rights, but in far more limited circumstances. If a wrongdoer acquires assets by doing wrong, he or she may be compelled to hold those assets in trust for the victim of the wrong. This is a property right to restitution of wrongful enrichment which is available only for some wrongs, most notably breach of trust, breach of fiduciary duty, and unlawful killing. For example, an agent who takes a bribe in breach of fiduciary duty will hold it in trust for the principal.[28] If one joint tenant unlawfully kills the other, the share of the estate acquired by way of survivorship will be held in trust for the deceased joint tenant's estate.[29] Restitution of wrongful enrichment is not available for every wrong and, when available, it is usually a personal right to restitution of the value of the enrichment, rather than a property right to restitution of the enrichment itself.

---

26 Smith, LD, 'The Province of the Law of Restitution' (1992) 71 Can BR 672, 694–99; McInnes, M, 'Disgorgement for Wrongs: An Experiment in Alignment' [2000] Restitution L Rev 516, 521–22. In *Gain-Based Damages*, Oxford: Hart, 2002, James Edelman distinguishes between two measures of damages: restitution of enrichment wrongfully taken from the victim and disgorgement of other profits obtained through wrongdoing.

27 *XL Petroleum (NSW) Pty Ltd v Caltex Oil (Australia) Pty Ltd* (1985) 155 CLR 448, 471.

28 *Attorney-General (Hong Kong) v Reid* [1994] 1 AC 324; [1994] 1 NZLR 1 (PC).

29 *Rasmanis v Jurewitsch* (1969) 70 SR (NSW) 407.

Wrongs are fundamentally different from other sources of rights, which Birks calls 'not-wrongs'.[30] In the category of wrongs, rights are created by breach of duty. Interference with a primary right produces a secondary right. In other categories, rights are created by events other than breach of duty. They are primary rights created by consent, unjust enrichment, or other events. For example, making a contract creates primary rights (to performance of the contract) by consent, while breach of that contract creates secondary rights (usually to receive compensation for loss) arising in response to the breach of those primary rights.[31]

There is a temptation to treat some not-wrongs as wrongs, which is similar to the temptation to treat rights arising by operation of law as if they arise by consent. This temptation is understandable. Consent and wrongdoing are the sources of most rights and duties and provide satisfactory justifications for their creation. In most cases, people become liable to do things either because they agreed to do them or because they did something wrong. It is harder to explain why innocent people should become liable without their consent.

In the absence of consent or a recognised breach of duty, a court may be tempted to say that rights are created by unconscionable conduct or fraud. For example, in *Taitapu Gold Estates Ltd v Prouse*,[32] the defendants became the registered proprietors of minerals that had been included by mistake in a transfer of land from the plaintiffs. According to Hosking J, the defendants held the minerals on constructive trust for the plaintiffs because, 'Equity regards it as unconscientious to retain what has been given and received in mistake'.[33] However, it could not be improper to retain the minerals unless there was an obligation to return them and an obligation cannot be created by the failure to perform it. The reasoning is circular. Far better and simpler to identify the true source of the obligation, which is the not-wrong of unjust enrichment.

Unjust enrichment

Unjust enrichment is the third main source of rights, but is far less significant than either consent or wrongs. It occurs when one person (the defendant) has been enriched at the expense of another person (the plaintiff) and is required to give up that enrichment or pay for it.[34] There are many different types of enrichment and many different reasons why enrichments are unjust and, therefore, reversible. The enrichment may consist of assets (such as money, goods, or interests in land), services (such as repairs, transportation, or legal advice), or expenses saved (such as payment of a credit card or tax bill). The enrichment may be unjust because it was conferred by mistake, under undue influence or duress, under a contract that became frustrated or was void, pursuant to an invalid statute, and so on.

30 Birks, P, 'Equity in the Modern Law: An Exercise in Taxonomy' (1996) 26 UWA L Rev 1, 40.
31 *Photo Production Ltd v Securicor Transport Ltd* [1980] AC 827, 848–50.
32 [1916] NZLR 825.
33 *Ibid*, 833.
34 *Pavey & Matthews Pty Ltd v Paul* (1987) 162 CLR 221, 256–57.

The only possible response to unjust enrichment is restitution of that enrichment or its value in money. In the absence of consent or wrongdoing, there is no justification for making the unjustly enriched person pay compensation or do anything other than give up or pay for that enrichment. The main form of restitution is a personal right to be paid the value of the unjust enrichment. If the enrichment consists of assets received by the defendant, then restitution may take the form of a property right to those assets. For example, the plaintiff may be entitled to rescind a transaction and thereby recover legal or equitable ownership of assets transferred to the defendant.[35] If the plaintiff pays money to the defendant by mistake, the defendant may hold that money in trust for the plaintiff.[36]

Although the law of unjust enrichment has a long history, the modern understanding of that subject is the product primarily of work done over the last few decades. There are still many areas of uncertainty and controversy to be resolved by judges and lawyers. One particularly pressing problem is determining the proper form of restitution. When are plaintiffs entitled to personal restitution of the value of unjust enrichment and when are they entitled to property restitution of the enrichment itself? It is not possible to answer this question intelligently without crossing the division between property and obligations and bringing together all rights created by unjust enrichment.

There are two sorts of errors made in relation to the category of unjust enrichment. The first, discussed above, is the tendency to treat rights created by unjust enrichment as if they were created by consent or wrongdoing. The second is the tendency to overuse the recently recognised category of unjust enrichment to explain rights that are created by other events. For example, in Canada, the division of family assets at the end of a de facto marriage is routinely explained as restitution of unjust enrichment, even when the defendant is not required to give up or pay for an enrichment received at the plaintiff's expense, but is required to share assets obtained from other sources.[37] Rather than distort the law of unjust enrichment, courts should investigate other possible sources of the plaintiff's right to share those assets, such as her or his detrimental reliance on the expectation of obtaining a share.

Other events

There are many sources of rights other than consent, wrongs, and unjust enrichment. Statutes are the most common of these other sources. Many statutes regulate the relationships between governments and their citizens and, therefore, form part of public law. However, a large and increasing number of statutes create rights and duties between private persons. For example, s 408 of the Residential

---

35 *Hunter BNZ Finance Ltd v CG Maloney Pty Ltd* (1988) 18 NSWLR 420, 431–33.

36 *Re Berry* (1906) 147 F 208 (CA); *Chase Manhattan Bank NA v Israel-British Bank (London) Ltd* [1981] Ch 105.

37 *Peter v Beblow* [1993] 1 SCR 980, 101 DLR (4th) 621. See Elias, above n 23, 157; Chambers, above n 12, Alberta L Rev 201–33, Trust LI 5–7; McInnes, M, 'The Measure of Restitution' (2002) 52 U Toronto LJ 163, 204–10.

Tenancies Act 1997 (Vic) states that a bond paid by a tenant to a landlord is held in trust for the tenant, pending payment over to the Residential Tenancies Bond Authority. Since that trust arises regardless of the wishes of landlord or tenant, in the absence of wrongdoing or unjust enrichment, it falls into the miscellany as a trust created by other events.

Statutes also affect the creation of rights by consent, wrongs, or unjust enrichment. For example, most legal property rights to land in a Torrens system are created, not by deed or other act, but by registration of a document in the appropriate form.[38] That method of creating rights is dictated by statute, in much the same way that common law, equity, and other statutes dictate the methods of creating contracts, declaring trusts, or making wills. People must use the methods prescribed by law if they wish to create rights by consent. Torrens statutes also allow rights to be created in the absence of consent since they can be created by registration of forgeries.[39]

Many statutes create public wrongs with public consequences, such as imprisonment, loss of privileges, or fines paid to the government. However, a breach of statute can also be a private wrong, creating rights and duties between private persons. For example, if a breach of the Fair Trading Act 1987 (NSW) causes loss to someone, the victim has a right to be compensated by the wrongdoer (under s 68). Although the duty and consequences of breach are created by statute, that right to compensation belongs in the category of wrongs along with all other rights created by breach of duty, according to the rules of common law, equity, or other statutes.

Court judgments also belong with the miscellany of other sources of rights and duties. They enforce rights created by consent, wrongs, unjust enrichment, or other events. Sometimes a judgment merely declares the existence of a right. However, judgments can also replace rights. For example, if a creditor obtains a judgment enforcing a contract debt, the judgment replaces the contract as the source of that debt. The creditor can then take steps to enforce the judgment debt within the jurisdiction or sue to enforce it in another jurisdiction.

Another important source of rights is detrimental reliance on expectations. This is the basis of several forms of estoppel and a reason why de facto spouses may be entitled to shared ownerships of the family home. It also explains why secret trusts and mutual wills are enforced despite non-compliance with the formalities required to make a valid testamentary disposition.[40] As a source of rights, detrimental reliance is close to consent. Promises are enforceable if made for consideration (thus forming a contract) or in a deed and sometimes when they are detrimentally relied upon. Contracts and deeds belong in the category of consent, but detrimental reliance falls outside that category. However, the day may come when all three are viewed as methods of creating rights by consent.

---

38 See, eg, Real Property Act 1886 (SA), ss 57, 67.

39 *Frazer v Walker* [1967] 1 AC 569 (PC); *Pyramid Building Society v Scorpion Hotels Pty Ltd* [1998] 1 VR 188 (Vic CA).

40 Chambers, above n 12, Alberta L Rev 189–96, (2001) 15 Trust LI 214, 226–31.

Rights created by operation of law may evolve over time into rights created by consent. For example, the equity of redemption arose because the Court of Chancery began to help mortgagors who had defaulted on payment of the mortgage loan. The court allowed them to redeem the mortgaged land even though their mortgagees were entitled to retain the land under the agreed terms of the mortgage. When the court's intervention became routine, the equity of redemption evolved into a property right created by operation of law.[41] It is now an accepted and well understood aspect of the modern mortgage and one of the rights created by consent when people choose to mortgage their land.

The constructive trust arising on a specifically enforceable contract of sale might be regarded in the same way. Even though the parties to the contract do not intend to create a trust, it will arise by operation of law so long as the contract is specifically enforceable. However, it is now well understood that most written contracts to sell or lease land are specifically enforceable and will produce a constructive trust or equitable lease.[42] In the same manner, an equitable mortgage can be produced by making a mortgage contract. In substance, these equitable property rights are now the product of consent.

Property rights can also be created by physical changes to things. For example, if a domestic animal gives birth, the offspring belongs to its mother's owner, absent agreement to the contrary. The owner of land will own new plants growing on the land and any goods permanently attached to the land. There are rules dealing with the ownership of goods that become indistinguishably mixed together, attached to other goods (accession) or land (fixtures), or made into new goods (specification). Although most of these changes occur with the owners' consent, the rules can reallocate property rights in the absence of consent. For example, if my paint gets applied to your wall, you will become the owner of the paint regardless of our wishes. A physical change to something can be a source of property rights in the absence of consent, wrongdoing, or unjust enrichment. An understanding of this method of creating rights will not help bridge the gap between property and obligations, but it is part of a complete understanding of the 'other' sources of rights.

There are two ways in which the miscellany of right creating events develops. The first, discussed above, occurs when the creation of rights by operation of law becomes predictable and begins to be used intentionally as a way to create rights. They then change from rights created by other events to rights created by consent. Secondly, the miscellany of other events evolves when patterns emerge connecting what had been regarded previously as unrelated sources of rights. The recognition of unjust enrichment in the 20th century was this sort of development. It did not change the sources of those rights, but separated them

---

41 Simpson, AWB, *A History of the Land Law*, Oxford: Clarendon, 2nd edn, 1986, 245.

42 *Bunny Industries Ltd v FSW Enterprises Pty Ltd* [1982] Qd R 712. The vendor or landlord is not a bare trustee for the purchaser or tenant, but beneficial ownership is shared by the parties: see Law Commission, *Transfer of Land: Risk of Damage After Contract for Sale*, London: HMSO, Law Com No 191, 1990, 4; *Kern Corp Ltd v Walter Reid Trading Pty Ltd* (1987) 163 CLR 164, 191–92.

from the miscellany in a new category.[43] A similar process may be taking place with respect to the variety of ways in which rights are created by detrimental reliance.

Continued development of the category of other events will not remove the need for that category. There will always be sources of rights that do not fit neatly in another category. We must avoid temptations to treat them as if they were created by consent, wrongs, or unjust enrichment. If they do not belong in one of the three nominate categories (or any other nominate categories that may develop in the future), it is better to say so plainly rather than distort the law or the facts or resort to legal fictions to make them fit. Rational development and proper application of the law depends on our abilities to clearly and accurately identify the sources of legal rights.

Other characteristics

Rights have characteristics other than their enforceability, content, and source, and we can classify them according to these other characteristics. For example, rights may be legal or equitable or may pursue a particular goal, such as compensation, restitution, or punishment. These distinctions are important. We need to understand them and be able to use them when necessary. This would also contribute to the integration of obligations and property. However, it is no substitute for a thorough understanding of the various sources of all rights.

CONCLUSION

The time has come to expand the law of obligations to include the whole of private law. In other words, it is time to end the isolation of both property law and trusts. This is not intended as criticism of the excellent work that has been done, and continues to be done, within the obligations framework. However, the exclusion of property law from that work limits it unnecessarily. It impedes the proper development of private law and our understanding of it.

The solution is not drastic. It requires only that we organise property and trusts in a way which allows us to compare them meaningfully with obligations. We should be able to say of every property right and trust, whether it is created by consent, wrongdoing, unjust enrichment, or some other event. Of course, this would not be a complete solution to our problem, but merely another step toward that goal. There is still much work to be done understanding and organising the rights within each of these four categories. This is especially true of rights created by other events.

We need not abolish tried and true methods of organising the law, but must equip ourselves (and our students) with the ability to shift from one method to

43 *Pavey & Matthews Pty Ltd v Paul* (1987) 162 CLR 221, 256–57.

another. This will help us see that many of the problems arising in the law of obligations also arise in the law of property. Those two bodies of law must be brought together and understood together, so that comprehensive, consistent, and just solutions can be found to those problems.

9

OWNING SECRETS: 'PROPERTY' IN CONFIDENTIAL INFORMATION?

*Megan Richardson**

> ... property ... and all the rest of the magic 'solving words' of traditional jurisprudence ...
>
> Felix Cohen[1]

INTRODUCTION

Are secrets 'property', and does it matter? The first question has troubled breach of confidence scholars throughout the history of the equitable doctrine.[2] The answer to the second has been largely assumed. In addressing both it would help if we had a better understanding of the reasons *why* confidential information is protected[3] – reasons which may vary depending on the kind of information and circumstances of use. So far, only limited and patchy attention has been given to mapping out the complex mix of rationales that lie behind the field of confidential information law in Anglo-Australian jurisdictions.

Related fields have not been so immune. There is an emerging literature on the diverse policies relevant to the formal intellectual property systems protecting patents, copyright and trade marks, with views about the proper scope of the law exchanged and debated. Judge-made doctrines of fraud, fiduciary obligation and more generally tort and contract have also been subject to searching scholarly inquiries (including in other chapters of this book). Indeed, as trade secret

---

* I am especially grateful to Michael Bryan, Robert Chambers, David Brennan, Brian Murchison, Yves Poullet, Andrew Robertson, Michael Spence, Wendy Gordon, and participants in an expert meeting on privacy, property and personality at the University of Edinburgh in November 2002 for generously sharing their ideas and thoughts on matters pertaining to this chapter.

1 'Transcendental Nonsense and the Functional Approach' (1935) 35 Col L Rev 809, 820.

2 See, for instance, Ricketson, S, 'Confidential Information – A New Proprietary Interest?' (1977) 11 Melb ULR 223, 289; Gurry, F, *Breach of Confidence*, Oxford: Clarendon, 1984, 46–56; Deutch, M, 'The Property Concept of Trade Secrets in Anglo-American Law: An Ongoing Debate' (1997) 31 U of Rich L Rev 313.

3 For property as a social institution, see Cohen, F, 'Dialogue on Public Policy' (1954) 9 Rutgers LR 357. Cohen and other American legal realists argued that law and policy are inextricably intertwined and that this should be openly acknowledged, ideas now fully accepted in the United States. Such ideas are only now entering mainstream Anglo-Australian jurisprudence: see, for instance, Gummow, J, 'Equity: Too Successful?' (2002) 77 ALJ 30, 43 (law without support in values is ineffective, static rather than dynamic).

protection develops a special character as a subcategory of intellectual property, as arguments are made for a separate tort of privacy, as government secrets are increasingly the subject of contract to the extent they are not under legislative control, the dilemma is whether there is any rational future for the breach of confidence doctrine.[4] I argue there are benefits to treating protection of confidential information under a single set of principles. One is the increased prospect that common policy will be identified and promoted, leading to greater harmony in the law. Another is easier facilitation of a flexible approach permitting those lawfully in possession of confidential information to control the manner and extent of its use, including its ability to be traded in the market. The conclusion entails discussion of what is meant by 'property' in information. Unlike most legal property scholars (but like many economists), I see the important characteristic of a property right as less exclusion than market alienability.

The structure of the rest of this chapter is as follows. The second part identifies possible philosophical reasons for protecting confidentiality. The third part examines them through the lens of Anglo-Australian breach of confidence cases. The fourth part, '"Property" in Confidential Information', focuses on implications for the questions of property in confidential information. The conclusion that the choice to treat information as 'property' should be left to those lawfully in possession of the information is derived from the same broad philosophical premises that are found to have framed the equitable doctrine.

WHY PROTECT CONFIDENTIAL INFORMATION?

The foundations of law in civilised society are variously said to be liberal, economic and more broadly utilitarian.[5] In keeping with these ideas, a taxonomy of possible confidentiality theories can be devised. Figure 1 identifies efficiency, liberalism, and social planning theory (concerned with achieving broader utilitarian outcomes than efficiency) as most likely to be relevant to the equitable doctrine.[6] The paragraphs that follow provide further elaboration and focus.

---

4 In the United States, for instance, privacy and trade secret misappropriation became separate torts in the earlier 20th century and moves are afoot to develop a distinct statutory regime for computer information transactions (a form of trade secret contract): see Uniform Computer Information Transactions Act 2001 (so far adopted in two States). Government secrets are regulated by legislation, contract and/or fiduciary obligation: see, for instance, *Snepp v United States*, 444 US 507 (1980) (constructive trust granted for profits from a book written in breach of employment contract terms by former agent). The breach of confidence doctrine ostensibly remains, but has been largely subsumed under fiduciary obligation: Gilles, S, 'Promises Betrayed: Breach of Confidence as a Remedy for Invasions of Privacy' (1995) 43 Buff L Rev 1.

5 A combination of values may be identified as served by law: see most famously, Rawls, J, *A Theory of Justice*, Oxford: OUP, rev edn, 1999, 118–23. His philosophy comes closest to social planning theory.

6 Cf with respect to intellectual property rights, Fisher, W, 'Theories of Intellectual Property', in Munzer, S (ed), *New Essays in the Legal and Political Theory of Property*, New York: Cambridge UP, 2001, 169, 169–73 (stressing efficiency, natural rights and social planning theories); and with respect to contractual non-disclosure, Duggan, A, Bryan, M and Hanks, F, *Contractual Non-Disclosure: An Applied Study in Modern Contract Theory*, Melbourne: Longmans Professional, 1994 (identifying economic, liberal and 'fairness' theories as potentially relevant).

Figure 1: taxonomy of theories

Classification	Description
Efficiency	Law should provide incentives for optimal investments in and access to resources so that maximum social value can be obtained.
Liberal natural rights	Law should reflect the idea that persons who expend labour derive a natural right to the fruits of their labour.
Kantian liberal	Law should ensure that people are not used as means to the ends of others.
Progressive liberal	Law should promote human flourishing, which is essential to personal and social development.
Social planning	Law should foster the achievement of a just and attractive culture.

From the time of Adam Smith, economists have found one purpose of a property system as making worthwhile 'the natural effort ... to better [one's] own condition' by granting to the labourer a right of possession and control over what is produced.[7] A second purpose, later identified by Ronald Coase, is to provide the basis for efficient trades in the market so that resources can reach their highest value use.[8] Thus it is claimed there can be social benefit to be gained from a system based around private property, identified in terms of a set of market alienable use-rights. Whether there is any right to exclude others from the resource is, however, on an economic approach dependent on how efficiency goals will be served. Such questions need not be foreclosed by the existence of property rights (except perhaps in limited cases, noting there may sometimes be advantages to a high

7 Smith, A, *An Inquiry into The Wealth of Nations* (1776), Campbell, RH and Skinner, A (eds), Oxford: Clarendon, 1976, IV v b, 540. See also Bentham, J, *The Theory of Legislation* (1802), Ogden, CK (ed), London: Kegan Paul, 1931, 109–22; Mill, JS, *Principles of Political Economy* (1848), Ashley, WJ (ed), London: Longman, 1929, 221ff.

8 Smith and the classical utilitarian economists referred to the efficiency of a contract system in fostering efficient market exchanges, but Ronald Coase pointed out that the market exchange system depends on property rights as its basis: see 'The Federal Communications Commission' (1959) 2 J L and Econ 1 and 'The Problem of Social Cost' (1960) 3 J L and Econ 1. See also Demsetz, H, 'Towards a Theory of Property Rights' (1967) 57 Am Econ Rev 347 (a primary function of property rights is 'that of guiding incentives to achieve a greater internalisation of externalities': 348). Modern information economists have stressed the impact of non-rivalry for optimal pricing and dissemination of information-based products: see generally, Shapiro, C and Varian, H, *Information Rules*, Boston, MA: Harvard Business School Press, 1999.

degree of security: registered patent rights for inventions a case in point).[9] Depending on how low the threshold is set for grant of a property right, with aims of efficient investment and enjoyment of resources, exclusivity may be determined more by contract and tort (or equitable wrong), whose main economic function is to substitute for contract when markets fail.[10] Remedies for breach are also important. In a market deemed effective enough for efficient trades still to occur, a 'property rule' (specific performance, injunction) has the perceived advantage of leaving the rights holder to contract or not for terms of use; in other cases a 'liability rule' (a monetary remedy) substitutes for the market by putting a price on the use if the breach continues – operating as a kind of compulsory licence.[11] That property rules also entail lower administrative costs for courts compared to liability rules is not irrelevant where efficiency is the goal. It has also been argued that there may be alternative, more efficient solutions to invoking the coercive force of the law, with attendant administrative costs. As Laurence Lessig recently observed, social norms provide one possibility, architecture (technology) another.[12]

Efficiency is a justification for trade secret protection. The reasoning is the same whether the law is a separate tort (as in the United States) or a more general confidentiality doctrine (as in other common law jurisdictions). A property right is supported in order that, first, investments will be made in developing commercially valuable information which is not yet public knowledge and, secondly, the information generated will find its highest value use.[13] The standard of confidentiality – or non-public domain status – is not particularly demanding. Thus the optimal scope of the exclusive right over a trade secret vis à vis others is to be found, if not in the terms of contracts with owners prepared to deal in their information in the market, then in the parameters of the misappropriation tort or wrong – both functioning as a kind of hypothetical contract. An example of such reasoning is found in an article by David Friedman, William Landes and Richard

---

9 The classical economists stressed the importance of a secure right of exclusion attaching to patented inventions: see especially Smith, above n 7, V I e, 754; Mill, above n 7, 932–33 ('in general an exclusive privilege, of temporary duration, is preferable; because it leaves nothing to anyone's discretion'). Copyright was generally treated as analogous. It should be noted at that stage the copyright claim, as the patent right, was dependent upon registration – it was only with the Copyright Act 1911 (UK) that this was abolished.

10 See Coase, above n 8, 'The Problem of Social Cost', 15ff and, for instance, Calabresi, G, *The Cost of Accidents*, New Haven, CT: Yale UP, 1970; Posner, R, *Economic Analysis of Law*, New York: Aspen Publishers, 5th edn, 1998, Ch 6.

11 The Coasian ideas were elaborated and extended by Calabresi, G and Melamed, AD, 'Property Rules, Liability Rules and Inalienability: One View of the Cathedral' (1972) 85 Harv LR 1089, observing that property rights need not close off possibilities for secondary markets, even where entitlements are protected. Thus the focus turns to remedies as second-order devices that may be adopted to achieve efficient outcomes.

12 Lessig, L, 'The Law of the Horse: What Cyberlaw Might Teach' (1999) 113 Harv L Rev 501, 508.

13 In general, legal tests for a 'trade secret' stress commercial value and absence of general knowledge: see, for instance, *Ansell Rubber Co Pty Ltd v Allied Rubber Industries Pty Ltd* [1967] VR 37, 49–50; *Restatement of the Law Third on Unfair Competition*, St Paul, MN: American Law Institute, 1995, § 39 (a 'trade secret' is information intended for commercial use that is sufficiently secret to provide 'an actual or potential economic advantage'); Agreement on Trade-Related Aspects of Intellectual Property Rights (1995), Art 39(2).

Posner on the economics of trade secret law.[14] They generally favour a trade secret owner's entitlement to prevent unauthorised use of the information by would-be free riders, provided there is sufficient notice of the claim, although they see no economic problem with the law's traditional exception for reverse engineering of a product on the market. Rather they argue this limit on the exclusive right promotes derivative innovation which all potential innovators should prefer: rational would-be owners and users behind a veil of ignorance would hypothetically contract for reverse engineering to be allowed.[15] Other lawyer economists have responded that better prospects for contracting coupled with compulsory licensing to deal with market failure would be a generally practical and superior alternative to free reverse engineering, which does not only promote derivative innovation and is not the only way to do so (and may also harm incentives for original innovation). But they do not challenge the basic economic rationales for trade secret protection. Several have observed that social norms and technology have to date proved inadequate to prevent substantial free-riding.[16]

Before Adam Smith, natural rights theorists dominated property discourse, and Smith was influenced by their views, becoming a supporter of 'natural liberty' as well as efficiency.[17] The essential claim of the natural rights school was of a God-given 'natural right' to the fruits of labour. Although references to God may seem alien in our more secular age, aspects of natural rights theory have received support in recent writings of intellectual property philosophers, including Justin Hughes and Wendy Gordon.[18] According to Locke, a leading proponent of the natural rights school,[19] mixing 'the labour of his body and the work of his hands' with the products of nature provides the basis for a union

---

14 Thus the authors take as their starting point that trade secret protection, as intellectual property protection more generally has the function of 'internalising the benefits of innovation': (1991) 5 J Econ Persp 61, 64.

15 *Ibid*, 70 (reverse engineering will often generate knowledge that makes improvements possible) and 71 (contracting for rights is likely to be precluded by transaction costs). See also at 65 (weaker trade secret protection increases the incentive to patent information, with a social benefit of mandatory disclosure).

16 See Reichman, J, 'Legal Hybrids Between the Patent and Copyright Paradigms' (1994) 94 Col L Rev 2432 (proposing a new 'portable trade secrets system' granting a limited-term guaranteed protection against reverse engineering traded for easy compulsory licensing); Richardson, M, 'Of Shrink-Wraps, Click-Wraps and Reverse Engineering: Rethinking Trade Secret Protection' (2002) 25 UNSW L Rev 748 (preferring contract as the default mechanism for trade secret use, and monetary remedies as a last-resort judicial compulsory licence). But see (contending a reverse engineering freedom is efficient in keeping prices down) Samuelson, P and Scotchmer, S, 'The Law and Economics of Reverse Engineering' (2002) 111 Yale LJ 1175.

17 Adam Smith's ideas about natural liberty, which he combined with arguments about economic welfare, owe much to the natural rights theorists of the 17th century: see generally Muller, J, *Adam Smith in His Time and Ours*, Princeton, NJ: Princeton UP, 1993, 17.

18 Hughes, J, 'The Philosophy of Intellectual Property' (1988) 77 Georgetown LJ 287; Gordon, W, 'On Owning Information: Intellectual Property and the Restitutionary Impulse' (1992) 78 Virg L Rev 149 (although primarily concerned to identify Locke's 'enough and as good' exception as a basis for a commons of information not subject to private property rights). For a rejection of Lockean labour theory (critiquing its romantic idea of authorship), see also Craig, C, 'Locke, Labour and Limiting the Author's Right' (2002) 28 Queens LJ 1.

19 Locke, J, *Two Treatises of Government* (1690), Carpenter, W (ed), London: Dent, 1924.

between person and property.[20] The property created or improved is an extension of the self. Such reasoning may be drawn on to explain and justify trade secret rights, offering a more explicitly moral set of justifications for exclusivity than the economic arguments. However, it does not necessarily support absolute exclusivity (contrary to popular belief). Locke premised his reasoning for private property rights on a residual commons of 'as good left, as that already possessed' for others to enjoy. Moreover, as the purpose of the Lockean property right was to allow for the reaping of rewards, waste was logically viewed as exceeding the bounds of 'just property'.[21] Rather, Locke argued, the more natural and appropriate course where largess beyond the power of immediate consumption was concerned was to trade property for other commodities or for money, the only 'lasting thing that men might keep without spoiling'.[22] Such reasoning fits well with the economist's positing of optimal rather than absolute protection and perception of property as importantly a tradable commodity. If the starting point for analysis is different in stressing natural rights not social welfare, there are similarities in the localising of property rights in 'fruits of labour' and the shape and texture of the rights found to result. It works well enough for trade secrets. But privacy protection is more challenging. With limited exceptions where reputation is the key, private information is hardly the 'fruits of labour' but is rather an integral part of the person. Other reasons for protection must be found.

In the United States, the tort of privacy invasion is quite commonly conceptualised in terms of a Kantian idea of human dignity,[23] explicated as a principle that no one should be treated as a means to another's end but only as an end.[24] In keeping with this, the United States privacy tort has been confined in its core fields of operation to offering a personal right and then only in cases where the conduct would be 'highly offensive to a reasonable person'.[25] (Curiously, other fields of tort law have not been treated so rigorously, with classical tort scholars drawing on Kantian ideas to enunciate a broad corrective justice principle 'obliging a person whose morally culpable behavior has violated another's autonomy to restore the latter as nearly as possible to his pre-injury position' – nor

20 See especially book II, Chapter v.

21 *Ibid*, 139.

22 *Ibid*.

23 Kant, I, 'Groundwork of the Metaphysics of Morals' (1785), Paton, H (ed), *The Moral Law*, London: Hutchinson, 1948.

24 See, for instance, Warren, S and Brandeis, L, 'The Right to Privacy' (1890) 4 Harv L Rev 193, 205 (the principle is one of 'inviolate personality'); Bloustein, E, 'Privacy as an Aspect of Human Dignity' (1964) 39 NY U L Rev 962; Sheppele, KL, *Legal Secrets*, Chicago, IL: Chicago UP, 1988. Sheppele also mounts a Kantian argument for trade secret protection as privacy (Chapter 12) but others have drawn the line at 'privacy rights' for commercial corporate interests.

25 The US privacy tort is said to extend beyond the core fields of 'intrusion upon seclusion', 'publicity given to private life', and false light publicity (overlapping with the tort of defamation) to encompass appropriation of names or likenesses (see Prosser, W, 'Privacy' (1960) 48 Calif L Rev 383). But this category appears to have more to do with protecting other interests: see, further, n 30 below. This is also the only category which is not subject to a highly offensive to a reasonable person standard. It is also the only category that recognises commercial (but not corporate) claims. In general, the US privacy tort may not be claimed by corporations: *Restatement of the Law Second: Torts*, St Paul, MN: American Law Institute, 1965, § 625I.

has such reasoning been limited to the United States.)[26] Kant himself supported the keeping of promises as an illustration of the duty not to treat others merely as 'an end he does not share',[27] and modern liberal scholars such as Charles Fried and Anthony Kronman have developed this aspect of Kantian philosophy into an influential theory of promising and contract,[28] a theory reflected in recent US cases where promises of confidentiality have been strongly enforced even notwithstanding the Constitution's powerful freedom of speech.[29] Some US courts have additionally found a right of publicity in personal names and likenesses on the basis that reputation, at least, may be viewed as fruits of labour which can be traded (in the same way as other intellectual property rights).[30] Thus, commentators have observed, a property right exists in private information albeit for limited purposes.[31]

There is no exact equivalent to the US privacy tort in Anglo-Australian jurisdictions where privacy protection is still subsumed under the doctrine of breach of confidence and dealt with quite differently.[32] In a recent article I suggested that such protection may be based less on Kantian human dignity than on another liberal perspective closer to the Anglo-Australian utilitarian tradition.[33] The perspective is rooted in John Stuart Mill's liberal-utilitarianism,

---

26 See, for instance, Dewees, D, Duff, D and Trebilcock, M, *Exploring the Domain of Accident Law*, New York: Oxford UP, 1996, 8 (although they see this as only one normative standard for articulating and assessing a modern system of tort law; efficiency and broader utilitarian justice are others). Cf Cane, P, *Anatomy of Tort Law*, Oxford: Hart, 1997 (seeing corrective justice as the key to understanding Anglo-Australian tort law).

27 Above n 23, 92 and *passim*.

28 Fried, C, *Contract as Promise: A Theory of Contractual Obligation*, Cambridge, MA: Harvard UP, 1981, 7 (the essence of the liberal ideal is 'respect for the person and property of others'); Kronman, A, 'Contract Law and Distributive Justice' (1980) 89 Yale LJ 472.

29 See *Cohen v Cowles Media Co* 501 US 663 (a promise to keep an informant's identity confidential enforced under Minnesota promissory estoppel law, notwithstanding the First Amendment's free speech guarantee). The majority held promissory estoppel was a law of 'general application', to which the press as the public were subject. But the policy that those making promises should keep them was clear (671–72).

30 See especially *Haelan Laboratories Inc v Topps Chewing Gum Inc*, 202 F 2d 866 (2nd Cir, 1953); *Uhlaender v Henricksen*, 316 F Supp 1277 (D Minn, 1970); *Zacchini v Scripps-Howard Broadcasting Co*, 433 US 562, 573 (1977) (the right of publicity, akin to copyright, provides incentives for entertainment). Canadian courts have followed suit in acknowledging a right of publicity: see Howell, R, 'Publicity Rights in the Common Law Provinces of Canada' (1998) 18 Loyola of LA Ent LJ 487. Cf the Australian doctrines of passing off and misleading or deceptive conduct under the Trade Practices Act 1974 (Cth) as applied to character merchandising. Although ostensibly misrepresentation is required, in practice, courts sometimes acknowledge copyright-like rights: see Richardson, M, 'Copyright in Trade Marks?' (2000) IPQ 66. English courts, however, have been generally reluctant to transform the passing off claim into a *de facto* publicity right: see Carty, H, 'Character Merchandising and the Limits of Passing Off' (1993) 13 LS 289.

31 See generally Berkman, H, 'The Right of Publicity – Protection for Public Figures and Celebrities' (1976) 42 Brooklyn L Rev 527; McCarthy, T, *Rights of Publicity and Privacy*, St Paul, MN: West Group, 2nd edn, 2001; Beverly-Smith, H, *Commercial Appropriation of Personality*, Cambridge: CUP, 2002.

32 Some Canadian provinces have enacted a privacy invasion tort, and New Zealand courts have explored the idea of a common law tort: see Fridman, G, *The Law of Torts in Canada*, Toronto: Carswell, 1990, vol 2, Chapter 9; Tobin, R, 'Invasion of Privacy' [2000] NZLJ 216.

33 Richardson, M, 'Whither Breach of Confidence: A Right of Privacy for Australia?' (2002) 26 Melb ULR 381.

which holds that '[i]n proportion to the development of his individuality, each person becomes more valuable to himself, and is therefore capable of being more valuable to others'.[34] Mill's reasoning implies there can be social benefits in allowing individuals (and collectivities – unlike Kant, Mill did not limit his arguments to human persons) the freedom to choose how to order their lives, including in maintaining a sphere of private information which concerned themselves alone. Not only should laws not interfere with 'the private life',[35] according to Mill, but they should actively protect it from the intrusions of others. The harm suffered by those who find their liberty invaded, as well as the consequential social harm, may be reason enough for the coercive sanction of the law. But if in addition the conduct involved a breach of promise or contract, the injustice of 'breaking faith' and disappointing expectations could only add to the utilitarian account.[36] Against such considerations, Mill acknowledged, there may sometimes be utilitarian justification for interference in individual liberty. That is, protection of other individuals or the public from 'the definite risk of damage'.[37] But the mere fact of wanting to control was never for Mill sufficient basis for interfering in another's protected sphere of liberty. Even in cases of definite risk of damage, an overwhelming case for intervention had to be made. Although the liberal-utilitarian perspective has been criticised for being neither truly liberal nor truly utilitarian, but a confusing mix between the two,[38] it gives primacy to liberal values as an instrument of utilitarianism in the broadest possible sense. Being utilitarian, it also offers a flexible tool for pragmatic decision making in Anglo-Australian courts. For instance, as social norms favouring free speech have become constitutionally entrenched, in the UK under the *aegis* of the European Convention on Human Rights, and in Australia through the implied freedom of political discussion found inherent in the democratic principles of the Australian Constitution, Mill's philosophy can be drawn on to support a balancing of

---

34 Mill, JS, 'On Liberty' (1859) in *Utilitarianism, On Liberty, Essay on Bentham*, Warnock, M (ed), London: Collins, 1962, 192. See further at 188 (individual facilities of observation, reasoning and judgment develop through being employed), 194–97 (diversity of individual experiments enables new truths to be uncovered – an argument Mill also brings in support of freedom of opinion and speech), 197ff (true happiness can only be found if individuals are allowed to choose for themselves: 'his own mode of existence is the best, not because it is the best in itself, but because it is his own mode'). On utilitarian benefits, Mill accepted that individual happiness sums to social welfare. But, more than that, he argued only truly free individuals could achieve the spiritual well-being that would make them good citizens, with 'genuine private affections and a sincere interest in the public good': 'Utilitarianism' in Warnock (ed), *ibid*, 265–66. Their conduct is thus *most* likely to be conducive of positive social welfare gains.

35 A term Mill uses for the first time in 'Utilitarianism' (published after 'On Liberty' in 1863) in seeking to connect his liberal-utilitarian arguments to social norms regarding justice: *ibid*, 303.

36 'Utilitarianism' *ibid*, 300ff – arguing that the intense sentiments involved when social norms of justice (as with a breach of faith) were violated necessitated a legal sanction. By contrast, lesser harms for Mill did not necessarily require the possibility of legal sanction. A 'moral' sanction might be sufficient: *ibid*, 213.

37 It seems Mill particularly had in mind conduct which constrains the freedom of others, although his thinking was not confined to that, encompassing also more material harms and public security: see 'On Liberty', in Warnock (ed), above n 34, 136–38.

38 Especially the excellent critique of Lyons, D, *Rights, Welfare and Mill's Moral Theory*, New York: OUP, 1994.

interests where liberal or at least utilitarian arguments can be found on both sides (something Kantian rights theory has proved incapable of doing, forcing US courts into dogmatic positions under which either privacy or free speech, but not both, can be acknowledged as implicated in actual cases).[39]

In general Mill may be viewed as an early social planning theorist. His liberal-utilitarian ideas have been adopted, along with those of Jeremy Bentham and Adam Smith, as a basis for modern economics. But modern efficiency theory reflects a constrained sort of utilitarianism at best. Thus Mill's broad focus on social benefit as the ultimate standard for assessing the value even of commercial property interests is typically in modern economics restricted to benefits that can be measured in money or money's worth.[40] And Mill's early acceptance that even property rights must always be subject to the broader public interest – especially where part of their origin is a common inheritance[41] – has been largely overlooked in mainstream economic discourse of the latter 20th and 21st centuries. Nevertheless, social planning theorists, such as William Fisher, Wendy Gordon, Neil Netanel,[42] and to a more limited extent myself,[43] have attempted to redress this imbalance by arguing for instance that intellectual property rights should be balanced against a 'commons' of shared information – or at least shared access – which must be kept available to all for reasons that may or may not have to do with efficiency (including the promotion of liberal ideas of freedom of speech and debate). Social planning theory may be applied both to trade secrets and private information, to yield a richer policy basis for legal decision making. But the most obvious application is government secrets where the stark conflict that may exist between individual freedoms and the public good, for a true utilitarian, requires a special attention to balancing public interests in national security and free public debate.

---

39 See Anderson, D, 'The Failure of American Privacy Law', in Markesinis, B (ed), *Protecting Privacy*, Oxford: OUP, 1999 and Richardson, above n 33 (the non-compromising character of the human dignity rationale for liberty has led to courts having to elect between privacy and free speech, generally preferring the second). For a recent case demonstrating the polarisation of the US Supreme Court, see *Bartnicki v Vopper*, 532 US 514 (2001). The minority and majority supported a right of private speech but the majority *per* Stevens J held this excluded teachers' union representatives whose conversation during collective bargaining negotiations was surreptitiously recorded and published in violation of anti-surveillance legislation, on the basis that 'one of the costs associated with participation in public affairs is an attendant loss of privacy': the court at 534. Only Breyer J (with O'Connor J), while concurring in the majority's result, accepted the need for balancing interests.

40 This is not the only constraint – another is the focus in assessing efficiency on 'willingness to pay', itself determined by existing resources: cf Dworkin, R, 'Is Wealth a Value?' (1980) 9 J Leg Stud 191.

41 Mill saw this as particularly relevant to land: '[t]he community has too much stake in the proper cultivation of land, and in the conditions annexed to the occupation of it, to leave these things to the discretion of a class of persons called landlords, when they have shown themselves unfit for the trust.' If not cultivation then access should be publicly available 'except to the extent necessary to protect the produce against damage, and the owner's privacy against invasion': above n 7, 234–35.

42 See, for instance, Netanel, N, 'Copyright and a Democratic Civil Society' (1996) 106 Yale LJ 283; Gordon, W, 'Authors, Publishers and Public Goods: Trading Gold for Dross' (2002) 36 Loy LA L Rev 159; and generally Fisher, above n 6, 172–73 and Netanel, N and Elkin-Koren, N (eds), *The Commodification of Information*, The Hague: Kluwer Law Int, 2002.

43 See above n 16.

WHAT COURTS SAY ABOUT THEIR POLICY REASONS

Anglo-Australian courts, unlike their American counterparts, generally have little to say about the policy reasons behind the laws they foster and promote. Nevertheless, there are subtle indications that some of the above policies are important to the framing of the equitable breach of confidence doctrine in all its different aspects.

Economic concerns seem to dominate in the trade secret cases, although hints of natural rights reasoning can be found as well. So, for instance, in the classic case of *Saltman Engineering Co Ltd v Campbell Engineering Co Ltd*,[44] where the equitable doctrine was re-established as independent of contract after a period of hiatus,[45] Lord Greene MR appeared to have economic incentives especially in mind in stressing the plaintiff's entitlement to benefit from the 'labour and calculation and careful draftsmanship' expended by the plaintiff in developing its design for the making of leather tools, being tools which it was clear would serve a 'useful purpose'.[46] The idea of a trade secret as fruits of labour, central to Lockean labour theory, is also evident in Lord Greene's identification of the original designer as having 'used his brain and thus produced a result which can only be produced by somebody who goes through the same process' and as distinguishing the finished product from 'materials which may be available for the use of anybody'.[47] For various found-to-be compelling reasons (and notwithstanding scant reference to prior case authorities), it was therefore decided that, while the defendant company would be entitled to draw the material from public sources, it was barred from dispensing 'with the necessity of going through the process which had been gone through in compiling those drawings' by breaching a confidence understood and consented to when the drawings were handed over or relatively soon thereafter.[48] Similarly, in the Australian case of *Franklin v Giddins*,[49] where the principle of *Saltman* was extended to cover surreptitious obtaining of valuable genetic information embedded in nectarine budwoods stolen from the plaintiff's nursery – taking it beyond the accepted scenario of information imparted and received 'in confidence' – Dunn J appeared to have avoidance of free-riding in mind. The judge observed (again after very limited citation of earlier cases) that '[t]he thief is unconscionable because he plans to use and does use his own wrong conduct to better his position in competition with the owner, and also places

---

44 [1948] 65 RPC 203 ('*Saltman*').

45 Vaisey J at first instance had held that without a contract no obligation of confidentiality could exist. The Court of Appeal disagreed, Lord Greene MR (with whom Somerville and Cohen JJ concurred) finding the generally applicable principle to be that the use of 'confidential information, directly or indirectly obtained from a plaintiff, without the consent, express or implied of the plaintiff', is an 'infringement of the plaintiff's rights': *ibid*, 213.

46 *Ibid*, 215.

47 *Ibid*.

48 *Ibid* and see also 213 (referring to the fact that the defendants knew the drawings were confidential 'at a comparatively early date', and that they were handed over only for the limited purposes of assessing whether an order for the manufacture of the tools might be accepted).

49 [1978] Qd R 72.

himself in a better position than that of a person who deals consensually with the owner'.[50] It may be noted that in both *Saltman* and *Franklin* the court referred to the plaintiff as having 'property' in, respectively, the drawings and budwoods.[51] However, apart from the obvious assumption that this was something the owner could deal with through the market, no great significance was attached to that denomination.

Even *Coco v AN Clark (Engineers) Ltd*,[52] the case that articulated the equitable basis of the breach of confidence doctrine, did not take this as a reason to abandon a robust concern with economic values. After specifying the 'normal' requirements for breach of confidence – contract aside – as unauthorised use of confidential information which had been imparted in confidence,[53] Megarry J suggested detriment was a further requirement (although acknowledging the requirement could not always be rigorously applied; in later trade secret cases even potential commercial value has proved sufficient). Further, the judge drew on tort law's 'reasonable man' as the benchmark for determining whether information was imparted 'in confidence'.[54] That standard in tort law has come to be seen as much about efficiency in requiring a balancing of costs and benefits under a hypothetical contract as about any broad idea of Kantian corrective justice. Indeed, there seems to be a great deal of economics and rather little corrective justice – Kantian or otherwise – in Megarry J's treatment of the equitable doctrine. For instance, the requirement of 'confidentiality', defined in *Saltman* as not 'public property and public knowledge',[55] was supplemented in *Coco*, obviously with trade secrets in mind, as setting an innovation threshold of 'originality or novelty or ingenuity' or the like.[56] The plaintiff failed to satisfy this threshold with his moped design, so lost in the interlocutory proceedings notwithstanding that an implied promise of confidentiality could be found: that the circumstances of disclosure were 'redolent of trust and confidence' was not in

---

50 *Ibid*, 80. The case, a first instance decision on an interlocutory application in the Queensland Supreme Court, has had doubtful authority since its pronouncement. But now it is largely accepted that surreptitious obtaining is, if not a breach of confidence, then the basis of an obligation not to breach by use: see below n 64ff.

51 *Saltman* [1948] 65 RPC 203, 213 (Lord Greene MR) (the defendants knew that they were given, for purposes of assessment and negotiating terms, 'drawings belonging to Saltmans. Saltmans had not in fact paid for them, but that did not alter the fact that they were Saltmans' drawings'); *Franklin v Giddins* [1978] Qd R 72, 78 (Dunn J) (common law damages for theft are inadequate – 'the consequence would be what has been described as "an involuntary sale to the converter". The plaintiffs would be divested of their title to the productive wood ...').

52 [1969] RPC 41 ('*Coco*').

53 *Ibid*, 47–48.

54 *Ibid*, 48: the test is whether 'any reasonable man standing in the shoes of the recipient of the information would have realised that upon reasonable grounds the information was being given to him in confidence, then this should suffice to impose upon him the equitable obligation of confidence'. In the Australian case of *Smith Kline and French Laboratories (Australia) Ltd v Secretary to the Department of Community Services and Health* (1991) 28 FCR 291, the Full Court of the Federal Court of Australia suggested the reasonable imparter's understanding of the recipient's intentions must also be considered (302–03). However, this seems to be covered by the words 'upon reasonable grounds' in Megarry J's formulation.

55 [1948] 65 RPC 203, 215 (Lord Greene MR).

56 [1969] RPC 41, 47 (Megarry J) (with the obvious parallel to copyright and patent law which prescribes standards of originality and novelty plus inventiveness, respectively).

itself sufficient for equity's intervention.[57] Further, it was clear that even had the design been confidential this might not have been sufficient for an injunctive remedy to be granted. Mindful of the possibility that a recipient of confidential information may contribute material from the public domain or add other confidential information, Megarry J suggested that the essence of the duty of confidence might be one of 'not using without paying, rather than of not using at all': a sort of compulsory licence.[58] (In fact *Seager v Copydex Ltd*,[59] cited by Megarry J for this proposition, involved the particular circumstance of parties who had attempted to agree terms of use but had failed to do so, a failure attributed largely to the owner's prevarication. Because enforcing the property right with an injunction would not improve the prospects of a voluntary arrangement the court seemed inclined towards a damages award, the amount calculated as what would be agreed between a willing seller and buyer.[60] The true proposition from that case – and the one followed in most cases – therefore seems to be that the owner has the first [but not the last] go in determining payment terms.)[61] Finally, it would seem that Megarry J's reason for not extending the equitable doctrine to surreptitious obtaining in his formulation of the 'normal elements' was not any special sanctity of the promissory obligation – found not to be sufficient anyway for non-confidential information – but simply the folly of legal protection for those who fail to take care of themselves.[62] The style of the cheaper cost avoider argument is familiar to economic analysis of tort law.

In the end Megarry J failed to persuade subsequent courts that surreptitious obtaining of confidential information is more easily avoided by those lawfully in possession of information, a position soon rejected in *Franklin v Giddins*.[63] And in *Attorney-General v Guardian Newspapers Ltd (No 2)*,[64] Lord Goff suggested an obligation of confidence may arise whenever 'confidential information comes to the knowledge of a person (the confidant) in circumstances where he has notice, or is held to have agreed, that the information is confidential' with the effect that 'it would be just in all the circumstances' that unauthorised use should be

57 *Ibid*, 51.

58 *Ibid*, 50.

59 *Seager v Copydex Ltd* [1967] RPC 349.

60 'Damages' were calculated according to what the willing buyer and seller would agree: see *Seager v Copydex (No 2)* [1969] RPC 250. See also *Cadbury Schweppes Inc v FBI Foods Ltd* (1999) 167 DLR (4th) 577 (where confidence was breached after termination of a licence, although the method used to calculate the compensation for information characterised as 'not very special' was different).

61 See Richardson, above n 16. Cf regarding copyright law, Ginsburg, J, 'Copyright and Control over New Technologies of Dissemination' (2001) 101 Col L Rev 1613 (reviewing US copyright cases and legislation).

62 *Coco* [1969] RPC 41, 47–48 (there can be no binding confidentiality obligation for information which is 'blurted out' in public) – and further *Malone v Metropolitan Police Commissioner* [1979] Ch 344, 376 (Megarry VC) ('a person who utters confidential information must accept the risk of any unknown overhearing that is inherent in the circumstances of communication ...' including those listening in on bugged telephone conversations).

63 See also *Francome v Mirror Group Newspapers Ltd* [1984] 2 All ER 408 (*Malone v Metropolitan Police Commissioner* distinguished on the basis that the surreptitious telephone tap was under a lawful police warrant).

64 [1990] 1 AC 109 ('*Guardian Newspapers*').

precluded.[65] The statement has become the core of the modern equitable doctrine. But, while establishing an appealingly simple set of principles based around confidential information, notice and unauthorised use, the formulation leaves out the undistributed middle inherent in the words 'as justice requires'. So, while Lord Goff at least appeared to contemplate that even accidental obtaining of private information, as with an 'obviously private diary' dropped in the street, might be sufficient for an obligation to arise, it is not so clear the same result would – or should – follow for trade secrets. As Megarry J had already pointed out in *Coco*, to impose an obligation not to use 'blurted out' information imposes an extra cost on those who might wish to use it (and a social cost as well if the use would lead to improvements) compared to before. Prospects of independent development are now more restricted since even subconscious use of information which once known cannot easily be forgotten suffices for breach of confidence to be found. The owner may be the cheaper cost avoider compared to a recipient forced to guard against such an unpredictable burden,[66] and sensitive decisions need to be made. Of course the problem is not restricted to accidental obtaining. Cases of inadvertent disclosures of confidential information (inadvertent at least as far as the recipient is concerned) have proved to be among the hardest for the equity courts to resolve.[67]

Some aspects of the case law seem more explicable as historical remnants of an earlier age than a living law economically attuned to the 21st century.[68] For instance, the traditional freedom to reverse engineer a product on the market – in *Saltman* given as an example of obtaining material from a public source – was in a recent English case of *Mars UK Ltd v Teknowledge Ltd*[69] explained simply as a right inherent in ownership of a physical product.[70] Such a rationale seems increasingly redundant in an age where information may be a primary source of value and the

65 *Ibid*, 281. Query whether Lord Goff had in mind a Kantian idea of corrective justice. A more utilitarian approach can be discerned in the observation that '[t]he existence of this broad general principle reflects the fact that there is such a public interest in the maintenance of confidences, that the law will provide remedies for their protection': *ibid*. See also his comments regarding government secrets, discussed below n 117.

66 Cf Friedman, Landes and Posner, above n 14, 69 (there is less economic justification for extending trade secret protection to accidental loss: 'it would be highly costly to competitors to have to sift the information they received in order to determine whether some of it might be information accidentally "mislaid"').

67 *Seager v Copydex* [1967] RPC 349 is an example. There the confidential information (about the plaintiff's carpet grip invention) was blurted out by the plaintiff inventor in discussions for marketing another product, with little notice for the defendant. The court's conclusion that the obligation arose, but the remedy should be restricted to damages, may be as much a response to the difficulty facing the defendant in preventing the disclosure as in negotiating licence terms with an unwilling seller: see especially 373 (Winn LJ).

68 To adopt the language of Gummow, above n 3.

69 [2000] FSR 138.

70 *Ibid*, 151 (even express notice could not override 'the buyer's entitlement to find out how his machine worked'). Contrast the policy focus of the US Supreme Court in *Bonito Boats Inc v Thunder Craft Boats Inc*, 489 US 141 (1989), SC 159–60 (precluding reverse engineering 'conflicts with the federal policy "that all ideas in general circulation be dedicated to the common good unless they are protected by a valid patent." *Lear, Inc v Adkins*, 395 US, at 668 ...') and at 160 ('reverse engineering is "an essential part of innovation"', often leading to 'significant advances in technology'). Cf Friedman, Landes and Posner, above n 14.

physical component trivial at best.[71] And the fictitious character of the reasoning that property rights in physical property *necessarily* encompass the information within begs the question whether any early economic justification for such an exception (for instance, the promotion of derivative innovation) has now been dissipated by greater possibilities for market-based solutions to derivative innovation.[72] Another example is the Australia case of *Maggbury Pty Ltd v Hafele Australia Pty Ltd*.[73] There the conclusion that a contractual provision prohibiting the use of a trade secret indefinitely might be held invalid as an unreasonable 'restraint of trade' relies on reasoning that predates 19th century economic liberalism.[74] In that case the terms of the restraint were clear enough, the parties sophisticated and well informed commercial corporations. There could be no misunderstanding as to meaning.[75] Nor was there evidence of inequality of bargaining power, as perhaps might be assumed in employee restrictive covenant cases where the restraint of trade doctrine is well established.[76] Rather the case involved information which was secret at the time of contracting but subsequently fell into the public domain when a patent was applied for. Simple generalised statements by the Australian High Court that the parties were 'in trade' and 'the activities restrained were part of that trade'[77] suggest an unnecessarily paternalistic role for the restraint of trade doctrine.[78] The only economic justification for applying a restraint of trade doctrine in a case such as this was the trade secret owner's relatively easier ability to control the happening of a supervening frustrating event (or at least insure against it).[79] Such cases aside, however, there seems a remarkable degree of support for economic analysis in Anglo-Australian breach of confidence-trade secret cases.

Privacy-breach of confidence cases are rationalised differently. The earliest ones might have suggested an economic and/or natural rights basis for protection, using the language of 'property' to explain this. In *Prince Albert v Strange*,[80] Lord Cottenham LC referred to Prince Albert's property right in his

---

71 Cf *Beta Computers (Europe) Ltd v Adobe Systems (Europe) Ltd* [1996] FSR 367, 373 (Lord Penrose) (information 'the dominant characteristic' of computer software provided under a shrink-wrap licence).

72 See Reichman and Richardson, above n 16.

73 (2001) 185 ALR 152.

74 For the origins of the restraint of trade doctrine in the English law of apprenticeship, see Carpenter, C, 'Validity of Contracts not to Compete' (1928) 76 U Penn L Rev 244. It later took on the role of a competition law in the period before extensive statutory regulation: see Atiyah, PS, *The Rise and Fall of Freedom of Contract*, Oxford: Clarendon, 1979, 697–701 (and even then, Atiyah points out, economically liberal 19th century courts generally upheld the contractual provision).

75 Unlike *Mustad & Son v Dosen* (1928) (CA, unreported) cited in *Cranleigh Precision Engineering Ltd v Bryant* [1964] 3 All ER 289, 298–99 (Roskill J) as authority that restraints would be narrowly construed.

76 See, for instance, *Faccenda Chicken Ltd v Fowler* [1987] Ch 117, 138 (Neill LJ); *Wright v Gasweld* (1991) 22 NSWLR 317.

77 (2001) 185 ALR 152, 167–68 (Gleeson CJ *et al*).

78 As observed in the dissenting judgment of Kirby and Callinan JJ.

79 Cf (frustration of contracts) Posner, R and Rosenfield, A, 'Impossibility and Related Doctrines in Contract Law: An Economic Analysis' (1977) 6 J Leg Stud 83.

80 (1849) 47 ER 1302.

private etchings in holding the defendant not permitted to publish them, or a catalogue about them, without his permission.[81] It was the author's exclusive entitlement, it was said, to keep the products of his work 'for his private use or pleasure'.[82] Similarly, in *Pope v Curl*,[83] *Thomson v Stanhope*,[84] and *Queensberry v Shebbeare*,[85] private and personal letters and manuscripts were treated as belonging to the author.[86] But these cases concerned tangible etchings, letters and other manuscripts, and the 'property' right referred to was common law copyright in unpublished works,[87] whose protection was established as lying with economics and natural rights.[88] The boundaries of common law copyright, later to be brought under the statutory copyright regime, were not then restricted to reproduction, adaptation and dissemination of the work.[89] Conceivably, at least, the law could extend to the mere unauthorised use of the work in question, for instance by disclosure of information contained within it. At the same time these early courts could already see a possible alternative basis for protection lying in breach of 'trust, confidence or contract'[90] – and as copyright took on a life of its own, so did breach of confidence as a vehicle for privacy protection.

Subsuming privacy protection under the breach of confidence doctrine was easy enough where information was imparted in confidence, the 'normal' scenario referred to by Megarry J in *Coco*.[91] For such cases, 20th century Anglo-Australian courts readily accepted the claimant's entitlement to be 'let alone'.[92]

---

81 *Ibid*, 1310–12, although also rather vaguely suggesting the ground could equally be 'breach of trust, confidence or contract': see further below n 90.

82 *Ibid*, 1312.

83 (1741) 26 ER 608.

84 (1774) 27 ER 476.

85 (1758) 28 ER 924.

86 See also *Exchange Telegraph Co Ltd v Gregory & Co* [1895] 1 QB 147 (common law copyright in material recorded on tickertape – the information more in the nature of a trade secret than private information).

87 Although not all cases required a tangible form: see *Abernethy v Hutchinson* (1826) 47 ER 1313, 1315 (Lord Eldon LC) (private lectures treated as property by analogy with copyright principles; although being delivered in oral form they were not 'literary compositions' for copyright purposes).

88 See, generally, Sherman, B and Bentley, L, *The Making of Modern Intellectual Property Law*, Cambridge: CUP, 1999, Ch 1. If anything, the authors may have, in stressing natural rights, underestimated the importance of economics in early common law copyright cases: see, for instance, *Pope v Curl* (1741) 26 ER 608, 608 (Lord Hardwiche LC: 'no works have done more service to mankind than those which have appeared in this shape, upon familiar subjects, and which perhaps were never intended to be published; and it is this that makes them so valuable'); *Abernethy v Hutchinson* (1826) 47 ER 1313, 1318 (suggesting the result might have been different had the plaintiff, under the terms of his employment, been 'precluded from publishing his own lectures for his profit').

89 See, generally, Scrutton, T, *The Law of Copyright*, London: William Clowes, 1896, 3–65.

90 *Prince Albert v Strange* (1849) 47 ER 1302, 1311–12 (Lord Cottenham LC). See also *Abernethy v Hutchinson* (1826) 47 ER 1313, 1315 and 1318 (Lord Eldon LC).

91 It was this limiting aspect that for a while, at least, led to the commonly accepted view that the English law did not recognise a 'right of privacy': see *Kaye v Robertson* [1991] FSR 62 (surreptitious filming of plaintiff in a hospital bed did not give a legal remedy. Curiously, breach of confidence was not even claimed, the apparent assumption being the action would be unavailable outside the normal scenario of *Coco*).

92 The expression adopted by Warren and Brandeis, above n 24, subsequently becoming the catchphrase for the US privacy tort.

However, unlike in their American counterparts, protection in Anglo-Australian courts was typically rationalised (to the extent any policy can be determined from the passing comments of the judges) in liberal-utilitarian terms focused on the individual as a social being. This is most clearly exemplified in the marriage secrets case *Argyll v Argyll*,[93] where the protection of confidential communications was said to encourage and preserve the marriage relationship, a union ideally based on mutual trust, intimacy and happiness.[94] Similarly, in the personal disclosure case of *Stephens v Avery*,[95] Browne-Wilkinson VC referred to the 'unconscionability' of breaching promised confidentiality between friends, as well as the privacy which 'every individual is entitled to enjoy' as reasons the plaintiff's highly sensitive information should have been kept out of the public domain.[96] Further evidence of the liberal-utilitarian approach is found in the recognition of collective interests in claiming confidentiality. Corporations, partnerships, and Aboriginal groups have successfully claimed breach of confidence when their sensitive information disclosed in confidence – being information they would not have wished to trade in because of what it reveals about themselves – was at risk of being revealed to the world.[97] And once the breach of confidence doctrine came to be accepted to encompass surreptitious obtaining following Lord Goff's pronouncement in *Guardian Newspapers*,[98] there was a perceived public as well as private interest in granting a degree of security to private information.[99] It was only because, consistent with Mill's ideal of a genuinely tolerant society, judges felt they should not 'apply their own personal moral views' that in the post-*Coco* era the detriment requirement for unauthorised use that Megarry J posited was, in the case of privacy claimants, reduced to a subjective standard of personal concern.[100] Conversely, courts acknowledged a

---

93 [1967] Ch 302.

94 *Ibid*, 322–29 (Ungoed-Thomas J), quoting *inter alia* from *Monroe v Twisleton* (1802) 170 ER 250.

95 [1988] 1 Ch 449. The case concerned the plaintiff's confidential disclosure to a then friend about a lesbian relationship with a Mrs Telling, a relationship which culminated in Mrs Telling's murder by her husband (and his conviction for manslaughter). The friend leaked the story to the second defendant newspaper.

96 *Ibid*, 456. For a feminist perspective on the social dimension of the case, see generally Wright, S, 'Confidentiality and the Public/Private Dichotomy' [1993] 7 EIPR 237.

97 *Schering Chemicals Ltd v Falkman* [1982] QB 1 (secrets concerning dangerous side-effects of a drug previously marketed by the company subject to equitable obligation); *John v Express Newspapers* (2000) 150 NLJ 342; *Foster v Mountford and Rigby Ltd* [1976] 29 FLR 233 (representatives of Pitjantjara tribe entitled to an injunction against the author and publisher of a book revealing tribal secrets). In the case of individuals, as well, commercially sensitive information has been treated as private and confidential: *Bolkiah v KPMG* [1999] 2 AC 222 (confidential disclosures made during a fiduciary relationship protected after the end of the relationship).

98 See, for instance, *Shelley Films Ltd v Rex Features Ltd* [1994] EMLR 34 (a case of surreptitious filming); *Hellewell v Chief Constable* [1995] 4 All ER 473, 476 (Laws J); *Australian Broadcasting Corp v Lenah Game Meats* (2001) 208 CLR 199 (*'Lenah Game Meats'*), 224 (Gleeson CJ), 272 (Kirby J), 289 (Callinan J).

99 See above n 65.

100 *Stephens* [1988] 1 Ch 449, 454 (Browne-Wilkinson VC) (in the absence of a generally accepted moral code, 'it would be wrong ... for any judge to apply his own personal moral views' as to what confidential information should be protected and what should not). See also *Guardian Newspapers* [1990] 1 AC 109, 138 (Lord Goff) (the example of a private diary shows the breadth of the action for privacy claimants).

real potential restraint on the protection available under the equitable doctrine, once confidentiality, notice and unauthorised use is found, as lying with the public interest in being informed on matters of legitimate public debate. The availability of a public interest exception to breach of confidence was thus endorsed.[101] But consistent with Mill's arguments, mere wanting to know on the part of the public was not enough to invoke the exception[102] – at least where pure privacy claims were concerned.

In recent years some difficulties have emerged in using the breach of confidence doctrine to protect claimed privacy interests. In the wake of the UK accession to the European Convention on Human Rights (which provides both for a right of privacy and free expression), actions have been brought by well known public figures, including Michael Douglas, Catherine Zeta Jones and Naomi Campbell, claiming their privacy rights have been invaded through unwanted publication by the media of stories about them. Although these cases were presented as privacy-breach of confidence claims, it was clear that at least part of the reason for mounting the claims was to maintain control over a public image rather than simply to keep personal information out of the public domain, which is the essence of a privacy claim. So in *Douglas v Hello! Ltd*[103] the complaint was not that the wedding shown by the defendant's pictures should be allowed to be kept private, but rather that the plaintiffs should be permitted to choose the venue for publication of pictures about the event as well as exercising a degree of control over how it was done. And in *Campbell v Mirror Group Newspapers*[104] the plaintiff's particular reason for objecting to publication of a story about her drug addiction treatment was her claimed entitlement to decide how to present herself to the public gaze. Such cases thus fell on the borderline of what might in the United States be described as a publicity right. But publicity is not a separate tort in Anglo-Australian law. And privacy, judged to be not about 'property',[105] became identified as the antithesis of such evident commercial interests. Reluctant to extend breach of confidence to grant a de facto publicity right in personal image, UK courts responded by introducing restrictions on the breach of confidence doctrine – first, as to the remedy available when privacy interests are 'sold' (in *Douglas* the plaintiffs in interlocutory proceedings were refused the injunction

---

101 See *Hellewell v Chief Constable* [1995] 4 All ER 473, 479 (Laws J). Cf *Guardian Newspapers* [1990] 1 AC 109, 281 (Lord Goff) (although mentioning triviality as an additional constraint); *Lenah Game Meats* (2001) 208 CLR 199, 275–76 (Kirby J) (the public interest also taking into account the constitutionally implied freedom of political discussion). See also Gleeson CJ, *ibid*, 224–25 (the Australian implied constitutional freedom of political discussion a qualification on the public interest exception).

102 See *Lion Laboratories Ltd v Evans* [1985] QB 526; *Guardian Newspapers* [1990] 1 AC 109, 138 (Lord Goff); *Ashdown v Telegraph Group Ltd* [2002] Ch 149, 170 (Lord Philips). In Australia, it has been suggested the defence may have a narrower focus, if such a defence exists (see especially *Smith Kline and French Laboratories v Department of Community Services* [1990] 22 FCR 73 ('*Smith Kline*'), 110–11 (Gummow J) – the question is simply of excluding protection to iniquity). But the weight of authority is broader: see Australian cases noted above n 101 and below n 118, and generally Richardson, above n 33.

103 [2001] 2 All ER 289 ('*Douglas*').

104 [2003] 1 All ER 224 ('*Campbell*').

105 *Douglas* [2001] 2 All ER 289, 319 (Sedley LJ) quoting also *Argyll v Argyll* [1967] Ch 302, 318–22 (Ungoed-Thomas J).

they sought to prevent publication of the pictures);[106] second, as to the entitlement to claim when publicity is manipulated (in *Campbell* the defendant was held free under the public interest exception to set the record straight after the plaintiff had publicly misrepresented her drug addiction);[107] and more generally, as to the ability to treat information as 'confidential' (the Court of Appeal in *Campbell* apparently endorsing a threshold test of whether the publication would be offensive to a reasonable person,[108] a test that in a climate of a mass-publication and readership of daily details of celebrities' lives – often with their consent – was something the plaintiff found impossible to satisfy).

At the time of writing, both cases are yet to reach an ultimate decision. In final proceedings in *Douglas v Hello! Ltd* a first instance judgment cast some doubt on aspects of the Court of Appeal's decision on the interlocutory injunction application. Lindsay J held that not only damages but an injunction against further publication of the wedding pictures would be available to the plaintiffs, citing privacy and trade secrecy as values protected under the equitable confidentiality doctrine.[109] The judge also refused to hold that the control the plaintiffs were seeking to exercise over information about them was an 'improper objective of the confidentiality doctrine'.[110] But damages are still to be assessed and *Hello!* has signalled it may appeal. In *Campbell* an appeal is pending, here from the Court of Appeal to the House of Lords. At one level, it may be argued, the problem to be addressed in both these cases lies not with the breach of confidence doctrine but with the limited and even negative protection accorded to reputational interests under Anglo-Australian law.[111] The broad suggestion at the interlocutory stage in *Douglas* that 'selling' privacy would lead to lesser confidentiality protection is a particular matter of concern, denying to the rights holder ultimate control over how valuable personal information is to be used. Even trade secrets which are protected because of their commercial value are not treated so preemptively, courts generally appreciating the economic and liberal reasons for giving the owner 'first go' in determining how the information will be exploited.[112] Also potentially of concern for those steeped in the liberal-utilitarian tradition of the equitable doctrine is the *obiter* comment of Sedley LJ in *Douglas* that now may be the time to abandon breach of confidence and, in the spirit of the Human Rights Convention, openly acknowledge the 'right' of privacy with (presumably) a tort of privacy invasion.[113] This was not ruled out for Australia

106 See especially [2001] 2 All ER 289, 234–35 (Sedley LJ). See also Brooks LJ at 314–15 and Keene LJ at 331.

107 *Campbell* [2003] 1 All ER 224, 239 (Lord Philips). See also *A v B plc* [2002] 2 All ER 435 (publication of sexual promiscuity by a professional footballer allowed on a balancing of interests, applying the public interest exception – while not going so far as the *Campbell* court in a blanket prohibition on confidentiality, the weighting gave emphasis to the footballer's public image and status as a role model).

108 *Campbell* [2003] 1 All ER 224, 237–38 (Lord Philips, finding support also in comments of Gleeson CJ in *Lenah Game Meats* (2001) 208 CLR 199, 226).

109 See *Douglas and Others v Hello! Ltd (No 3)* [2003] 3 All ER 996, especially at 1044–61 and 1074–75 (Lindsay J).

110 *Ibid*, [216].

111 Although Australian courts have gone further than their English counterparts: see above n 30.

112 See above n 61.

113 [2001] 2 All ER 289, 317–20.

either by Gummow and Hayne JJ in the recent case of *Australian Broadcasting Corp v Lenah Game Meats Ltd*, but here it was rightly noted that such a development would not necessarily lead to more privacy protection, and may involve less if the US experience is taken as a guide.[114] Later courts have generally maintained their reliance on breach of confidence (coupled with torts such as trespass to the person) as the vehicle for privacy protection.[115] However, the suggestion in *Campbell* that the 'confidentiality' of claimed private information might yet entail a standard of offensiveness to a reasonable person sits better with the US privacy tort than the traditional equitable doctrine.[116] It is too soon to tell (especially given the pending appeal to the House of Lords) whether an offensiveness threshold will be part of the doctrine's future operation.

The utilitarian basis of the breach of confidence doctrine when applied to protect government secrets is plain from Lord Goff's statement in *Guardian Newspapers* (the 'Spycatcher' case, involving directly the subject of claimed government secrets) that in cases of government secrets the Crown has to establish not only that the information to be published is confidential but also that publication would be detrimental in the sense that 'it is in the public interest that it should not be published'.[117] In the case of government secrets the public interest in protecting confidentiality has become the essence of the claim and must be proved directly. As Mason J observed in the Australian Government secrets case, *Commonwealth v John Fairfax & Sons*,[118] equity: 'acts, or is supposed to act, not according to the standards of private interest, but in the public interest. This is not to say that equity will not protect information in the hands of the government, but it is to say that when equity protects government information it will look at the matter through different spectacles.'[119] The prospect of a utilitarian balancing of interests is also most obvious in government secret cases, especially where the

---

114 (2001) 208 CLR 199, 252–58 (uncommitted to whether the future will see a tort of privacy invasion in Australia, but clear that if it did it would not be available to the plaintiff corporation). Gleeson CJ and Callinan J preferred to rely on the breach of confidence doctrine (although differing on whether the information as to the plaintiff's abattoir operations, conceded to be non-confidential, should be treated as confidential). Kirby J held that an interlocutory injunction did not require a specific substantive cause of action.

115 See generally *Wainwright v Home Office* [2002] QB 1334 (CA) approved on appeal [2003] UKHL 53; *Douglas v Hello! (No 3)* [2003] 3 All ER 996, 1061–62 (Lindsay J). It also appears to have been assumed in *Campbell* that breach of confidence was the appropriate basis. For some endorsement of a privacy tort, see Queensland case *Grosse v Purvis* [2003] QDC 151, although contrast New Zealand case *Hosking v Runting* (HC, unrep, 30 May 2003) – both currently under appeal.

116 Cf *Douglas v Hello!* [2003] EWHC 786, [189] (Lindsay J), concluding that the Court of Appeal in *Campbell* 'cannot have intended' to adopt such a restriction, given its inconsistency with the *Saltman-Coco* confidentiality test. Interestingly, in the United States the restriction does not apply where publicity rights are concerned (see above n 25).

117 [1990] 1 AC 109, 283 (elaborating as follows: 'although in the case of private citizens there is a public interest that confidential information should as such be protected, in the case of government secrets the mere fact of confidentiality does not alone support such a conclusion, because in a free society there is a continuing public interest that the workings of government should be open to scrutiny and criticism').

118 (1980) 147 CLR 39 (*'Fairfax'*).

119 *Ibid*, 51–52.

public interest exception is raised.[120] Indeed, as Mason J observed in *Fairfax*, the entire question of whether maintaining government secrecy is in the public interest calls for a balancing of interests (the onus lying with the claimant). And 'there will be cases in which the conflicting considerations will be finely balanced, where it is difficult to decide whether the public's interest in knowing and in expressing its opinion, outweighs the need to protect confidentiality'.[121] In fact, the cases are few in which government secrets have been protected under the equitable doctrine.[122]

Lately, governments have turned to contract to improve their chances when their information is in danger of being revealed (especially by former secret agents). In *Attorney-General v Blake*,[123] a contractual confidentiality clause was successfully invoked against notorious double agent and 'self-confessed traitor' George Blake to draw back profits from his book *No Other Choice*, published many years later, notwithstanding the information contained within it was said to be no longer confidential. The public interest in protecting information accepted to be fully in the public domain was apparently not in issue. The possibility that the book's real revelation lay in Blake's motives for his betrayal and those of others like him was not considered – the government's legitimate interest in claiming these as government secrets thus left unexplored.[124] Nor was there any suggestion that the equitable public interest exception might find a parallel in contractual secrecy cases (although there is Australian authority in support)[125] or that freedom of speech should be accommodated.[126] Instead the main question for the House of Lords was whether, at the plaintiff's election, a disgorgement remedy rather than

---

120 Defined in *Fairfax* as designed to protect the community from 'destruction, damage or harm': *ibid*, 56–57. See also *Lenah Game Meats* (2001) 208 CLR 199, 224–25 (Gleeson CJ), 275–76 (Kirby J).

121 (1980) 147 CLR 39, 52 (Mason J).

122 A telling example is the UK Government's attempts to use the equitable doctrine to prevent publication of the *Spycatcher* book by ex-MI5 agent Peter Wright, criticising the organisation, in a series of cases around the world. For a mixture of reasons including failure to satisfy the public interest requirement and the simple fact that much of the information was already in the public domain (so was not confidential), the claims only succeeded in the UK against the first newspaper to serialise the book and failed elsewhere: see, generally, Patfield, F, '*Spycatcher* Worldwide' [1989] 11 EIPR 201. The most restrictive approach was revealed in the High Court of Australia, where it was held that the British Government was claiming a foreign public interest, cognisance of which was barred under Australian private international law: *Attorney-General (UK) v Heinemann Publishers Australia Pty Ltd* (1988) 165 CLR 30. Query whether the same result would be reached in the current political climate of collaborative efforts to combat international terrorism.

123 *Attorney-General v Blake* [2001] 1 AC 268.

124 Alternatively, a basis might be found in an ongoing fiduciary obligation. However, any fiduciary obligation Blake may have had was held extinguished at first instance and on appeal: *Attorney-General v Blake* [1997] Ch 84; [1998] Ch 439, a position not questioned by the majority in the House of Lords. See, however, [2001] 1 AC 268, 291–92 (Lord Steyn).

125 *A v Hayden* (1984) 156 CLR 532. See also *Esso Australia Resources Ltd v Plowman* (1995) 183 CLR 10, 31–32 (Mason CJ).

126 Contrast the New Zealand case of *Attorney-General for England and Wales v R* [2002] 2 NZLR 91, where freedom of speech was given as a reason not to grant an injunction for breach of a contractual confidentiality clause between the British Government and a former member of the SAS, whose book *Bravo Two Zero* was strongly critical of government actions taken in the Gulf War. Interestingly it was noted a monetary remedy (including account of profits) would be available: *ibid*, 98 (Keith J), 124–25 (Tipping J) and 133 (McGrath J).

an injunction or specific performance remedy might be available for breach of contract in cases where the plaintiff suffers 'no financially measurable loss'.[127] In answering yes, or at least sometimes, the House of Lords referred to the 'Crown's legitimate interest in preventing Blake profiting from the disclosure of official information, whether classified or not, while a member of the service and thereafter'[128] and drew an analogy with the remedies available for invasion of a property right.[129] The idea that remedies for contract could be tailored to profit-capturing ends is interesting.[130] But the conclusion raises the broader question of why, when private claimants may find themselves penalised for seeking to turn their privacy rights into tradable property rights, governments should be permitted to treat *their* sensitive information as – in effect – property, substituting themselves for someone who wrongly seeks to profit from its disclosure.[131] This brings us back to the questions of property in confidential information.

'PROPERTY' IN CONFIDENTIAL INFORMATION?

Legal property theorists from the time of Felix Cohen's famous 'Dialogue on Private Property'[132] have generally maintained that property entails in essence a right to exclude.[133] Support for this is found in the writings of classical philosophers, including Locke, Smith, Bentham and Mill. But as we have seen, while classical philosophers generally argued for some exclusivity of rights to the fruits of labour on various grounds, they were less enamoured of the idea of

---

127 *Attorney-General v Blake* [2001] 1 AC 268, 278 (Lord Nicholls).

128 *Ibid*, 287–88, citing *Snepp v United States*, 444 US 507 (1980), where a constructive trust was awarded over profits from publication by an ex-CIA agent held subject to an ongoing fiduciary obligation, as a comparable in its facts.

129 *Ibid*, 632–34, 639, although ostensibly the government's right was characterised as 'personal' only (*ibid*, 637: 'it is not clear why it should be any more permissible to expropriate personal rights than it is to expropriate property rights'). For a critique of this characterisation see further below.

130 There is some academic support for such an approach: see, for instance, Birks, P, 'Profits of Breach of Contract' (1993) 109 LQR 518; Phang, A and Lee, P-W, 'Rationalising Restitutionary Damages in Contract Law' (2001) 17 JCL 240. Contrast Burrows, A, 'No Restitutionary Damages for Breach of Contract' [1993] LMCLQ 453 and Hedley, S, 'Very Much the Wrong People: The House of Lords and the Publication of Spy Memoirs' [2002] 4 Web J Current Leg Issues (generally unenthusiastic about discretionary remedialism).

131 In fact the general entitlement of private claimants to obtain an account of profits for breach of the equitable obligation, irrespective of the initial character of the information (and their own treatment of it), seems to be assumed: see *Attorney-General v Blake* [2001] 1 AC 268, 639 (Lord Nicholls: '[I]f confidential information is wrongly disclosed in breach of a non-disclosure agreement, it would be nothing short of sophistry to say that an account of profits may be ordered in respect of the equitable wrong but not in respect of the breach of contract which governs the relationship between the parties').

132 (1954) 9 Rutgers L Rev 357.

133 See, for instance, Harris, J, *Property and Justice*, Oxford: Clarendon, 1996; Penner, J, *The Idea of Property in Law*, Oxford: Clarendon, 1997; Merrill, T, 'Property and the Right to Exclude' (1998) 77 Neb L Rev 730; Merrill, T and Smith, H, 'What Happened to Property in Law and Economics' (2001) 111 Yale LJ 357. Contrast, however, Gray, K, 'Property in Thin Air' (1991) 50 CLJ 252, observing that property rights do not in practice generally determine exclusivity. Rather '[t]he precise allocation of "property" in excludable resources is left to be determined – is indeed constantly formulated and reformulated – by various kinds of social and moral consensus ...' (295).

absolute exclusivity than modern legal theorists may suppose. As noted earlier, Locke accepted the need for a common pool of shared resources kept available to all; and Mill would always subject the exclusivity of private property (especially resources drawn from a common pool) to the utilitarian ideal of promoting the public good. For different reasons modern economists have also questioned whether absolute exclusivity is necessary. Rather, they suggested, it is a particular *manner* in which fruits may be reaped – through not just possessing, occupying and enjoying the resource but rather treating it as a commodity which can be traded in the market – that belongs to an owner and is the true signpost of a 'property' right.[134] Thus Coase observed '[w]e may speak of a person owning land and using it as a factor of production but what the land-owner in fact possesses is the right to carry out a circumscribed range of actions'.[135] And because Coase read cases, he saw that courts did not view property rights as neat packages of rights to exclude but rather as entailing, for the most part, contingent exclusivity to be resolved by lawmakers when rights come into conflict. The same may be seen of rights which conflict with the broader social interest.

As the breach of confidence cases surveyed in this chapter have shown, the exclusivity of confidential information is not premised on property but is rather determined by contract and equity.[136] In *Blake*, Lord Nicholls may have reiterated the standard legal view that '[p]roperty rights are superior to contractual rights in that, unlike contractual rights, property rights may survive against an indefinite class of persons'.[137] But the equitable confidentiality obligation has long extended to third parties, bound subject to notice, without this depending on a property right. And in *Guardian Newspapers* Lord Goff asserted a general obligation for those who obtain confidential information subject to notice, without feeling the need to resolve the question of property in confidential information.[138] In fact, those kinds of confidential information for which the 'property' label is sometimes used – trade secrets – are often less exclusive than the kinds for which it is not. In the case of trade secrets, there is at best a presumption against interference and sometimes not even that. Reverse engineering is still an accepted exception to trade secret protection and the status of accidental obtaining is not entirely clear. (The public interest exception may also apply, being not restricted

---

134 Merrill and Smith argue that there are economic benefits to absolute or at least general exclusivity as the test of a property right: see above n 133, 389ff (arguing for the efficiency of bright lines of exclusion in cases where 'information about rights is costly to acquire and process'). The reasoning explains why some classes of property may be more absolute – as, for instance, with the registered intellectual property systems. Query whether it does more than that.

135 'The Problem of Social Cost', above n 8, 44.

136 Cf the Australian case of *Moorgate Tobacco Co Ltd v Philip Morris Ltd (No 2)* (1984) 156 CLR 414, 438 (Deane J: '[l]ike most heads of exclusive equitable jurisdiction, [the equitable doctrine's] rational basis does not lie in proprietary right. It lies in the notion of an obligation of conscience arising from the circumstances in or through which the information was communicated or obtained').

137 *Attorney-General v Blake* [2001] 1 AC 268, 283. Cf Ricketson, above n 2, 308, although preferring the language of enforceability to exclusivity to elucidate this right as one that may only give rise to a monetary remedy.

138 [1990] 1 AC 109, 281–82 (Lord Goff).

by the category of information concerned.) Further, that the remedy for breach may be limited to a monetary award implies even greater scope for compelled use for efficiency ends than the limited free use exceptions would allow. In general, the label 'property' for trade secrets seems largely to refer to the economist's sense of rights that may be traded in the market (in first instance by the owner, or if markets fail then under the *aegis* of the law). As was said in one early case '[t]his information ... is something that can be sold. It is property, and being sold to the plaintiffs it was their property'.[139] The same conception of property – as about 'selling' – can be seen in the privacy and government secrets cases. It is the freedom to market alienate that distinguishes trade secrets from these kinds of information, although some recent cases suggest government secrets (but not yet privacy?) may exhibit inchoate trading capacities.

In some respects these decisions may be criticised. The identification of a trade secret as property may be accepted as appropriate, signalling its status as a commodity, or thing, capable of being traded to its highest value use (in economic terms at least). That government secrets may, at least sometimes, be treated as property at the election of the putative owner at least acknowledges that the state can be trusted to decide such matters for itself. But the question of the freedom to commodify privacy, and thus trade it in the market, has not yet been satisfactorily resolved. On the one hand, it may in the future be argued that commodifying and trading in private information is akin to selling oneself into slavery, something even Mill found abhorrent to the liberal-utilitarian ideal.[140] On the other hand – and in my view preferably – the act of 'selling privacy' may be seen as an exercise in liberty quite unlike the special case of selling into slavery.[141] For any loss of privacy through the trading process is exchanged for control over personal reputation or, at the very least, money (or its equivalent) bringing the power to acquire and use resources in the future – being, as Locke said many years ago, the only 'lasting thing that men might keep without spoiling'.[142] Of course, one cost of

---

139 *Exchange Telegraph Co v Gregory Co* [1895] 1 QB 147, 153 (Lord Esher MR). See also *Smith Kline* [1990] 22 FCR 73 119–20 (Gummow J) (confidential information may be characterised as property for certain purposes – such as assignment, creation of a charge, holding in trust, and devolution upon bankruptcy).

140 'On Liberty' above n 34, 235–36 ('by selling himself into slavery [a person] abdicates his liberty; he forgoes any future use of it beyond that single act. He therefore defeats in his own case the very purpose which is the justification of allowing him to dispose of himself'). Kantian liberals have similarly argued against commodification of personal material, seen as too integral to the person to be capable of alienation without loss of dignity: see, for instance, Radin, MJ, 'Market Inalienability' (1987) 100 Harv L Rev 1849. For a well argued response that this is only if commodification occurs involuntarily, see Duxbury, N, 'Do Markets Degrade?' (1986) 59 Mod L Rev 331.

141 Slavery should be treated as in a special category of its own given the complete and utter loss of liberty that results, by definition, from the status of being a slave. Mill understood this: see above n 140. Cf Duxbury, above n 140, 339–40 with respect to the sale of human organs: 'it is misleading to equate the sale of human tissues and organs with slavery. Whereas a right entirely to deprive oneself of autonomy would obviously serve to negate rather than enhance individual liberty, a right to sell human organs and tissues – irrespective of whether one considers it objectionable – extends the range of individual choices and opportunity.'

142 Above n 22.

choosing the property status is that this entails acceptance of the limitations as well as benefits of property rights – in particular, possibilities for compulsory licensing. But provided the putative owner's choice is real, not coerced or misinformed,[143] there are sound liberal as well as utilitarian arguments for permitting property rights to be established in private information.

As to the second question posed at the beginning of this essay – does it matter whether confidential information is property? – the answer must be qualified assent. At best property rights, conceived in terms of market alienability, are of instrumental and limited importance. The various economic, liberal and utilitarian claims for and against protection in actual cases are not solved by attaching a 'property' label to the information concerned. Their concerns still need to be addressed. Moreover, if one were seeking to find a unifying thread to the equitable breach of confidence doctrine, the language of property could not assist. Rather, the theme would likely be the one courts have identified from the beginning – promoting trust and confidence, understood now to extend even as between those who may be strangers, within an anonymous and crowded community. Promoting trust and confidence cannot explain why only confidential information is protected.[144] Nor can it explain other particular aspects of the law. One theme of this chapter has been that trade secrets, private information and government secrets are not and should not be treated exactly alike for important policy reasons. But abstaining from 'unconscientious behavior'[145] may still be the glue that binds the equitable obligation together, reflecting that there is at least some common policy. Acknowledgment of this need not necessitate a Kantian philosophical approach either. Mill also appreciated that the ability to trust in the conduct of others is 'the most vital of interests', finding here justification for the binding force of promising and contract.[146] Curiously, the personal and social value of trust is something modern economic/utilitarian scholars are only now beginning to explore.[147]

143 See, generally, Trebilcock, M, *The Limits of Freedom of Contract*, Cambridge, MA: Harvard UP, 1993, Chapter 2 – rejecting anti-commodification arguments on economic as well as liberal grounds, and suggesting the important issues are rather the reality of information and consent.

144 See, for instance (trade secrets), *Coco* [1969] RPC 41, 51.

145 The expression preferred over unconscionable behaviour by Gummow and Hayne JJ in *Lenah Game Meats* (2001) 208 CLR 199, 245.

146 'Utilitarianism', above n 34, 310.

147 See, for instance, Bowles, S and Gintis, H, 'Social Capital and Community Governance' (2002) 112 Economic J F419.

10

CONTRACT RIGHTS AS PROPERTY RIGHTS

*Ralph Cunnington**

INTRODUCTION

The nature of a contractual obligation has given rise to much debate over the years. For the legal economists who advocate the efficient breach theory of contracting, a contract is nothing more than a disjunctive obligation, requiring the contractor either to perform the contract or undergo the stipulated penalties.[1] If this is the nature of a contractual obligation then a contract is little more than an insurance policy; an agreement to pay a certain sum if an event takes place or fails to take place. The remedies are merely pecuniary. However, as Buckland succinctly stated over 50 years ago, 'One does not buy a right to damages, one buys a horse'.[2] Pollock made similar observations: 'A man who bespeaks a coat of his tailor will scarcely be persuaded that he is only betting with the tailor that such a coat will not be made and delivered within a certain time. What he wants and means to have is a coat, not an insurance against not having a coat.'[3]

The question arises, if contractual obligations are more than merely disjunctive obligations, what are they? Daniel Friedmann has suggested that 'contract rights' are akin to 'property rights' and as such should yield restitutionary damages.[4] It is relatively uncontroversial to suggest that restitutionary damages are available for interferences with property rights. Recently in *Attorney-General v Blake*, Lord Nicholls said that 'damages at common law for violations of a property right may be measured by reference to the benefits wrongfully obtained by the defendant'.[5] Indeed, restitutionary damages are an obvious remedy for breach of proprietary rights since the ownership of property includes the right to profit from the use of

---

* I would like to express my gratitude to His Honour Justice WMC Gummow, Professor Harvey Teff, Ms Janet Ulph, and Assistant Professor Jason Neyers for their valuable comments on earlier drafts of this chapter. All errors are mine alone.

1 See Pollock, F, *Pollock-Holmes Letters*, de Wolfe Howe, M (ed), Cambridge: CUP, 1942, vol 1, 177. Also see: Holmes, OW, 'The Path of the Law', in *Collected Legal Papers*, New York: Harcourt Brace, 1920, 167, 175; Holmes, OW, *The Common Law*, de Wolfe Howe, M (ed), London: Macmillan, 1968, 235; Posner, R, *Economic Analysis of Law*, Boston, MA: Little, Brown, 2nd edn, 1977, 89–90.

2 Buckland, FF, 'The Nature of Contractual Obligation' (1944) 8 CLJ 247, 249–51.

3 Pollock, F, *Principles of Contract*, London: Stevens, 3rd edn, 1881, 19.

4 Friedmann, D, 'Restitution of Benefits Obtained Through the Appropriation of Property or the Commission of a Wrong' (1980) 80 Col LR 504.

5 [2000] 3 WLR 625, 635. See also Lord Nicholls at 639. See also *Surrey County Council v Bredero Homes* [1993] 1 WLR 1361, 1365 (Dillon LJ), 1371 (Steyn LJ).

that property.[6] Thus any appropriation of that right should give rise to an award of restitutionary damages.

More controversial is Friedmann's thesis that contract rights are rights akin to property rights. The truth of such an assertion depends on one's definition of property, a notoriously nebulous concept. If the defining feature of property rights is that they can be asserted against an indefinite class of persons then it would be quite difficult to argue that contract rights are property rights. However, if a broader definition is adopted which includes *choses in action* then contracts could be recognised as a form of property.[7]

In this chapter it will be asked whether contractual rights can be equated with property rights, thus yielding restitutionary damages when breached.[8] In the first part of the chapter the development of the tort of inducing breach of contract will be traced. It will be suggested that the right recognised in *Lumley v Gye* was akin to a property right, potentially yielding restitutionary damages. As such, it is difficult to justify contractual rights having a proprietary status against third parties while not having such a status between the original contracting parties. In the second part of the chapter it will be asked whether contract rights can be regarded as property rights and whether this connection serves any useful purpose. Friedmann's theory on contract rights as property rights will critically be examined. In conclusion it will be contended that both Friedmann's theory and the tort of inducing breach of contract identify a need for greater protection of contractual interests. However, such protection is not best provided by piecemeal measures or a blurring of the categories of contract rights and property rights. Instead there should be an open recognition of the need for restitutionary damages as a tertiary remedy for breach of contract in circumstances where compensatory damages are inadequate and equitable remedies are unavailable.

---

6 See Weinrib, E, 'Restitutionary Damages as Corrective Justice' (2000) 1 Theoretical Inquiries in Law 1.

7 *Foskett v McKeown* [2000] 3 All ER 97, 126 (Lord Millett), 108–09 (Lord Hoffmann), 114 (Lord Hope). Lord Millett spoke of an insurance policy as being a bundle of contractual rights which constitute a chose in action.

8 The term 'restitutionary damages' has been adopted in this chapter to simplify terminology by recognising all gain-based awards as 'restitutionary damages'. (See Law Com No 247, 1997, paras 3.82–3.84; Burrows, A, 'We do this at Common Law but that in Equity' (2002) 22 OJLS 1, 12). As Birks has noted, the underlying Latin *'restituere/restitutio'* indicates that the word 'restitutionary' can include both 'give up' and 'give back' (see Birks, P, 'Equity in the Modern Law' (1996) 26 UWA L Rev 1, 28; Heumann, H and Seckel, E, *Handlexikon zu den Quellen des Römischen Rechts*, Graz: Akademische Druck- u. Verlagsanstalt, 11th edn, 1971, 515). Therefore it is apt to cover gain-based awards for breach of contract. However it is recognised that this position is controversial and that many would argue that a more appropriate label would be 'disgorgement damages' or an 'account of profits'. See: Lord Nicholls in *Attorney-General v Blake* [2000] 3 WLR 625, 638 (*'Blake'*); Doyle, S and Wright, D, 'Restitutionary Damages – The Unnecessary Remedy?' (2001) 25 Melb ULR 1, 13–20; Edelman, J, *Gain-Based Damages*, Oxford: Hart, 2002, 65–112. Sustained debate on this point is beyond the scope of this chapter.

THE TORT OF INDUCING BREACH OF CONTRACT

At present, English law does not recognise breach of contract as a civil wrong in the tortious sense.[9] The law of contract provides a cause of action and the claimant may recover damages for the loss sustained. The absence of a remedy in the law of tort is undoubtedly due to the theoretical foundations of the English economy. English law of contract is based upon free market principles which encourage parties to freely negotiate contracts with minimal State intervention. This necessitates limitations on the remedial consequences of breach in order to encourage parties to enter into contractual relations. As a consequence there is no tort known in English law for breaching one's own contract. However, the desire to ensure that contracting parties are left free to act independently has led to the creation of a tort for inducing breach of contract.

Origins of the tort

The tort of inducing breach of contract has its roots in the medieval law of tort which gave a right of action to an employer if his servants were forcibly abducted.[10] Although this action had its foundations in liability for physical injury, it was extended to cases of enticement where no independent wrong had been done to the servant.[11] In 1349 an additional remedy for the enticement of servants was introduced by the Ordinance of Labourers.[12] This statute was enacted following the Bubonic Plague in response to the huge shortage of labour. The Act created a system of compulsory labour which prevented labourers from leaving their service until the agreed term had been completed. Furthermore, chapter two of the Ordinance provided that anyone retaining a labourer in breach of the Ordinance was liable to imprisonment. This enactment did not replace the pre-existing common law action for injuring another person's servants through violence. It was an additional statutory remedy which required no proof of violence. Initially the actions were kept distinct. However, over time the distinction between the actions became eroded as the lawyers and judges took little trouble to distinguish between them. By the end of the 18th century the courts were allowing an action at common law for the procurement or enticement of another person's servant without any proof of violence.[13]

---

9 Birks, P, 'Rights, Wrongs and Remedies' (2000) 20 OJLS 1, 27–36 has argued that breach of contract should be classified as a wrong in his taxonomic analysis of private law. Birks contrasts wrongs (breaches of duty) with not-wrongs. Consent based causes of action such as mistaken payments are not-wrongs whilst breaches of contract are wrongs. Birks' analysis provides a convincing justification for differential treatment between those who commit wrongs and those who commit not-wrongs. Wrongdoers can be mistreated. Not-wrongdoers should not be mistreated. As such, remedies for breach of contract are to be more defendant focused. Although such a theory is attractive it would certainly be wrong to suggest that English law presently recognises breach of contract as a tortious wrong.

10 See Ibbetson, D, *A Historical Introduction to the Law of Obligations*, Oxford: OUP, 1999, 66; Jones, G, '*Per Quod Servitum Amisit*' (1958) 74 LQR 39.

11 Sayre, F, 'Inducing Breach of Contract' (1922) 36 Harv LR 663, 664–65.

12 23 Edw III. See also the Statute of Labourers, 25 Edw III.

13 See, eg, *Blake v Lanyon* (1957) 6 TR 221; *Pilkington v Scott* (1846) 15 M & W 657.

Thus the tort of procuring or enticing another person's servant was born. The tort has its roots in ancient trespass actions and 14th century compulsory labour law. Clearly, these foundations should have meant that the tort was highly restricted within its peculiar framework; however the tort has since received a very expansive interpretation in later cases.

Lumley v Gye

The leading case in this area was the 19th century decision in *Lumley v Gye*.[14] The plaintiff, Lumley, had a contract with Johanna Wagner for her exclusive services as an opera singer. However, Wagner was lured away from the contract by the defendant who offered a higher fee to sing at his theatre. The defendant had been aware of the terms of the contract between Lumley and Wagner but had offered an alternative contract regardless. The plaintiff sued for damages and the Court of Queen's Bench decided by a majority that he had a good cause of action.

There were two questions to be answered by the court in the case:[15]

(1) Was Miss Wagner a servant? If so, the actions of the defendant may fall within the action for procurement or enticement of another's servant under the Statute of Labourers.[16]

(2) Was the 'enticement' principle broad enough to cover all those involved in contracts for personal service even though they could not be called servants?

Although the majority of the court refused to confine the action for enticement to 'servants' as defined by the Statute of Labourers, Coleridge J delivered a highly convincing dissenting judgment. He declared that:

> in respect of breach of contract the general rule of our law is to confine its remedies by action to the contracting parties, and to damages directly and proximately consequential on the act of him who is sued; that, as between master and servant, there is an admitted exception; that this exception dates from the Statute of Labourers, and both on principle and according to authority is limited by it.[17]

Coleridge J therefore held that the action for enticement could not be extended beyond the Statute of Labourers. Furthermore, he decided that an opera singer was not a servant within either the letter or the spirit of the Statute of Labourers.[18]

The judgment of Coleridge J is to be commended as being the most accurate statement of the law. He noted that the general rule of contract law is to confine its remedies by action to the contracting parties.[19] The one exception which the learned judge identified was the limited action under the Statute of Labourers

14 (1853) 2 E & B 216.
15 Sayre, above n 11, 667.
16 25 Edw III.
17 (1853) 2 E & B 216, 246.
18 *Ibid*, 266–67.
19 *Ibid*, 246.

which facilitated compulsory labour. Since no equivalent form of compulsory labour exists today it would seem that the Act should no longer have application. It is submitted that neither the wording nor the spirit of the Statute of Labourers lends support to the extension of the principle beyond its original ambit of compulsory labour relations.

However, the majority of the Court of Queen's Bench disagreed with Coleridge J. They refused to confine the action for enticement to 'servants' as defined in the Statute of Labourers and increased the application of the tort beyond its original statutory intention. Compton J speaking for the majority declared: 'I think that we are justified in applying the principle of the action for enticing away servants to a case where the defendant maliciously procures a party, who is under a valid contract to give her exclusive personal services to the plaintiff for a specified period, to refuse to give such services during the period for which she had so contracted, whereby the plaintiff was injured.'[20] The common law tort of maliciously procuring a breach of contract was thus created. However, as Sayre[21] recognised, the tort, as defined by Compton J,[22] was confined to cases where:

(1) the defendant's action was malicious;

(2) there existed a valid and binding contract between the plaintiff and the person induced to breach it; and

(3) this contract was one to render exclusive personal services for a specified period.

Erle J refused to so confine the tort and he declared much more general grounds of liability. For him: 'The procurement of the violation of a right is a cause of action in all instances where the violation is an actionable wrong ... He who maliciously procures a damage to another by violation of his right ought to be made to indemnify, and that whether he procures an actionable wrong or a breach of contract.'[23]

It is interesting that Erle J sought to remove any distinction between breaches of contract and other actionable wrongs. He clearly viewed contractual breaches as being equivalent to actionable wrongs. However, as has been recognised, breaches of contract are not civil wrongs in the tortious sense. There exists no tort of breaching a contract. It is true that some breaches of contract are also actionable, concurrently, as torts.[24] This can be seen from the example of a surveyor, Anna, who causes her client, Colin, financial loss by negligently writing a report. Under the current law, Colin could sue Anna in tort for negligent mis-statement or in

---

20 *Ibid*, 231.

21 Sayre, above n 11, 664–65, 669.

22 With whom Wightman J agreed.

23 (1853) 2 E & B 216, 233.

24 *Henderson v Merrett Syndicates Ltd* [1995] 2 AC 145; *Saunders v Edwards* [1987] 1 WLR 1116; *Edler Auerbach* [1950] 1 KB 359. Also see Cane, P, *Anatomy of Tort Law*, Oxford: Hart, 1997, 153–55.

contract for breach of contractual duty of care. The choice of cause of actions is Colin's. However, the tortious action in such a case is in negligence which is independent of the contract.

It is very difficult to ascertain exactly why Erle J reaches the conclusion that the procuring of a breach of contract is as deserving of liability as the procuring of an actionable tort. It is possible that the learned judge believed that breach of contract was an actionable tort. This was certainly not inconceivable in 1853. Alternatively Erle J may have recognised that breaches of contract were not actionable as civil wrongs but believed that they should be. Such a proposal has radical implications. The remedies available for breach of contract are fairly limited in comparison to those available for torts. Specific performance and injunctions are occasionally available in contract but they are secondary remedies. The primary remedy is compensatory damages,[25] and following *Attorney-General v Blake* there is limited availability of an account of profits.[26] This can be contrasted with the remedies available for tortious wrongdoing. For certain torts exemplary damages can be awarded to punish the defendant for cynical wrongdoing.[27] Furthermore, restitutionary damages are sometimes available, most notably for actions in trespass,[28] and for passing off.[29] If the procuring of a breach of contract really is as deserving of liability as the procuring of an actionable tort then it is arguable that more far-reaching remedies are required for breach of contract. However, further comment on this is unnecessary at this stage since Erle J did not even consider the issue explicitly. It will be returned to in later analysis when comparing the remedies available in tort with the obligations imposed on contracting parties by the law of contract.

The defence counsel in *Lumley v Gye* also submitted the argument that extension of the third party tort was unnecessary because the plaintiff had recourse against Miss Wagner for breach of contract.[30] Erle J dismissed this argument because there was no certainty that the remedy on the contract would provide adequate damages. He gave several examples of such circumstances. First, the measure of damages could be restricted. Secondly, the creditor could become bankrupt. Thirdly, the damages awarded against the defendant may not take account of consequential losses caused by the plaintiff's having to miss deadlines and breach contracts with other people. Under these circumstances Erle J believed that 'he who procures the damage maliciously might justly be made responsible beyond the liability of the contractor'.[31]

---

25 *Johnson v Agnew* [1980] AC 367, 400. See also Viscount Haldane LC in *British Westinghouse Electric and Manufacturing Co Ltd v Underground Electric Railways Co of London Ltd* [1912] AC 673, 689. It is also the general position accepted by the Law Commission in its Consultation Paper No 132, *Aggravated, Exemplary and Restitutionary Damages*, 1993 at 159, para 7.7.

26 [2000] 3 WLR 625, 638–42 (Lord Nicholls).

27 *Rookes v Barnard* [1964] AC 1129.

28 *Penarth Dock Engineering Co Ltd v Pounds* [1963] 1 Lloyd's Rep 359; *Bracewell v Appleby* [1975] Ch 408.

29 *My Kinda Town Ltd v Soll and Grunts Investments* [1982] FSR 147 (Ch D); [1983] RPC 407 (CA).

30 In fact a separate action was taken: *Lumley v Wagner* (1852) 1 De GM & G 604.

31 (1853) 2 E & B 216, 234.

The suggestion that the procurer of a breach of contract might justly be made responsible beyond the liability of the contractor is subject to much criticism. It seems perverse that third parties are made subject to more extensive remedial obligations than are the contractors themselves. Parties to a contract are bound by it in a way that third parties are not and surely this necessitates more extensive liability for contracting parties than for third parties. It is also noteworthy that the examples given by Erle J of inadequate contractual damages are all of the plaintiff's own doing. Howarth has pointed out that restrictions on the level of damages in the contract action must have been agreed upon by the plaintiff.[32] The risk of the deal putting the plaintiff into bankruptcy is also the plaintiff's own fault and the lack of an action for consequential damages is a matter for negotiation with the third party.[33] The fact that the examples of inadequacy of damages are all of the plaintiff's own doing undermines Erle J's reasoning on why the plaintiff needs a remedy against the inducer in addition to his remedy in contract.

The decision in *Lumley v Gye* is subject to a great number of criticisms and the grounds for doubting the decision are still valid today. However, the decision of Erle J was later confirmed by the House of Lords in *Allen v Flood*.[34]

Further developments in the tort

Following the decision in *Lumley v Gye*, the tort of inducing breach of contract has been developed by the courts.

Intention

It is clear that, for the *Lumley v Gye* tort to be established, the defendant must have intended to interfere with the plaintiff's contractual rights.[35] Compton J, in *Lumley v Gye*, spoke of the defendant 'maliciously' procuring a party to breach its contract of personal service with the plaintiff.[36] The requirement of malice does not necessitate ill-will or an illegitimate motive behind the defendant's actions.[37] It merely implies that the defendant must have knowledge of the contract.[38] The

32 But see Robertson, A, 'On the Distinction between Contract and Tort', Chapter 6 of this volume. Robertson questions the realism of expecting contracting parties to negotiate around default rules.

33 Howarth, D, *Textbook on Tort Law*, London: Butterworths, 1995, 475.

34 [1898] AC 1.

35 See Markesinis, BS and Deakin, SF, *Tort Law*, Oxford: Clarendon, 4th edn, 1999, 471–74; Howarth, above n 33, 479–84. Contrast the approach of the Californian Supreme Court: *J'Aire v Gregory*, 24 Cal 3d 799, 598 P 2d 60, 157 Cal Rptr 407 (1979). See comments on non-uniformity of US law in Dowling, D, 'A Contract Theory for a Complex Tort: Limiting Interference with Contract Beyond the Unlawful Means Test' (1987) 40 Miami LR 487, 519.

36 (1853) 2 E & B 216, 231.

37 *Quinn v Leathem* [1901] AC 495, 510 (Lord MacNaghten).

38 *Stratford v Lindley* [1965] AC 269. Recklessness is not sufficient (*Cattle v Stockton Waterworks Co* (1875) LR 10 QB 453), although recklessness as to consequences is sufficient if the defendant knowingly creates a risk and is indifferent as to whether or not the breach happens (*Torquay Hotel Co Ltd v Cousins* [1969] 2 Ch 106).

nature of the intention required for the tort is a matter of some controversy. Weir has suggested that the defendant must be shown to have intended to harm the claimant.[39] Such a requirement of intention to harm has also been recognised by the High Court of Australia.[40]

Howarth has argued that a clear line should be drawn between the defendant who merely intends the act that causes a breach of contract, and the defendant who intends and wants the contract to be broken.[41] This would mean that merely assisting the breach would not give rise to tortious liability. The issue was considered by the Court of Appeal in *Millar v Bassey*.[42] The case concerned the singer Shirley Bassey who was sued by the plaintiffs on the grounds that, by deliberately breaching her contract with her record company Dreampeace, she had made it impossible for Dreampeace to perform their contract with the plaintiffs. It was alleged that Shirley Bassey knew about the contract made with the plaintiffs and was aware that her own breach of contract with Dreampeace would have caused their contract with the plaintiffs to be broken. At first instance the claim was struck out as disclosing no cause of action. However, the decision was reversed in the Court of Appeal and the plaintiffs were allowed to proceed in their claim.

Beldam LJ delivered the judgment that most clearly supported liability in such cases. He declared that he found 'difficulty in understanding the distinction drawn between "inducing and causing" Dreampeace to break its contracts with the appellant and "procuring" those breaches'.[43] For him: 'if it is actionable to cause loss to the plaintiff by enticing or persuading another to break his contract with the plaintiff, can it be said to be inarguable that it is actionable to cause such loss by voluntarily and deliberately refusing to perform a contract knowing that such refusal will make it impossible for the other party to fulfil his obligations to the plaintiff? I do not think so.'[44]

Beldam LJ suggested the recognition of a very expansive basis for liability which would severely restrict liberty to trade.[45] Inevitably, such liability would make commercial parties highly reluctant to breach their own contracts for fear of inducing the breach of another contract. This presents a bizarre situation in which contracting parties are deterred from breaking their own contracts, not because of remedies available in contract law, but because of the risk of tortious actions by third parties.

The inconsistency of remedies in English contract law is clear from this analysis. It is absurd that the performance interest of contracts is better protected

---

39 Weir, T, *Economic Torts*, Oxford: Clarendon, 1997, 14.

40 *Northern Territory of Australia v Mengel* (1997) 185 CLR 307, 342.

41 See Howarth, above n 33, 479–84. Also see Weir, above n 39, 35–42.

42 [1994] EMLR 44.

43 *Ibid*, 49–50.

44 *Ibid*, 55.

45 See comments of Peter Gibson LJ: [1994] EMLR 44, 64. Also see Carty, H, *An Analysis of the Economic Torts*, Oxford: OUP, 2001, 52–53; Sales, P and Stilitz, D, 'Intentional Infliction of Harm by Unlawful Means' (1999) 115 LQR 411, 434; Fleming, JG, *The Law of Torts*, Sydney: LBC, 9th edn, 1988, 761–62; Cane, P, *Tort Law and Economic Interests*, Oxford: Clarendon, 2nd edn, 1996, 119–20.

by third party tortious actions for indirect interference than by first party contractual actions. There is no reason in logic or law why the performance interest of contracts should be protected against interference from third parties but not protected from interference by the contracting parties themselves. It is submitted that the protection offered to the performance interest of contracts by the third party tort demonstrates the sanctity of the performance of contracts in English law. However, to maintain consistency throughout the law it is surely necessary for the performance interest to be better protected from interference by the contracting parties.

'Indirect' Interference with contract

The general tendency of the courts has been to extend the remit of the tort since *Allen v Flood*. The tort has been significantly extended in terms of what constitutes an inducement to breach the contract. In *Lumley v Gye* the defendant persuaded the contracting party to breach her contract with the plaintiff. The persuasion was a direct inducement to breach the contract. However, in subsequent cases it became apparent that there was liability for 'indirect' inducement to breach contracts.[46]

The first significant case on 'indirect' inducement to breach a contract was *DC Thomson & Co Ltd v Deakin*.[47] In that case the defendant union objected to Thomsons' refusal to employ union labour. The union had no members employed at Thomsons. Therefore, they operated a scheme of 'blacking'. This involved them instructing their members who worked for one of Thomsons' major suppliers, Bowaters, to refuse to work on contracts with the plaintiff. Bowaters ceased to supply the plaintiff, which caused them great difficulties. The Court of Appeal decided in favour of the defendants, but this was only because the employees had not breached their contracts with Bowaters since they had never asked the employees to work on contracts for the plaintiff. Thus the requirement that unlawful means be used was not established.[48]

The development of the tort of interference with contractual performance is a significant sign of the court's willingness to protect contractual performance. A defendant can now be liable for the tort without having directly interfered with the contract in question and without even breaching a supply contract. Furthermore, it now seems that once the tort of interference with contractual performance is established, either party to the contract can bring an action without it necessarily being the person against whom the defendant was

46 The development of the tort to include indirect interference with contract has been criticised by Carty, above n 45. She argues, at 80–84, that indirect interference with contracts should be subsumed within the more recently acknowledged tort of unlawful interference with trade.

47 [1952] Ch 646.

48 See *JT Stanford & Son Ltd v Lindley* [1965] AC 269, where it was held that a union instruction which induced its members to breach their employment contracts was sufficient to constitute unlawful means for the tort of indirect interference. Also see *Mekur Island Shipping v Laughton* [1983] 2 AC 570; *Wooley v Dunford* (1972) 3 SASR 243. See also Sales and Stilitz, above n 45, 434.

aiming.[49] These cases are completely inconsistent with the efficient breach theory of contract. Indeed, the cases demonstrate that contracts cannot be regarded merely as disjunctive obligations. The efficient breach theory demands the facilitation of breaches of inefficient contracts. The tort of interference with contractual performance does not provide such facilitation. Instead it demands compensation from any third party who aims to promote economic efficiency by inducing a breach of contract. The tort can thus be seen as an expression of the court's willingness to protect the performance interest of contracts by using remedies to supplement ordinary contractual damages.

Justification

The common law recognises a limited justification defence for the tort of inducing breach of contract. However, it is not possible to lay down any general rule as to the nature of this defence.[50] The writers of *Clerk & Lindsell on Torts* have noted that the defence appears to be limited to the 'fulfilment of a "moral duty" which appeals to the "good sense of the tribunal"'.[51] Heydon also suggests that the plaintiff can rely on some private interest such as an interest in the liberty to trade. However, he notes that this will almost always be outweighed by the plaintiff's contractual rights unless it can be coupled with some public interest.[52] It is no justification to demonstrate that an association has only sought to pursue its duty of improving the wages of its members,[53] or of preventing breaches of industrial agreements.[54]

The availability of the justification defence in English law is highly restricted. A more liberal interpretation of the defence has been taken by the courts in other Commonwealth jurisdictions.[55] However, the restrictions placed on the defence in

---

49 See *Falconer v Aslef* [1986] IRLR 331.

50 *Glamorgan Coal Co v South West Miners' Federation* [1903] 2 KB 545, 574–75 (Romer LJ). Romer LJ did however provide what he described as a frequently approved test for justification: '... regard might be had to the nature of the contract broken; the position of the parties to the contract; the grounds for the breach; the means employed to procure the breach; the relation of the person procuring the breach to the person who breaks the contract; and to the object of the person in procuring the breach.' This test was approved in *British Industrial Plastics v Ferguson* [1938] 4 All ER 479, 510; *Grieg v Insole* [1978] 1 WLR 302, 340–41. Also see Heydon, JD, *Economic Torts*, London: Sweet & Maxwell, 2nd edn, 1978, 38; Heydon, JD, 'Defence of Justification in Cases of Intentionally Caused Economic Loss' (1970) 20 U Tor LJ 139, 161–71.

51 Brazier, MR (ed), *Clerk & Lindsell on Torts*, London: Sweet & Maxwell, 17th edn, 1995, 23–37, citing *Glamorgan Coal Co v South West Miners' Federation* [1903] 2 KB 545, 574 (Romer LJ). Also see *Pritchard v Briggs* [1980] Ch 388, 416–17 (Goff LJ); Dobbs, D, 'Tortious Interference with Contractual Relationships' (1980) 43 Ark LR 335, 343.

52 Heydon, above n 50, 46. See *Grieg v Insole* [1978] 1 WLR 302, 333. See *US Knupp v Bell* (1966) 58 DLR (2d) 256.

53 *South Wales Miners' Federation v Glamorgan Coal Co* [1905] AC 239.

54 See *Read v Friendly Society of Operative Stonemasons* [1902] KB 88; *Smithies v National Association of Operative Plasterers* [1909] 1 KB 310, 337.

55 Compare the New Zealand case of *Pete's Towing Services Ltd v Northern Industrial Union of Workers* [1970] NZLR 32, 48–51; in Australia *Latham v Singleton* (1981) 2 NSWLR 843; *Building Workers Industrial Union v Odco* [1991] 29 FCR 104. A more traditional approach is taken in Canada: *Posluns v Toronto Stock Exchange* (1968) 67 DLR (2d) 165; *Pacific Western Airlines v British Columbia Fedn of Labour* (1986) 26 DLR (4th) 87, 91–92.

English law demonstrate that the English courts view the contracting party's interest in performance and the public interest in security of transactions as more important than an interest in liberty to trade.[56] This is very important. If the party's interest in performance is viewed as being more important than liberty of trade as between contracting parties and third parties why is it not also more important between the contracting parties themselves?

The impact of the tort

The tort has undoubtedly had a significant impact on the law of obligations. Several specific implications can be highlighted.

Protection of the performance interest

The tort of inducing breach of contract has a significant role to play in protecting the performance interest of contracts. The notion of a performance interest has been well defined by Professor Coote. He writes: '... what distinguishes an effective contractual promise from any other is that it is intended to, and does in fact, confer on the promisee an enforceable legal right to have the promise performed.'[57] Accordingly, performance of the action promised is what the promisee ought to be entitled to receive. If that is not received the promisee is entitled to claim damages that provide an adequate substitute for performance.

To understand the decision in *Lumley v Gye* it is important to know the background to the case. In Professor Waddams' excellent article on the case he draws attention to a similar dispute which arose four years earlier.[58] A famous opera singer, Lind, had been tempted away from her contract with a Drury Lane theatre and had gone to sing at Lumley's theatre. The Drury Lane theatre brought an action for damages against Lind which led to a jury award of £2,500.[59] Lumley escaped any action and made a very handsome profit out of the deal, even after indemnifying Lind and paying her fee.[60] *Lumley v Gye* was heard against the background of the *Lind* case which showed that contracts were inadequately protected against cynical breaches induced by third parties.

Of course this cynical disregard for the performance interest of contracts would have raised no problems for the efficient breach theorists. Holmes and Posner both contend that the duty to perform a contract is imaginary.[61] However, the position of the Court of Queen's Bench in *Lumley v Gye* was quite different. Erle J declared that: 'He who maliciously procures a damage to another by

---

56 Heydon, *Economic Torts*, above n 50, 46.

57 Coote, B, 'The Performance Interest, *Panatown*, and the Problem of Loss' (2001) 117 LQR 81. See also Friedmann, D, 'The Performance Interest in Contract Damages' (1995) 111 LQR 628; Coote, B, 'Contract Damages, *Ruxley*, and the Performance Interest' [1997] CLJ 537, 540–43.

58 Waddams, SM, 'Johanna Wagner and the Rival Opera Houses' (2001) 117 LQR 431.

59 *The Times*, (1848) February 23, 8b.

60 Waddams, above n 58, 433.

61 See above n 1.

violation of his right ought to be made to indemnify, and that whether he procures an actionable wrong or a breach of contract.'[62] In this context, Erle J clearly viewed performance of the contract as a right belonging to the plaintiff.[63] If this wasn't his understanding then his comments make no sense because the plaintiff has not been deprived of anything other than performance of the contract. Lumley still had recourse against Miss Wagner on the contract and he brought a separate action for this.[64] Therefore, the only right which required indemnification from a third party was the right to performance, a right which the efficient breach theorists deny exists.

Erle J held that the third party tort was necessary because there was no certainty that the remedy on the contract would provide adequate damages.[65] The real problem, as the *Lind* case identified, is that compensatory damages do not always provide adequate protection to the performance interest of contracts. This has recently been recognised in a number of cases including *Attorney-General v Blake*,[66] and *Alfred MacAlpine Construction Ltd v Panatown Ltd*.[67] It is submitted that the right to performance of a contract is a right worthy of protection because of the commercial desirability of preserving the security of transactions.[68] One of the central functions of contractual damages is to promote and facilitate security of transactions. This is because contracts are of benefit to society in allowing individuals to submit their own will to the will of others, thus allowing them to benefit from co-ordination and constructive action.[69] The law of contract provides a facilitative institution for this practice.[70] Without security of transactions, contracting parties are not able to plan their future commercial activity. As a result, commercial activity is stifled, with significant social and economic repercussions. Far from being economically inefficient, protection of the performance interest of contracts by means of the tort promotes economic

---

62 (1853) 2 E & B 216, 233.

63 Also see *Hill v Van Erp* (1995) 188 CLR 159, 197, where Gaudron J said that the tort of interference with contractual rights: 'is no different from trespass, conversion, detinue and slander of title which, as I pointed out in *Hawkins v Clayton* (1988) 164 CLR 539, 594, are directly concerned with the protection of legal rights'.

64 *Lumley v Wagner* (1852) 1 De GM & G 604.

65 (1853) 2 E & B 216, 234.

66 [2000] 3 WLR 625, 638 (Lord Nicholls). See also *Experience Hendrix LLC v PPX Enterprises Inc Edward Chalpin* [2003] EWCA Civ 323, [20] (Mance LJ), [53] (Peter Gibson LJ).

67 [2000] 3 WLR 946, 971 (Lord Goff), 1016 (Lord Millett). See Coote, above n 57; Loke, AFH, 'Damages to Protect the Performance Interest and the Reasonableness Requirement' [2001] Singapore Jnl Leg Stud 259.

68 Bagshaw, R, 'Inducing Breach of Contract', in Horder, J (ed), *Oxford Essays in Jurisprudence*, Oxford: OUP, 4th series, 2000, 134 argues that 'the protection of contracts against third parties increases the security of contracts, and by thus making it easier for a party to rely on his or her contract assists the institution in extending the range of choices' open to human beings.

69 See Fried, C, *Contract as Promise*, Cambridge, MA: Harvard UP, 1981, 7; Finnis, J, *Natural Law and Natural Rights*, Oxford: Clarendon, 1980, 325; Raz, J, 'Promises in Morality and Law' (1981) 95 Harv LR 916, 933; Danforth, J, 'Tortious Interference with Contract: A Reassertion of Society's Interest in Commercial Stability and Contractual Integrity' (1981) 81 Col LR 1491, 1509 and 1511–14.

70 See Jackman, I, 'Restitution for Wrongs' [1989] CLJ 302, 318–21; Friedmann, D, 'The Efficient Breach Fallacy' (1989) 18 LS 1, 7–8.

efficiency by providing stability to economic markets and by minimising transaction costs involved in contractual breach.[71]

Recognition of a right in rem

It is clear that the performance interest of contracts is an interest worthy of protection but this, in itself, tells us little about the nature of that interest. Some judges and academics have asserted that there were no proprietary rights involved in *Lumley v Gye*.[72] However, it is important to note that the right recognised in *Lumley* appeared to be a right *in rem* – a right good against the world. Anson, writing in 1879, recognised this and doubted the correctness of the decision for that very reason.[73] As a right *in rem*, the right resembles a property right, and may give rise to the special protection of restitutionary damages. This will be considered in greater detail in the second part of this chapter.

Inconsistent remedial responses

As has been noted in the preceding analysis of the tort, protection of the performance interest of contracts has been provided by a tortious remedy against a third party rather than by improved remedies for breach of contract. Indeed, the tort of inducing breach of contract has been incrementally extended far beyond its roots and now provides a general remedy against third parties who intentionally induce breaches of contract.[74] Although it is clear that the performance interest of contracts requires better protection, it is questionable whether the best solution is to provide recovery against third parties. As Cane has recognised, while 'popular morality no doubt supports liability for breach of contract, it is less clear that it supports liability for persuasion of breach of contract by conduct which is not independently unlawful'.[75]

The position appears even more perverse when it is realised that third parties are subject to more extensive liability in tort than are the parties themselves in contract. The contract rules of remoteness do not apply to the tort. In contract, the rule in *Hadley v Baxendale* requires that the loss be 'within the reasonable contemplation of the parties' at the time of contracting.[76] The rule in tort is much less strict; loss need only be 'reasonably foreseeable' at the time of breach.[77] Although attempts have been made to suggest that the rules of remoteness are the

---

71 McChesney, F, 'Tortious Interference with Contract versus "Efficient" Breach: Theory and Empirical Evidence' (1999) 28 Jnl Leg Stud 131, 143–59.

72 See Cane, above n 45, 124; *Perre v Apand Pty Ltd* (1999) 198 CLR 180, 245 (Gummow J).

73 Anson, WR, *Principles of the English Law of Contract*, Oxford: Clarendon, 1879, 199.

74 For criticism of this extension see Weir, above n 39, 41; Carty, above n 45, 85; Dobbs, D, 'Tortious Interference with Contractual Relationships' (1980) 34 Ark LR 335, 376.

75 Cane, above n 24, 150.

76 (1854) 9 EX 341, 355 (Alderson B). See also *Victoria Laundry (Windsor) Ltd v Newman Industries & Co Ltd* [1949] 2 KB 528; *Koufos v Czarnikow Ltd* [1969] 1 AC 350, 386 (Lord Reid), 413 (Lord Pearce), 423 (Lord Upjohn).

77 *Overseas Tankship (UK) Ltd v Morts Dock and Engineering Co Ltd, The Wagon Mound (No 1)* [1961] AC 388.

same in contract and tort when the damage claimed is economic loss, the issue remains uncertain.[78] Furthermore, even less stringent tests for remoteness are applied to intentional torts. The remoteness rule for deceit is that all the losses directly flowing from the wrong are recoverable.[79] It is unclear which test is applied to the tort of inducing breach of contract. American law favours recovery of all losses directly flowing from the tort.[80] By analogy with the law on deceit this may be the appropriate test in England. Whether the test for remoteness be that of 'reasonable foreseeability' or that of 'direct consequences' it is apparent that the damages recoverable may be greater than in contract.

Furthermore, when awarding damages for the tort of inducing breach of contract the court is not restricted to awarding only the expectation interest. It is arguable that restitutionary damages may be available for the tort of inducing breach of contract.[81] This will be considered later in the chapter. However, at this point it is sufficient to state that it is incongruous for such remedies to be available against third parties when they are not available against the contracting parties themselves.[82] Finally, it appears inconsistent that the right to performance of a contract is a right akin to a proprietary right against third parties but not a right akin to a proprietary right between the contracting parties themselves.

CONTRACT RIGHTS AS PROPERTY RIGHTS

Following the recognition of a right akin to a proprietary right in *Lumley v Gye* it has been suggested that contract rights are a form of property. The problem with assessing the accuracy of such an assertion is that 'property' is an illusive concept which is neither self-explanatory nor clearly defined. Indeed, Kevin Gray in his seminal article titled 'Property in Thin Air' argues that: 'Perhaps more accurately than any other legal notion it was "property" which deserves the Benthamite epithet, "the rhetorical nonsense – nonsense upon stilts".'[83]

For Gray, a resource can be propertised only if it is 'excludable'.[84] The owner of the resource must be able to exercise regulatory control over the access of

---

78 *Parsons (Livestock) Ltd v Uttley Ingham & Co Ltd* [1978] QB 791, 801–03 (Lord Denning MR), 806 (Scarman LJ); *The Commonwealth v Amann Aviation Pty Ltd* (1991) 174 CLR 64, 116 (Deane J). See Edelman, J, 'The Meaning of "Damages": Common Law and Equity', Chapter 3 of this volume; Tilbury, M, 'Remedies and the Classification of Obligations', Chapter 2 of this volume.

79 *Doyle v Olby (Ironmongers) Ltd* [1969] 2 QB 158, 167 (Lord Denning MR); *Smith New Court Securities Ltd v Scrimgeour Vickers (Asset Management) Ltd* [1996] 4 All ER 769, 777 (Lord Browne-Wilkinson), 791–92 (Lord Steyn).

80 *Vaught v Jonathan L Pettyjohn & Co* 1919, 104 Kan 174, 178 O 623; *Martin v Sterkx* 1920, 146 La 489, 83 So 776. See Keeton, WP, *Prosser & Keeton on Torts*, St Paul, MN: West Group, 5th edn, 1984, 1003.

81 *Federal Sugar Refining Co v United States Sugar Equalisation Board* 268 F 575 (1920) (SDNY). See further below.

82 See Jackman, I, *The Varieties of Restitution*, Leichhardt, NSW: Federation Press, 1998, 119.

83 Gray, K, 'Property in Thin Air' [1991] CLJ 252, 305. Also see Dowling, D, 'General Proposition and Concrete Cases: The Search for a Standard in the Conflict between Individual Property Rights and the Social Interest' (1985) 1 J Land Use & Envtl L 353, 358–65.

84 Also see Weinrib, above n 6.

strangers to the benefits inherent in the resource.[85] Something similar to the requirement of excludability was recognised by the High Court of Australia in refusing to classify a grazing licence as property. In *R v Toohey ex p Meneling*,[86] Mason J considered the speech of Lord Wilberforce in *National Provincial Bank Ltd v Ainsworth*.[87] He noted that a degree of permanence and stability is required before a right can be admitted to the category of property. This was not present on the facts of *Toohey* because the grazing licence was terminable at will by the Crown. Therefore, it was the Crown who could exclude access to the grazing rights not the holder of the licence. As such the licence did not constitute property in the hands of the licence holders. However, ordinary contracts do possess characteristics of excludability. The tort of inducing breach of contract demonstrates this as do specific remedies for breach of contract. As Gray notes, 'the test of excludability throws into severe doubt the validity of any sharp dichotomy between contract and property'.[88]

Since the creation of the tort of inducing breach of contract, the identification of contract rights as property rights has become popular amongst academics[89] and the courts, particularly in the United States. This has led to the development of theories contending that restitutionary damages should be awarded for breach of contract. One such theory, expounded by Daniel Friedmann,[90] will be analysed in greater depth below. Before embarking on this analysis it is necessary to consider how the courts have understood the nature of contractual rights.

The US approach

The courts in the United States began to treat contract rights as property rights following the decision in *Lumley v Gye*.[91] Initially the American courts were very reluctant to recognise the tort of inducing breach of contract. The decision in *Lumley v Gye* was rejected by many State courts because it enabled recovery for interference with contractual relations other than that of master and servant.[92] However, most of these decisions have been subsequently overruled,[93] and the

---

85 [1991] CLJ 252, 268.

86 (1982) 158 CLR 327, 342–43.

87 [1965] AC 1175, 1247–48.

88 Gray, above n 83, 302.

89 See Smith, S, 'Towards a Theory of Contract', in Horder, J (ed), *Oxford Essays in Jurisprudence*, Oxford: OUP, 4th series, 2000, 123; Bagshaw, above n 68, 137; Epstein, RA, 'Inducement of Breach of Contract as a Problem of Ostensible Ownership' (1987) 16 Jnl Leg Stud 1; McChesney, above n 71.

90 Above n 4.

91 Keeton, above n 80, 978–1004. Also see Dobbs, DB, *Law of Remedies*, St Paul, MN: West Group, 2nd edn, 1993, vol 3, 170–78; Danforth, J, 'Tortious Interference with Contract: A Reassertion of Society's Interest in Commercial Stability and Contractual Integrity' (1981) 81 Col LR 1491, 1500–08.

92 See, eg: *Boyson v Thorn*, 98 Cal 578, 33 P 492 (1893); *Glencoe Sand and Gravel Co v Hudson Bros Commission Co*, 138 Mo 439, 40 SW 93 (1897); *Swain v Johnson*, 151 NC 93, 65 SE 619 (1909).

93 See *Imperial Ice Co v Rossier*, 18 Cal 2d 33, 112 P 2d 631 (1941); *Downey v United Weatherproofing Co*, 1953, 363 Mo 852, 253 SW 2d 976; *Bryant v Barber*, 237 NC 480, 75 SE 2d 410 (1953).

tort is now recognised almost everywhere in the US. Prosser remarks that, since *Lumley v Gye*, the US courts have 'laid emphasis upon the existence of the contract, as something in the nature of a property interest in the plaintiff or a right *in rem* good against the world'.[94] The significant factor about the decision in *Lumley v Gye* was that a contractual right, which is a form of personal right, was enforced against a third party. It is a basic tenet of private law that personal obligations create rights *in personam*, that is, rights against an individual person or a group of persons. However, in *Lumley v Gye*, a personal right was enforced against a party outside of the contractual relationship. This was the enforcement of a right *in rem* – a right good against the whole world.

As Charles Carpenter notes, the authorities 'have been wont to call it a property right'.[95] This can be seen in the Texan case of *Raymond v Yarrington*,[96] where the court declared that: 'It seems to us that where a party has entered into a contract with another to do or not to do a particular act or acts, he has as clear a right to its performance as he has to his property, either real or personal; and that knowingly to induce the other party to violate it is as distinct a wrong as it is to injure or destroy his property.' Likewise the District Court in North Carolina has asserted that contract rights are property rights. In the case of *Munchak Corp v Riko Enterprises*,[97] it was held that a contract between a North Carolina corporation and a professional basketball player was a property right.[98]

The US courts have also allowed the recovery of restitutionary damages in an action for money had and received as a result of the tort of inducing a breach of contract. In *Federal Sugar Refining Co v United States Sugar Equalisation Board*,[99] the plaintiff had contracted to sell a quantity of sugar to the Norwegian Government. It was alleged that the defendant induced the Norwegian Government to repudiate its contract with the plaintiffs and buy the same quantity of sugar from them at a higher price. The defendants were able to do this because they were the only authority with the power to issue licences for the export of sugar from the United States. The plaintiff sought to recover the profit made by the defendant and this claim was upheld by the court. Judge Meyer said: 'The action is not for damages for breach of contract, but for the profit which the defendant is alleged to have made as the result of its alleged wrongful acts.'[100]

The English approach

The above cases all provide support for the proposition that a promisee's interest under a contract is a property interest potentially yielding restitutionary damages

94 Keeton, above n 80, 981.

95 Carpenter, CE, 'Interference with Contractual Relations' (1928) 41 Harv LR 728, 733.

96 96 Tex 443; 72 SW 580; 73 SW 800 (1903).

97 368 F Supp 1366 (MDNC, 1973).

98 Following the decision in *Carolina Overall Corp v East Carolina Linen Supply Inc*, 8 NC App 528; 174 SE 2d 659 (1970). Also see *SC Posner Co v Jackson*, 233 NY 325; 119 NE 573 (1918), where the New York Court of Appeals held that a contract with a premier dress designer was a property right; *Goldman v Harford Road Building Association*, 150 Md 677; 133 A 843 (1926).

99 268 F 575 (SDNY, 1920).

100 *Ibid*, 583.

where a breach is induced by a third party. However, the cases and opinions are mostly from the US and there is far less English authority for the proposition. Indeed, Jackman has opined that, in English law, a contractual interest is not a property interest.[101]

Jackman's theory declares that restitutionary damages should be used to disgorge the defendant's gain in order to protect people from both institutional and personal harm. To this end, restitutionary damages are justified for the protection of the facilitative institutions of property, relationships of trust, and confidence. Jackman believes that restitutionary damages should not be available for breaches of contract because the facilitative institution of contract already receives adequate protection from compensatory damages.[102] In recommending this, Jackman is ostensibly distinguishing the protection of property rights from the protection of contractual rights.

However, the English cases regarding the tort of inducing breach of contract present a major obstacle to Jackman's theory. It was noted earlier that, in *Lumley v Gye*, Erle J viewed performance of the contract as a right belonging to the plaintiff. The language used by the learned judge certainly suggests that the institution of contract is as deserving of protection by tortious and restitutionary remedies as the institution of property. Bagshaw has recently sought to use the justifications for the protection of private property as reasons for defending the *Lumley v Gye* tort.[103] He contends that the same reasons for protecting property interests apply to protecting contract interests from third parties. In other words, contract interests are as deserving of protection as property interests.

The 19th century case of *Lightly v Clouston*[104] also presents a difficulty for Jackman.[105] In that case it was held that the plaintiff was entitled to waive his action for the tort of seduction by inducing the plaintiff's employee to break his contract of service. The plaintiff was allowed to bring a restitutionary action of *indebitatus assumpsit* for work and labour done by his apprentice against the person who tortiously employed him. Jackman notes that *Lightly v Clouston* predates *Lumley v Gye* and suggests that this case was an 'illegitimate extension of the doctrine'.[106] Although the doctrine of waiver of tort has been criticised,[107] Goff and Jones suggest that, following the US case of *Federal Sugar Refining Co*,

---

101 'Restitution for Wrongs' [1989] CLJ 302. This approach was subsequently followed by Burrows, A, *The Law of Restitution*, London: Butterworths, 1993, 403 (however, following *Attorney-General v Blake*, this support was excised from Burrows, A, *The Law of Restitution*, London: Butterworths, 2nd edn, 2002, 486).

102 [1989] CLJ 302, 320.

103 Bagshaw, above n 68, 134.

104 (1808) 1 Taunt 112. See also *Foster v Stewart* (1814) 3 M & S 192.

105 [1989] CLJ 302, 310.

106 [1989] CLJ 302, 311. See also Winfield, PH, *The Law of Quasi-Contracts*, London: Sweet & Maxwell, 1952, 98–100; Salmond, JW, *The Law of Torts*, London: Stevens & Haynes, 3rd edn, 1912, 145–46.

107 See Hedley, S, 'The Myth of "Waiver of Tort"' (1984) 100 LQR 653, 676–78; Goff (Lord Goff of Chievely) and Jones, G, *The Law of Restitution*, London: Sweet & Maxwell, 5th edn, 1998, 775–78; *Hospitality Group Pty Ltd v Australian Rugby Union Ltd* [2001] 110 FCR 157, 198 (Emmett J).

restitutionary damages for the tort of inducing breach of contract might be available.[108] Indeed, such a view has recently been supported by Emmett J in the Federal Court of Australia in *Hospitality Group v Australian Rugby Union*.[109] Further support for the availability of restitutionary damages is provided by the recent analogies that have been drawn by the House of Lords between the tort of inducing breach of contract and liability in equity for dishonest assistance.[110] The remedies for dishonest assistance are compensation and an account of profits. By analogy it could be argued that restitutionary damages should be available for the tort of inducing breach of contract.

Despite disapproving of the decision in *Lightly v Clouston*, Jackman conceded that possibly 'contract, like property, is a type of facilitative institution, and it may be that tort has a role to play in providing institutional protection for contracts, as well as for property, at least where the interference with contractual relations was deliberately acquisitive'.[111] In other words, despite his contention that contract rights are not property rights he argues that they may be deserving of further institutional protection. If it is admitted that contracts are deserving of protection through a tortious action there seems to be no logical reason why the claimant cannot elect through waiver of tort to seek restitutionary damages rather than pursue a compensatory claim. In summary, Jackman claims that contract rights can be distinguished from property rights and, as such, restitutionary remedies are not required for the infringement of contractual rights. However, his admission that contract rights may require the protection of tort is significant and will be returned to later in this chapter.

It is submitted that, although Jackman is correct in asserting that there is little English authority for equating contract rights with property rights, some authority does exist. The cases of *Lumley v Gye* and *Lightly v Clouston* have already been discussed.[112] More recently, Steyn LJ remarked in *Surrey County Council v Bredero Homes* that there was scope for further development in the law of restitution for invasion of 'property rights'.[113] It was his opinion that the word 'property' in this context should be interpreted in a wide sense. Indeed, if we are considering property in a wide sense then it is utterly uncontroversial to speak of contract rights as property rights. In *Foskett v McKeown* the House of Lords

---

108 Goff and Jones, 780.

109 [2001] 110 FCR 157, 198–99.

110 *Royal Brunei Airlines Sdn Bhd v Philip Tan Kok Ming* [1995] 2 AC 378, 387 (Lord Nicholls); *Twinsectra Ltd v Yardley* [2002] 2 WLR 802, 838–39 (Lord Millett).

111 Jackman's recommendation that tortious recovery should only be permitted when the interference with contractual relations is 'deliberately acquisitive' is open to objection. In the past it has never been considered relevant to ask whether the defendant's breach was cynical (see *Surrey CC v Bredero Homes* [1993] 3 All ER 705, 715). Furthermore, as Burrows, A and McKendrick, E, *Cases and Materials on the Law of Restitution*, Oxford: OUP, 1997, 402 remark, there is an acute practical difficulty in drawing the line between cynical and non-cynical breaches of contract. It should be noted that Jackman's position has since become even more restrictive. This sentence has been excised from his reproduction of the article in *The Varieties of Restitution*, above n 82, 119.

112 *Lumley v Gye* (1853) 2 E & B 216; *Lightly v Clouston* (1808) 1 Taunt 112; *Foster v Stewart* (1814) 3 M & S 192.

113 [1993] 3 All ER 705, 715.

recognised that an insurance policy was a bundle of contractual rights which constituted a chose in action.[114] As such it may be argued that English law does recognise contractual rights as a form of property in its wide sense.

Friedmann's theory

Having recognised that there is the potential for the recognition of contract rights as property rights it is necessary to consider whether Friedmann's theory could be usefully applied. For Friedmann, 'contract interests may give rise to interests that come within the ambit of "property" for purposes of restitution'.[115] On the face of it Friedmann's thesis is very attractive. It is well established that restitutionary damages are available for interferences with property rights.[116] Therefore, if contract rights could be equated with property rights, restitutionary damages could be available for breaches of contract on the basis that such a breach is an infringement of a proprietary interest.[117] This might provide much needed protection to the performance interest of contracts.

Despite the attraction of Friedmann's theory it is not wholly convincing. An immediate problem with the theory is that it appears to contradict the very authority that Friedmann uses for equating contract rights with property rights. Friedmann lists six illustrations and considers whether the plaintiff in each illustration should be permitted to make a restitutionary recovery. His general rule is that the defendant's profit should be disgorged if the profits are made directly by the misappropriation of a property/contract right belonging to the plaintiff. However, in illustration three, Friedmann opines that restitutionary damages should not be awarded.[118] This illustration involves an employee who, in breach of contract, leaves his employer to work for another employer at a higher salary. Friedmann recommends that restitutionary damages should not be awarded against the employee in such circumstances because such a claim might force him back to his former employer. For Friedmann, recognition of 'such claims would create undesirable impediments to social and economic mobility'.[119]

However, the cases on which Friedmann bases his theory are cases concerning employer/employee relations. *Lumley v Gye*,[120] *Munchak Corp v Riko Enterprises*,[121]

---

114 [2000] 3 All ER 97, 108–09 (Lord Hoffmann), 114 (Lord Hope), 126 (Lord Millett).

115 Friedmann, above n 4, 513.

116 See *Attorney-General v Blake* [2000] 3 WLR 625, 639 (Lord Nicholls); Jackman, above n 70, 305–11. Weinrib, above n 6, says that, 'because property rights give proprietors the exclusive right to deal with the thing owned, including the right to profit from such dealings, any gains resulting from the misappropriation of property are necessarily subject to restitution. Gains from dealings in property are as much within the entitlement of the proprietor as the property itself'.

117 Also see Carpenter, CE, 'Interference with Contractual Relations' (1928) 41 Harv LR 728, 742, who argues that, if contract interests are treated as property, there seems to be no sufficient reason for distinguishing between contract interests and property interests when considering liability.

118 Above n 4, 519–21.

119 Above n 4, 520. See also Palmer, G, *The Law of Restitution*, Boston, MA: Little, Brown, 1978, vol 1, 445.

120 (1853) 2 E & B 216.

121 368 F Supp 1366 (MDNC, 1973).

and *Lightly v Clouston*[122] all concerned contracts for personal service. These cases are key authorities for establishing the principle that a 'contract right' is a 'property right'. Nonetheless, Friedmann follows the opinions expressed by Woodward,[123] in holding that restitutionary damages should not be awarded either against the breach of contract[124] or against the inducement to breach the contract.[125] He argues that, for the purposes of the property approach, it cannot be said that the employee's labour still belongs to the employer after the employee has broken his contract of employment. However, Friedmann does not adequately substantiate this point. He appears to suggest that, because the remedy of specific performance is not available, it cannot be said that the employer still retains a property interest in the employee's labour.[126] However, there seems to be no reason why the property interest in the labour should be tied to the availability of specific performance. A property interest in the cause of action might lie in the availability of specific performance, but the property interest in the employee's labour does not. This highlights a further problem with Friedmann's analysis caused by the circularity of defining property in terms of proprietary consequence. This will be commented on further below.

Friedmann's theory claims to provide a basis upon which restitutionary damages can be awarded within the framework of property law.[127] However, the reasoning of Friedmann suggests that he does not adopt a property approach but merely seeks to award restitutionary damages as a remedy akin to equitable damages under Lord Cairns' Act. Perhaps his comments subsequent to the discussion of specific performance provide some explanation of his approach. He recognises that the courts' refusal to order specific performance for employment contracts is because they do not wish to compel contracts for personal service. However, he says that there are broader interests which might require the refusal of restitutionary damages, such as the avoidance of waste and the promotion of mobility and the full personal development of the employee. These broader interests are clearly not considerations of property law but are considerations of public policy.[128]

Friedmann's theory of the 'property approach' to restitutionary damages has provided a useful contribution to the area of law. However, it is submitted that he has used the property approach to provide a legitimising veil for what is really a discretionary mechanism for the award of restitutionary damages. Friedmann's theory is really a policy-driven approach. This can be seen clearly from his comments with regard to contracts of personal service. However, the artificiality

122 (1808) 1 Taunt 112.

123 Woodward, F, *The Law of Quasi-Contracts*, Boston, MA: Little, Brown, 1913, 284.

124 Above n 4, 519–21.

125 Above n 4, 528–29.

126 A similar point was recently made by the Supreme Court of Canada in *Bank of America Canada v Clarica Trust* (2002) 211 DLR (4th) 385. See also, Waddams, SM, *The Law of Damages*, Toronto: Canada Law Book, 3rd edn, 1997, ¶ 9.200.

127 Above n 4, 556–58.

128 Friedmann himself refers to the considerations as policy: above n 4, 528.

of the 'property approach' can be seen most clearly when considering the 'inherent limitations'[129] of Friedmann's theory.

Friedmann recognises that, while the approach is based on the assumption that certain interests qualify as property, it does not itself provide a means of determining whether a particular interest ought to be recognised as property. The theory draws on the third party inducing breach of contract cases to justify equating contract rights with property rights. However, the line of authority used is not conclusive on the issue as was recognised earlier in this chapter. Even if it is accepted that certain contract interests qualify as property it is difficult to determine which contract interests are property. Donald Dowling has said that, 'whether a contract consists primarily of property aspects is an insoluble jurisprudential puzzle. It is not an issue that can be conclusively proved'.[130] Friedmann himself admits that 'any reasoning to the effect that an interest should be deemed property in order to prevent unjust enrichment would be circular'.[131] It is arguable that this is exactly what the property approach does. Friedmann has fallen into the trap of defining property in terms of the proprietary consequences that should be yielded. Such an approach has regularly been adopted both by the courts[132] and by academics.[133] However, this is surely circular. Defining property in terms of remedial consequence is, in the words of Kevin Gray, 'tautologous' and 'incestuous'.[134] It is an instrumental approach lacking principled justification. As such, it does little to provide a coherent framework for better protection of the performance interest of contracts.

Another major limitation of the property approach identified by Friedmann is that it requires an 'appropriation' of a property interest. This requirement involves a showing of use, consumption, or exploitation of another's property. Appropriation in this sense does not apply to the mere infliction of damage. Therefore damage without additional acts will not give rise to liability in restitution, even if the person who inflicted the damage has made a profit as a result of the act. This presents a major limitation to the availability of restitutionary damages under Friedmann's 'property approach'. He suggests that, in cases beyond the reach of the 'property approach', his second approach, based on principles of deterrence, may become relevant.[135] This may be so, but the great merit of the 'property approach' was that it legitimised an award of restitutionary damages on conventional property law principles. A supplementary approach

---

129 Above n 4, 557.

130 Dowling, above n 35, 505.

131 Above n 4, 557.

132 *Millennium Productions Ltd v Winter Garden Theatre (London) Ltd* [1948] AC 173; *Smith Kline & French Laboratories (Australia) Ltd v Secretary, Department of Community Services and Health* (1990) 95 ALR 87, 135; *Hoystead v Federal Commissioner of Taxation* (1920) 27 CLR 400, 423.

133 Waddams, S, 'Breach of Contract and the Concept of Wrongdoing' (2000) 12 Sup Ct LR 1, 29; Calabresi, G and Melamed, AD, 'Property Rules, Liability Rules and Inalienability: One View of the Cathedral' (1972) 85 Harv LR 1089.

134 Gray, K, 'Property in Thin Air' [1991] CLJ 252, 301.

135 Above n 4, 551–56. See Emmett J who endorses these two grounds for restitutionary damages in *Hospitality Group Pty Ltd v Australian Rugby Union Ltd* [2001] 110 FCR 157, 198.

based on deterrence is largely discretionary and defeats the very object of the 'property approach'.[136]

AN OPEN APPROACH

By trying to fit contract rights into the straightjacket of property rights Friedmann has argued that restitutionary damages should be available for certain infringements of contract rights. Friedmann's theory is based on the recognition that compensatory damages do not always provide adequate protection to the performance interest of contracts. This can be seen from his comments with regard to his illustration two. This illustration concerns a defendant who undertakes to transfer certain property to the claimant on a certain date, but in breach of contract transfers the property six months late and in the meantime derives profit from its use.[137] Friedmann recognises that compensatory damages will normally be adequate on these facts. However, in some exceptional circumstances damages may not be recoverable at all. Friedmann proposes that restitution ought to be available in such cases.[138]

It is undoubtedly true that compensatory damages do not always provide adequate protection to the performance interest of contracts. This is the very reason why specific performance and injunctions are awarded. Such equitable remedies are only available when compensatory damages are inadequate.[139] As stated above, the right to performance of a contract is a right worthy of protection because of the commercial desirability of preserving the security of transactions. However, such concerns do not provide justification for a theory that blurs the categories between contract rights and property rights. Contract rights could be equated with property rights if property rights are interpreted in a very wide sense to include all debts, contractual rights and causes of action.[140] Unfortunately, such an interpretation empties the word 'property' of any real meaning. It could even be suggested that contracts exhibit characteristics of excludability, and thus resemble property rights in the narrow sense. The right recognised in *Lumley v Gye*

---

136 See Weinrib, E, *The Idea of Private Law*, Cambridge, MA: Harvard UP, 1995, 39–42. In his discussion of coherence and justification, Weinrib recognises that the justification of a private law obligation is undermined by 'the competing presence in the same legal relationship of different goals'. Friedmann's 'property approach' is based upon a desire to develop a coherent and principled means for awarding restitutionary damages. However, this goal is frustrated if a largely discretionary deterrent approach is simultaneously adopted.

137 Above n 4, 518–19.

138 Also see Friedmann's comments with regard to illustration one, above n 4, 516. He recognises that restitutionary damages will not be necessary where the compensatory damages are adequate.

139 *Falcke v Gray* (1859) 4 Drew 651; *Sky Petroleum Ltd v VIP Petroleum Ltd* [1974] 1 All ER 954; *Ashton v Corrigan* (1871) LR 13 EQ 76; *Decro-Wall International SA v Practitioners in Marketing Ltd* [1971] 1 WLR 361; *Beswick v Beswick* [1968] AC 58; *Coulls v Bagot's Executor and Trustee Co Ltd* (1967) 119 CLR 460, 503–04.

140 See Smith, L, 'Disgorgement of the Profits of Breach of Contract: Property, Contract and "Efficient Breach"' (1994–95) 24 Can Bus LJ 121, 130; *Lipkin Gorman v Karpnale Ltd* [1991] 2 AC 548, 574 (Lord Goff); *Nokes v Doncaster Amalgamated Collieries Ltd* [1940] AC 1014, 1033 (Lord Atkin).

appeared to be a right *in rem* – good against the world. But such a line of reasoning is not convincing. Contract rights are generally rights *in personam*; they are rights between the promisor and promisee. They are not rights *in* the contract.[141] The inducing breach of contract cases are anomalous, but it has been argued that these cases are best explained on the basis that the courts were seeking to protect the performance interest of contracts. Proprietary remedies were required to protect the contract interest. However, to argue that contracts are property on this basis is to commit once again the 'incestuous tautology' of defining property in terms of the proprietary consequences that should be yielded.

It is true that the end does not always justify the means. The 'end' of providing adequate protection to the performance interest of contracts does not justify the 'means' of labelling contract rights as property rights. Such an approach may have the appeal of building on pre-established case law. However, as demonstrated by the analysis of Friedmann's theory, it is only a piecemeal measure to address a serious problem. Furthermore, it lacks coherence and is internally inconsistent.[142]

An open recognition of restitutionary damages for breach of contract is required. Such an open recognition of restitutionary damages may be possible following the House of Lords decision in *Attorney-General v Blake*.[143] Indeed, recently in the case of *Esso Petroleum Co Ltd v Niad Ltd*,[144] the Vice Chancellor has adopted a flexible approach to the *Blake* requirement of the plaintiff having a 'legitimate interest in preventing the defendant's profit making activity'. This suggests that the availability of restitutionary damages for breach of contract may be more widespread than initially expected. However, in *Blake* itself Lord Nicholls insisted that restitutionary damages should only be 'exceptionally'[145] available and it must be expected that subsequent courts will follow this guidance.[146]

It is submitted that a restrictive approach to the availability of restitutionary damages should not be taken. There is no justification for allowing the recovery of restitutionary damages for infringements of proprietary rights while not allowing restitutionary damages for breach of contract. The basis for this bold assertion is stated succinctly by Ames in his seminal article 'Purchaser for Value without Notice'.[147] Ames argues that the common law rules of property apply equally to

---

141 See Smith, above n 140, 131; Chambers, R, 'Integrating Property and Obligations', Chapter 8 of this volume.

142 See Weinrib, above n 136, 39–42.

143 [2000] 3 WLR 625.

144 [2001] EWHC Ch 458.

145 See *Experience Hendrix LLC v PPX Enterprises Inc Edward Chalpin* [2003] EWCA Civ 323, [24]. Mance LJ suggested that this 'exceptional' qualification might only apply to a full disgorgement of profits (account of profits) as awarded in *Blake* itself. The same qualification was not necessarily required for an award of damages of the nature ordered in *Wrotham Park*. Mance LJ appeared to be distinguishing between two gain-based measures of damages – what Edelman, above n 8, 65–112 has described as restitutionary damages (*Wrotham Park*) and disgorgement damages (*Blake*). A full discussion of this is beyond the scope of this chapter.

146 [2000] 3 WLR 625, 638. An account of profits was refused at first instance in the following recent cases: *World Wide Fund for Nature (formerly World Wildlife Fund) v World Wrestling Foundation Entertainment Inc* [2002] FSR 32; *AB Corp v CD Co* [2002] 1 Lloyd's Rep 805.

147 Ames, JB, 'Purchaser for Value without Notice' (1887) 1 Harv LR 1, 9–10.

ownership of obligations as to ownership of things. The only difference is in the mode of enjoyment. The owner of a thing, such as a house or a horse, has a right *in rem*. The owner of an obligation, such as a promisee under a contract or a *cestui que trust*, only has an *in personam* right against the promissor. Ames declares that, 'the general duty resting upon all mankind not to destroy the property of another, is as cogent in favour of an obligee as it is in favour of the owner of a horse'.[148] Therefore contract rights are as deserving of the court's protection as ordinary property rights.

This reasoning has been followed much more recently by Lionel Smith.[149] He cites Hohfeld[150] in stating that the *only* difference between personal and proprietary rights is that personal rights are enforceable against a single person (and proprietary rights are enforceable against people generally).[151] He emphasises that the difference between the two rights does not depend upon whether there is a tangible subject matter. For example, copyrights and patents are proprietary rights but there is no physical thing to show for the right. Nor does the difference depend on the value of the rights. One person may have a proprietary right in a worthless pebble while another person has a personal right in a substantial debt. Neither does the difference turn on the scope of the rights. A trustee has common law proprietary rights in the subject matter of the trust, but they are of a very limited nature and not for his own benefit. On the other hand, someone who holds a contractual licence to occupy a house has a personal right which is as broad in scope as a freehold title.

This raises the question of why restitutionary damages should be available for the infringement of proprietary rights but not for the infringement of a personal obligation. In the field of unjust enrichment no such property requirement exists and it is anomalous to have such a restriction on the availability of restitutionary damages for wrongs.[152] As Lionel Smith states: 'The way rights are protected should reflect differences in the rights.'[153] The only difference between proprietary and personal rights is that a personal right can be enforced against one person or a group of persons while a proprietary right can be enforced against a large group of potential defendants. Although this is a significant difference it is difficult to understand why this justifies personal rights, such as contractual rights, being protected by a narrower range of remedies.[154]

It is submitted that there is no justification for this difference in remedial response. Instead of attempting to fit contract rights into the straightjacket of property rights there should be an open recognition of restitutionary damages for breach of contract where compensatory damages are inadequate and equitable

148 *Ibid*, 10.

149 Above n 140.

150 Hohfeld, WN, *Fundamental Legal Conceptions*, Westport, CT: Greenwood, 1964.

151 Above n 140, 131.

152 See Edelman, J, 'The Meaning of "Damages": Common Law and Equity', Chapter 3 of this volume.

153 Above n 140, 132.

154 Also see Weinrib, E, 'The Juridical Classification of Obligations', in Birks, P (ed), *The Classification of Obligations*, Oxford: OUP, 1997, 52–54.

remedies are unavailable. This proposal has been developed by the writer elsewhere.[155] A full exposition of this framework is beyond the scope of this chapter and it can merely be summarised here. The proposal is based on an extension of the pre-established framework for awarding equitable damages under Lord Cairns' Act.

It is well established that, when compensatory damages are inadequate to protect the performance interest of a contract, the courts are prepared to grant either specific performance or an injunction.[156] In some circumstances, however, these remedies are unavailable for either jurisdictional or discretionary reasons.[157] If the claimant were to be left with his compensatory damages the performance interest of the contract would remain unprotected. Therefore, the courts have been willing to award equitable damages on a restitutionary basis to such claimants.[158] Since specific performance or injunctive relief has been refused these damages are better understood as an alternative to full equitable relief rather than as a substitute. As such, it is submitted that there is no reason why the availability of equitable damages should be tied to the continuing jurisdiction of the court to grant full equitable relief. The jurisdictional restrictions placed on the availability of specific performance and injunctive relief are peculiar to the nature of the remedies sought and should not be applied to the availability of equitable damages, which are very different in nature.[159] It is therefore suggested that the courts should openly recognise what they have already been doing under the veil of equitable damages. Restitutionary damages should be awarded as a tertiary remedy for breach of contract. By this, the writer means that restitutionary damages should be awarded, subject to general equitable considerations,[160] whenever compensatory damages are inadequate and full equitable relief is unavailable. Such an approach was taken by the Court of Appeal in the recent case of *Experience Hendrix LLC v PPX Enterprises Inc Edward Chalpin*, where Mance LJ recognised that an award of restitutionary damages was appropriate where it was

---

155 Cunnington, R, 'Equitable Damages: A Model for Restitutionary Damages' (2001) 17 J Cont L 212, 234–39.

156 *Falcke v Gray* (1859) 4 Drew 541; *Decro-Wall International SA v Practitioners in Marketing Ltd* [1971] 1 WLR 361; *Beswick v Beswick* [1968] AC 58.

157 *Co-operative Insurance v Argyll Stores (Holdings) Ltd* [1998] AC 1; *Johnson v Shrewsbury & Birmingham Rly* (1853) 3 DM & G 914; *Ryan v Mutual Tontine Westminster Chambers Association* [1893] 1 Ch 116; *Patel v Ali* [1984] Ch 283; *Kelsen v Imperial Tobacco Co Ltd* [1957] 2 QB 334.

158 See, eg, *Wrotham Park v Parkside Homes* [1974] 1 WLR 789; *Jaggard v Sawyer* [1995] 1 WLR 269; *Gafford v Graham* (1999) 77 P & CR 73. Cf *Experience Hendrix LLC v PPX Enterprises Inc Edward Chalpin* [2003] EWCA Civ 323, [35] (Mance LJ).

159 See *Surrey County Council v Bredero Homes* [1993] 3 All ER 705, 715 (Steyn LJ); Cunnington, above n 155, 236.

160 One relevant equitable consideration might be that the plaintiff has acted in a high-handed manner (*Mountford v Scott* [1975] Ch 258; *Walters v Morgan* (1861) 3 DF & J 718), justifying refusal of equitable damages. Alternatively, damages may be denied because the plaintiff has delayed excessively in bringing an action (*Bracewell v Appleby* [1975] 2 WLR 282, 286). Equitable damages, awarded on a restitutionary basis, might also be refused on the ground that they would cause severe hardship to the defendant or a third party. Such a discretion already lies with the court in respect of specific relief (*Patel v Ali* [1984] Ch 283). The case law on the considerations that should be relevant to the court when exercising their equitable discretion is already well established.

too late for either specific performance or an injunction to offer any effective remedy.[161]

There are many merits to this approach as compared with the property approach. First, it is developed from a pre-existing body of case law. The courts have been awarding equitable damages on an alternative basis ever since the decision of Brightman J in *Wrotham Park v Parkside Homes Ltd*.[162] It is only a small step to acknowledge that such damages cannot be explained by the fictitious 'lost opportunity to bargain' theory and are better explained as awards of restitutionary damages.[163] Secondly, the law relating to equitable damages has already established a body of case law to determine when compensatory damages are inadequate and restitutionary damages are required. Thus the approach offers a pre-established and coherent framework for awarding restitutionary damages. Such an approach is surely preferable to the Procrustean attempt to classify contract rights as property rights.

CONCLUSION

In the first part of this chapter the tort of inducing breach of contract was examined. It was suggested that the recognition and development of the tort since *Lumley v Gye* has demonstrated that the performance interest of contracts is an interest worthy of protection by the courts.[164] Furthermore, the development of the tort has demonstrated that the performance interest is not adequately protected by compensatory damages.[165] The right to performance of a contract is a right worthy of protection because of the commercial desirability of preserving the security of transactions.

It was submitted that the torts of inducing breach of contract and interference with contractual relations have developed to increase the protection of the performance interest of contracts when compensatory damages are inadequate. The tort has thus developed to fill a lacuna in the law.[166] However, the tort can only operate when the breach of contract has been induced or caused by a third

---

161 [2003] EWCA Civ 323, [36]. Mance LJ, *ibid*, [45], described the sum he was awarding as being based on the approach adopted by Brightman J in *Wrotham Park*. Although there is some ambiguity, it seems that Mance LJ recognised this as a restitutionary measure [25–26].

162 [1974] 1 WLR 798.

163 This explanation was originally formulated by Sharpe, R and Waddams, S, 'Damages for Lost Opportunity to Bargain' (1982) 2 OJLS 290, and was accepted by Lord Nicholls in *Attorney-General v Blake* [2000] 3 WLR 625, 635. See criticisms of the theory in Burrows, A, *The Law of Restitution*, London: Butterworths, 2nd edn, 2002, 477; Birks, P, 'Profits of Breach of Contract' (1993) 109 LQR 518, 520; Cunnington, above n 155, 225–28; Edelman, J, 'The Compensation Strait-Jacket and the Lost Opportunity to Bargain Fiction' [2001] Restitution LR 104.

164 *Lumley v Gye* (1853) 2 E & B 216, 233. The efficient breach theory of contract should accordingly be rejected.

165 *Ibid*, 234. This need for better protection of the performance interest was also recognised more recently by the House of Lords in *Attorney-General v Blake* [2000] 3 WLR 625, 636. Lord Nicholls declared that it is 'well established that an award of damages, assessed by reference to financial loss, is not always "adequate" as a remedy for a breach of contract'.

166 See comments of Erle J in *Lumley v Wagner* (1853) 2 E & B 216, 234.

party. Thus the lacuna in the law still exists for contracts that have been broken by a contracting party without any external influence. The tort merely provides partial and sporadic protection for the performance interest of contracts. This is unsatisfactory and the possibility that restitutionary damages could be recovered against third parties but not against defaulting parties creates a perverse situation which is an affront to both common sense and logic.

Some commentators have suggested that the right recognised in *Lumley v Gye* was akin to a property right, potentially yielding restitutionary damages against defaulting parties. Such damages for breach of contract could provide a solution for this lacuna in the law. Friedmann has used the cases concerning the tort of inducing breach of contract to formulate a theory that ties the availability of restitutionary damages to the identification of an appropriation of a property interest. By adopting an expansive view of property to include contract interests, Friedmann's theory enables the award of restitutionary damages for breach of contract within English law.

However, it has been argued that Friedmann's 'property approach' to restitutionary damages is an instrumental approach, which hides the award behind the legitimising veil of property law. Friedmann's main concern is to provide an alternative measure for contract damages where compensatory damages are inadequate.[167] It is submitted that there is no need to attempt to classify contract rights as property rights. Contract rights are as deserving of adequate remedial protection as property rights. Friedmann's objectives would be better achieved by an open approach to the award of restitutionary damages for breach of contract which does not seek to legitimise them by reference to principles of property law.

---

167 See, eg, Friedmann's comments with regard to illustration one, above n 4, 516. He recognises that restitutionary damages will not be necessary where the compensatory damages are adequate. See also illustration two, *ibid*, 518–19. Friedmann recognises that compensatory damages will normally be adequate. However, in some exceptional circumstances damages may not be recoverable at all. Friedmann proposes that restitution ought to be available in such cases.

Index